ENCOUNTERS IN PLACE

Detail from *Captain Cook's interview with the natives in Adventure Bay, Van Diemen's Land, January 29, 1777.* Artist thought to be J. Webber (see p.34)

ENCOUNTERS IN PLACE

Outsiders and Aboriginal Australians 1606-1985

D.J. MULVANEY

University of Queensland Press

First published 1989 by University of Queensland Press
Box 42, St Lucia, Queensland, Australia

Typeset by University of Queensland Press
Printed in Australia by Griffin Press Limited, Adelaide

To protect the National Estate

The University of Queensland Press
acknowledges the support and
encouragement of the Australian
Heritage Commission

Cataloguing in Publication Data

National Library of Australia

Mulvaney, D.J. (Derek John), 1925– .
 Encounters in place, outsiders and Aboriginal
 Australians 1606–1985.

 Bibliography.
 Includes index.
 ISBN 0 7022 2153 8.

 (1). Aborigines, Australian — History. 2. Historic
 sites — Australia. (3). Aborigines, Australian
 — Land tenure. (4). Aborigines, Australian
 — First contact with Occidental civilization.
 I. Title.

994'.0049915

British Library (data available)

Library of Congress

Mulvaney, Derek John.
 Encounters in place : outsiders and aboriginal Australians,
 1606-1985 / D.J. Mulvaney.
  p.   cm.
 Bibliography: p.
 Includes index.
 1. Australian aborigines — History. 2. Australian aborigines —
 — Foreign influences. 3. Australia — Discovery and exploration.
 4. Historic places — Australia. 5. Australia — Antiquities.

 I. Title.

GN665.M83 1988   994'.0049915 —— dc19   88-17605

ISBN 0 7022 2153 8

Contents

Illustrations

Maps

Black and White Plates

Colour Plates — Aboriginal Perceptions of Contact *Following page 126*

Foreword

Emeritus Professor Mulvaney's book makes a significant contribution to our understanding of Australia's cultural heritage. Encounters between peoples of different cultures have been an important element in the development of every society, with ideas and artefacts being transferred from one to the other. Archaeological evidence and the Dreaming indicate many such encounters between the different Aboriginal societies in Australia over the past forty thousand years. More recent interactions between Aboriginal groups in the North and outsiders, such as Macassans, Chinese and Papuans, have resulted in many aspects of that other society being adopted into Aboriginal culture. The past two hundred years since European settlement have, however, had a profoundly disruptive effect upon a way of life that had largely been isolated for many millennia.

John Mulvaney looks at these recent encounters, their impact on Aboriginal society and the evidence which these events have left on the landscape. From 1606, when William Jansz encountered Australia's shore, Professor Mulvaney traces modern contacts between Aboriginal groups and explorers, travellers, traders and settlers and relates how these episodes affected Aboriginal culture.

The fascinating accounts of the relationship between the Macassan trepang traders and peoples in Arnhem Land in the chapter "Praus to Carpentaria", between Papuans, Torres Strait Islands and Aboriginal people of Cape York in "Across Torres Strait", and between Afghans and Aborigines at Marree provide a dimension to Australia's multicultural heritage of which few of us are aware.

Encounters in Place recognises many of the grimmer episodes since European settlement, such as massacres and battlegrounds (for example the clashes at Cullinlaringo and Battle Mountain), frequently the tragic result of a lack of understanding between different cultures. Equally tragic, later official policies to move Aboriginal groups to reservations and remove children from their parents imposed a humiliating lack of individual freedom and disrupted family life. The chapters "Two Innovative Missions" and "The Cootamundra Home for Girls" portray different facets of this phase of Aboriginal history.

Encounters between Aboriginal groups and settlers were not always hostile. The book also acknowledges some of the more positive events and the achievements of Aboriginal people within modern Australian society, such as in the chapter "The Peppers of Ebenezer" and in "Epitaphs of Friendship". The continuity and resurgence of Aboriginality is expressed in "Freedom Ride to Moree" and in the chapter on the return of Uluru to its traditional owners.

A member of the Australian Heritage Commission for six years from its inception, John Mulvaney's belief in and concern about this country and its peoples shine out. He writes with elegance, clarity and a generous humanity. Anyone concerned about the future of Australia will find much to inform and more to cause question about our previously accepted beliefs and understandings.

Professor Mulvaney brings considerable scholarship to this account. His pioneering archaeological exploration of Australia's Aboriginal prehistory over the past thirty-five years, published in *The Prehistory of Australia*, was at a time when that prehistory was pushed back from ten to forty thousand years; combined with his longstanding interest and contribution to recent Aboriginal history, it brings great erudition to *Encounters In Place*.

A significant aspect of this book is its emphasis on place. The physical and symbolic remains of past encounters are important social and historical elements of Australia's heritage. The Australian Heritage Commission has recognised the significance of these places by listing many of them in the Register of the National Estate. Having reached our Bicentenary, it is important to acknowledge these events of the past two hundred years, as well as those which went before, for they helped fashion the society we have today.

The Commission is delighted to be associated with the University of Queensland Press in this publication.

Pat Galvin, Chairman,
Australian Heritage Commission

Preface

Somewhere between half a million and a million people were spread unevenly across Australia's 7,682,300 square kilometres in 1788, according to present estimates. They spoke well over two hundred mutually distinct languages and they were affiliated loosely into several hundred groupings, termed tribes by Europeans. There were occasions when upwards of 500 to 1,000 people assembled for ritual obligations, but usually they lived in bands of from 20 to 50 people, depending upon local conditions.

The first documented alien visitors to Australian shores, almost four centuries ago, therefore found an inhabited continent. These newcomers judged both the land and its inhabitants unattractive, so they largely left the country alone for over a century. The first uncomprehending visitors were Dutch sailors employed by a trading company who saw a people whose economy was neither commercial nor agricultural. These Aborigines regulated their lives without calendars, chronometers or books, yet observed formal and complex rules of etiquette and relationship. They believed that their ancestors originated in a timeless Dreaming. It was then, they knew, that landforms, creatures and humankind were created, or emerged from the landscape.

Dutch mariners were governed by a different and more prosaic world vision. They counted in units of time back for almost six thousand years from the seventeenth century which was the date of their own Creation time, according to their Book of Genesis literally interpreted, and they assumed their racial and cultural superiority. Later white Australians, the descendants of the British invaders of AD 1788, wrote their own mythology of the heroic landtaking of this sun-drenched "virgin" country. They measured time clinically in their journals and, later, in radiocarbon 14 laboratories. They ascertained pragmatically that the first Aboriginal colonists occupied the continent over 40,000 years ago, possibly considerably more.

This span of at least two thousand human generations across such a vast continent witnessed dramatic changes in the land and its societies. In the face of fluctuating climates, contrasting environments, creative insights and cultural innovations, populations increased, people shifted residence and countless meetings occurred between groups of people when ideas or goods were exchanged. Such encounters between neighbours became ritualised over time and were adjusted to seasonal cycles of water and food abundance, and economic and cultural needs. Kinship relationships, economic drives and linguistic affiliations fostered ceremonial gift exchange networks, linked morally by obligations, and physically by traditional Dreaming paths and trade routes. Prominent landform features, trackways and places where ritual encounters occurred, or where human activities modified the landscape by creating archaelogical sites, became celebrated for their Dreaming origins. Their very existence, and the songs, dances and stories which belonged to them, provided daily visual and oral confirmation of the reality of their mythological past.

This immense saga of challenge, response, and encounters within continental space, is retold by Aboriginal people, who feel bound to their territory and their sacred places by an intense feeling of belonging and identification. This book recounts something of encounters of a different kind — those later contacts, so many of them fatal, which have occurred during the four centuries since the rest of the world discovered the original Australians.

Places are selected for the significance of the face-to-face meetings which they typify or symbolise. Europeans were not the only agents of change during this period of contact. Other people interacting with Aboriginal societies included Afghans, Chinese, Japanese, Macassans, Papuans and Pacific Islanders. Manifestations of these encounters survive and provide a valuable material heritage for modern Australians of all races.

These studies are an outsider's version of some of these interactions, set into place and time. The existence of a visible and definable place meriting listing in the Register of the National Estate is a prerequisite for inclusion. (The convention adopted for reference to these places is "in the Register".) Representativeness is another criterion. It would prove easy to fill the book with sad killing grounds across the continent, for example, and every mission or government settlement featured importantly in the lives of particular groups of people. The selection included will not represent the choice of many readers. It is a personal attempt to weave a thematic history around physical evidence, while also providing chronological and geographical representativeness.

Its aim also is to foster greater respect for places and material relics as documents of Australian history. A mature Australian culture should identify with these monuments or symbolic sites and conserve them; the conscience-stirring places as well as sites of legendary heroic deeds. Above all, it must accept the reality that many races contributed to our culture, long before it was enriched by migrants during the past forty years. Aborigines were here first; Papuans and Indonesians influenced cultural diversity even before Europeans, who came predominantly from Great Britain and Ireland, fanned out across the continent. By the time of Federation, Afghans, Chinese and Melanesians had increased that diversity. The interaction of such peoples with the Aborigines, and representative symbolic and material manifestations of those contacts form the focus of this book.

Because the Register of the National Estate figures so prominently in this work, its functions and purpose require some explanation. The Australian Heritage Commission Act 1975 was passed with the support of all political parties. The Act required the Heritage Commission to identify and register significant places in what was termed a Register of the National Estate. The Act defined such places as being

> components of the natural environment of Australia or the cultural environment of Australia, that have aesthetic, historic, scientific or social significance or other special value for future generations as well as for the present community.

By 1987, 8,290 places were listed in the Register of the National Estate, ranging in size from a single cottage to national parks covering thousands of square kilometres. Frequently, places possessing environmental and cultural values coincide, especially places significant for Aboriginal people. The Kakadu and Uluru National Parks are obvious examples. The importance of the Register is that it alerts all Australians to the existence of places which, it is hoped, a mature community would wish to keep as a heritage for the future.

Relevant attributes taken into account in any assessment of places nominated on grounds of Natural Environment include the exceptional quality, representativeness or diversity of an ecosystem, landform, or feature; its demonstration of botanical or geological evolution; the habitat of an endangered species; aesthetic qualities; and association with celebrated persons or significant scientific discoveries.

Attributes taken into account for listing places of non-Aboriginal cultural significance, including the Built Environment, concern the quality, rarity or representativeness of a feature. They may exemplify a way of life, technology or function no longer practised or becoming rare; possess strong associations with important persons or symbolise an event or a social era; represent major creative and/or technical achievements; exhibit significant townscape values, or preserve humanly modified landscapes, both aesthetically attractive or stark and eroded. The housing and lifeways of the humble are as worthy of entry in the Register, as are grand houses and manicured estates.

Aboriginal places also may be assessed for Register listing on the quality or representativeness of their cultural and/or environmental features. These may include traditional sites of significance, when nominated by or with the approval of local Aboriginal communities; places showing artistic creativity, such as rock paintings; sites of potential or demonstrated scientific and archaeological importance; and contact sites, those places which symbolise or exemplify interaction between Aborigines and other races. These latter places are the focus of this series of episodes in cross-cultural relations.

CHAPTER ONE

The Protocol of Aboriginal Encounters

Before any encounter may be set into historic context, it is necessary to establish the protocols of the living Aboriginal culture. Only in this way is it possible to understand Aboriginal responses to contact situations. Every instance of early racial contact took place upon Aboriginal land, but few of the newcomers acknowledged this reality. The rules governing relationships in Aboriginal society were highly structured, placing strict obligations both on the hosts and on the visitors. Rituals of diplomacy governed different situations, but speed was never a priority. There were behavioural codes for appropriate relations between meetings of close kin or when marriage bestowals were initiated; and rules for establishing or reaffirming friendly relations between affiliated groups; or between strangers; codes governing the settlement of disputes, and responses to the approach of potential enemies; or of known foes. They all required time for the courtesies to be ascertained, or for the community to assemble. Some occasions were for males or females only, while others required the attendance of the whole community. Individuals also were responsible for special roles which could not be performed by others.

A mutual ignorance of behavioural rules and individual roles produced many unfortunate misunderstandings in stressful early inter-racial contact situations. Other problems arose because the foreign visitor, sitting high in the saddle, assumed a superiority in status or culture matching his physical elevation. He automatically imposed his social rules, rather than deferring to his host. He often rejected sincere gestures of hospitality, because he thought the offerings or their mode were repugnant.

Take the custom of offering wives to overnight visitors as a token of friendship. Europeans witnessed the meeting of two antagonistic groups in Central Australia. "As usual on such occasions", they reported of the host group, they "sent some of their women over to the strangers' camp, but the fact that the use of the women was declined by the visitors at once indicated that the mission . . . was not a friendly one. The women are offered with a view to conciliating . . . if they accept the favours . . . the quarrel will not be pursued any further''. Rejection by a European of such hospitality also would signal animosity. Acceptance, on the other hand, would impose an obligation for some future service, about which the European would be unaware.

Explorers or settlers seeking new pastures normally were in a hurry and became impatient of ritualised exchanges, or conversed with an inappropriate person. In mutual linguistic ignorance, both parties resorted to sign language, but gesticulations often conveyed the wrong meaning. Consequently, it was easy for the newcomer to appear grossly insulting, to cut corners in diplomacy and to fail to comprehend the underlying reciprocal nature of Aboriginal society. Many instances of Aboriginal antagonism doubtless resulted from European violations of traditional behaviour.

Charles Sturt elaborated another factor in confrontation, surprise, which resulted in impulsive action. His advice was never to arouse fear. ''If I had rushed on these poor people, I should have received their weapons, and have been obliged to raise my arm against them, but, by giving them time to recover from their surprise, allowing them to go through their wonted ceremonies, and, by pacific demonstrations, hostile collisions have been avoided.''

A remarkable characteristic of Aboriginal social organisation was its pan-Australian uniformity or patterning. One feature, its local territoriality, might seem to negate this and foster parochialism. William Thomas, working with the Yarra people around 1840, expressed the view that ''all tribes beyond the district of their friends are termed wild blackfellows''. Even so, despite a fear or distrust of unknown people, networks of ceremonial gift exchange stretched across the continent, linked by ancestral Dreaming paths and sacred centres. Participation in these cycles imposed long term reciprocal obligations.

Across Australia large scale ritual gatherings occurred periodically, determined by seasonal conditions and food availability, when initiation, bride bestowal, or mortuary ceremonies cemented social bonding. These were accompanied by dance, song and artistic exuberance, and the exchange of gifts which often possessed economic and technological importance. Depending upon the region and the importance of the ceremony, numbers attending varied between a few dozen to 1,000 people. At such gatherings, standardised camping arrangements were followed strictly, in the siting of each group's living area. When Aborigines were induced to live on European settlements, this latter necessity often was ignored, at cost to the social fabric.

Anywhere in Australia, once a group approached another group's territory for such ceremonial purposes, any existing grievances or disputes between those communities had to be resolved first. This often involved ritualised and noisy combat, at times ending in injury. Before matters could proceed, also, the kin or classificationary relationship and status of any new arrival had to be established with the host group. It all required much time and debate. The approach of Europeans, on the other hand, who ignored all these niceties, must have violated numerous rules, causing grave offence and creating total bewilderment.

Northeastern Arnhem Land customs during the 1920s offer helpful insight.

Anthropologist Lloyd Warner concluded that "the fundamental principle underlying all the causes of . . . warfare is that of reciprocity: if a harm has been done to an individual or a group . . . they must repay . . . by an injury that at least equals the one they have suffered".

An encounter between affiliated Arnhem Land groups in the Caledon Bay area in 1942, intended to settle grievances. During this ceremonial, known as a makarrata, the aggrieved persons hurled spears at the offenders. Serious injury rarely resulted, as they dodged the spears and the dispute usually ended when one or two men received thigh wounds. The groups then resumed normal relations. (Donald F. Thomson, copyright Mrs D.M. Thomson)

Such reciprocal pay-back situations must have been frequent during white settlement, but any Aboriginal resistance which wounded a settler prompted deadly and often random reprisals. Equally relevant was Warner's conclusion, that if a woman was stolen by an Aborigine, "only the return of the woman and a ceremonial fight, or the stealing of another woman, will satisfy . . . self-esteem, unless the clan has retaliated by killing or wounding one of the enemy clansmen. The same feeling is instigated by the improper viewing of the totem — an insult and an injury to the whole clan." Herein, surely, rest the explanations for many incidents which Europeans claimed were unprovoked.

Through the reciprocal exchange networks, goods circulated for hundreds of kilometres, passing from hand to hand with solemnity. When major ceremonies were planned, messengers (elders) were sent on long circuits, bearing ritual paraphernalia ("message sticks") as their credentials. Through the existence of these networks, and this system of personal communication, a dynamic mechanism existed to transport news or objects along traditional pathways. Explorers were surprised to find metal or other European items far beyond the frontier of settlement. Some also marvelled at the absence of visible inhabitants along their routes. This continental mechanism for spreading news, warnings, or objects, explains the situation which explorers experienced. A remarkable documented example is the spread of the Mudlunga (Molonga/Tjitjingalla) ceremonial dance. During a period of about twenty-five years from the early 1890s, this spectacular dance and related songs spread from northwest Queensland to Alice Springs, through the Lake Eyre Basin to reach the South Australian coast. A number of important ceremonial exchange centres are listed in the Register of the National Estate, including the Mt William hatchet stone quarry in central Victoria. Under the strict control of one clan, its products circulated throughout western Victoria and the Riverina.

When the anthropological pioneers Baldwin Spencer and Frank Gillen returned to Alice Springs in 1901, to resume their anthropological collaboration after a five-year absence, their experiences provided two separate cameos of traditional behaviour. The first happened on the day after their arrival and concerned their own ritual acceptance by the elders. They related the incident as follows.

> . . . a deputation of eight of the elder men, who had decorated themselves with bands of white pipe-clay, came into our camp to welcome us formally. It was a solemn ceremony. First of all they squatted on the ground in silence. Then, after a short pause, the head man of the Alice Springs group told us that they were very glad to see us again . . . and that we were welcome to their country. We acknowledged their welcome with a present of tobacco.

Here, then, was a racial encounter without stress, for it accorded entirely with the traditional pattern. The visitors expected to be received and had gifts ready for the deputation. The elders also prepared with symbolic body painting. It was a leisurely meeting, at which the Aboriginal hosts set the pace and the appropriate local clan leader acted as spokesman. By accepting the gifts, the host Aborigines accepted an obligation to reciprocate in some manner.

A comparable ceremony, in reverse, occurred in Canberra during 1982, when a group of Arnhem Land Anbarra people travelled there in order to honour the Australian Institute of Aboriginal Studies. This involved staging a ROM ceremony, an elaborate ritual of diplomacy performed to cement friendly relations. Beautifully decorated totemic poles, associated ritual objects and dances, were presented in public and the visitors also received gifts as an acknowledgment of continuing obligations. The preparation of the regalia and related ritual activities required considerable investment of time by the Anbarra, both at home and in Canberra. As in the previous episode, the key to its success was that traditional mores were followed carefully and both sides made appropriate arrangements beforehand.

In earlier contact times, much confusion and some fatal disputes might have been avoided if Europeans had attempted to adapt to customary behaviour. It is probable that some other races showed greater tolerance in such matters. The influence which Macassan trepangers exerted on Arnhem Land communities may be such a case. The mythologies and rituals of Cape York and Torres Strait Islander peoples suggest interaction with Papuan societies. Relations were not always mutually harmonious, but some cross-fertilisation of ceremonial life occurred, reflecting common expectations. These are the subject of subsequent chapters.

Spencer and Gillen also were the unwitting witnesses to a ritualised encounter between two affiliated Aranda groups, who had grievances to settle before normal relationships could be re-established. In a careful analysis of this incident, Sylvia Hallam showed that it illuminates the complexities of a functioning traditional society. The episode foreshadows many of the problems posed by European contact situations, so it is quoted at length. Aborigines, Spencer and Gillen explained,

> have to be . . . very careful to attend to certain points of etiquette on approaching a strange camp or on coming into the country of another local group: otherwise they might be received and greeted as enemies . . . . One afternoon . . . there was a sudden commotion . . . due . . . to the fact that word had been brought in that a party of armed strangers was approaching . . . . The visitors, as usual, sat down quietly about half a mile

away from the main camp. There were some thirty of them, all full-grown men and all armed with shields, spears and boomerangs and wearing in their hair curious flaked sticks called inkulta . . . the wearing of these sticks is the sign that the men mean to kill some one if they can . . . . After about half an hour, during which time no notice had apparently been taken of the visitors, though, in reality, the local men had provided themselves with their weapons and gone to the spot where visitors were received, one or two of the older local men went to them, squatted down on the sand in front of them, and invited them to come up. After being thus invited they formed themselves into a solid square and approached at a fairly quick run, every man with his spear aloft and all of them adopting the curious high knee-action which is so characteristic of the movements of natives during ceremonial performances. As they came near . . . they were met by some of the older women of the local group . . . they danced and yelled at the top of their voices . . . the visitors scarcely took any notice of them, and it proved to be all part of a well-understood method of procedure — it was only a kind of preliminary welcome to men who belonged, in some cases, to the same part of the country as did the women . . . . At the same time three men, each armed, appeared on the top of the hill close by gesticulating wildly, as if to show the visitors that they were quite prepared to fight if necessity arose. All of this however was mostly make-believe . . . . As soon as they had passed through the small gap leading on to the ceremonial ground, they were joined by a number of the local men, all carrying arms; and then, forming in a column four deep, and led by the chief man amongst the visitors, they all ran round and round with spears aloft and high knee-action. When this little reception dance was over, the two parties separated; the local people retired to the rocks on the hillside close by, while the visitors squatted on the level ground. For a few minutes nothing was done or said, and all this time the local people, men, women and even children, were gathering on the ceremonial ground. Then without a word the leader of the visitors went round his party, collected all the flaked sticks from their heads . . . and solemnly presented them to the head man of the local group. This was as a sign that the visit was meant to be purely a friendly one. The head man made a fire and at once burnt them . . . .

This ritualised Aranda meeting at Alice Springs in 1901 was described by Spencer and Gillen. The strangers are advancing on the host group in mock warlike formation. (Baldwin Spencer no. 786, courtesy Museum of Victoria)

After this things began to get decidedly more lively . . . . It was more than three of the younger men could stand, to see, sitting quietly in front of them, a guest who, in their opinion, had not mourned properly when death had robbed him recently of one of his numerous fathers-in-law . . . . Three of the aggrieved sons-in-law suddenly jumped up taunting the visitor as an arrant coward who was afraid to do his duty, and ended up without any warning by hurling their boomerangs at him. . . . He warded the weapons off easily . . . he first of all retaliated by throwing his own boomerang and then pranced down the flat to where his accusers stood. He embraced the oldest of the three, and then they sat down together on the ground with their arms round one another, some of the other men coming up to watch the performance. The accused man loudly expressed his determination to cut himself on the shoulder, right through to the bone, while the other man, instead of taunting him further . . . tried to soothe him and begged him not to injure himself too much. The final result was that he slightly cut his shoulder with a stone knife, and thereby completely re-established friendly relationships between himself and his accusers. . . . Accusations of all kinds were bandied about from one individual to another until there was probably not a single man, visitor or host, who had not been accused of doing something which he ought not to have done. Then the women took a hand for half an hour . . . [until] . . . the disturbance suddenly fizzled out.

As in the previous encounter reported by these two anthropologists, both parties were prepared for the meeting, and decorated and armed themselves accordingly. Although they were affiliated groups and understood their kin and classificatory relationships, these had to be re-ascertained and played out in public. Both parties allowed time for preparation and assembly, keeping their distance meanwhile. The encounter was then staged with much noise and movement, but old people were recognised as the leaders. Any possibility of massive conflict was resolved symbolically, by the public burning of the flaked sticks. Then it was time for the lesser personal and clan feuds to be acted out by the more aggressive young men. Injuries sustained were more symbolic than serious. Once these lengthy preliminaries were disposed of, amicable relations resumed and the real ceremonial activities could commence.

The relevance of this incident to understanding European encounters is considerable. Difficulties arose, as Hallam elaborates, when a contact was not properly arranged. The white visitors might be unexpected, and the two parties also were so unrelated that it was impossible to ascertain any appropriate affinity and status, or to assign modes of behaviour. One option was for the Aborigines to ignore the newcomers (so explorers reported deserted encampments). Another possibility was to rattle spears or shout in warlike fashion in the hope of frightening the newcomers away. In Victoria during 1838, E.J. Eyre's party encountered "much alarmed" people, who "set fire to the grass to windward of us, hoping to drive us off . . . all the time making the most horrible noises and grimaces". There was no violence. Major Mitchell unknowingly experienced both responses on his expedition to Queensland in 1846. Armed bands frequently approached in a threatening manner, on one occasion with bodies painted. Yet nothing violent happened. In the Barcoo River region the expedition noticed remains of fires and mussel shells "in heaps like cart loads", but they saw nobody. Even eight days later, beside lagoons abounding in wildfowl and discarded shells "as to resemble snow covering the ground", they met no one.

After communities became accustomed to the presence of Europeans, there were later occasions when they attempted to formalise relations. At a personal level, a few obviously sympathetic persons were assigned formal classificatory status. George Grey was possibly the first celebrity so regarded, around 1840 in southwestern Western Australia. Alfred W. Howitt, in Gippsland during the eighties, and Frank Gillen, at Alice Springs during the nineties, were others. Usually, however, their peaceful ritual mode of approach to Europeans (armed, gesturing and body-painted, for example) was misunderstood. They were rebuffed as intruders or assailants.

It must be remembered, also, that many contacts involved the Aborigines' first sight of white people. Their dramatic appearances by sea from a sailing ship, or by land on horseback, must have been traumatic experiences, perhaps even Dreaming events involving semi-divine beings, or people returned from the dead. Their clothing, carts, livestock and explosive guns, all must have proved frightening or mysterious. When Kimberley people first saw camels coming over a sandridge, "they were terror-stricken", reported L.A. Wells in 1896. Impulsive reactions might be expected, sometimes violent. At other times, spontaneous nervous responses could be attributed wrongly by the newcomers to low intelligence. Mitchell recounted two interesting reactions on his Queensland expedition. As the Aborigines he met understood neither himself nor Yuranigh, his Wiradjuri guide, they simply repeated every word spoken to them. On another occasion, a frustrated elder "burst into tears, finding himself incapable either in words or deeds for a meeting so uncommon".

It is tragic that Aboriginal intentions and responses were misunderstood on so many occasions. To most settlers, if Aborigines were armed and noisy, an attack was feared imminent; if nobody was visible, the treacherous cowards were lurking in the bush waiting to attack. It was best to anticipate the worst and have a rifle ready. This combination of ethnocentric contempt for an "inferior" race, fear of "savage" violence and a total lack of understanding of the social basis of Aboriginal law, resulted in many encounters proving fatal. Beyond those psychological factors lurked the matter of conscience. Europeans occupied Aboriginal lands and displaced people without alternative recompense. It was this "suffocation of conscience" which, W.E.H. Stanner believed, makes racial relations in Australia "the history of indifference".

Cape
Keerweer

CHAPTER TWO

Confrontation near Cape Keerweer

Unequivocal historical evidence establishes that Europeans first met original Australians in the Torres Strait region. The associated events foreshadowed the fatal course of racial contact. By a remarkable coincidence, explorers from Protestant Holland and Catholic Spain both sailed those waters during 1606. They voyaged in opposite directions and in complete ignorance of each other. Possibly Portuguese vessels had visited a century earlier. If so, no material traces affecting contacts with Aborigines are known, and so secretive were the Portuguese about their voyages, that evidence for their presence in Australian waters has to be inferred indirectly.

Around March, 1606, Willem Jansz navigated his tiny yacht *Duyfken* on an easterly route from Java, along the southern New Guinea coast. Unfortunately his journal is lost, but surviving fragmentary reports indicate that he almost entered the western entrance to Torres Strait, but failed to grasp its importance. Just before reaching its many-islanded sea, he swung his course southward, thereby meeting the western tip of Cape York. Probably this earliest recorded European landfall was at Pennefather River. *Duyfken* coasted south until reaching the point of return. Jansz named it Cape Keerweer (or Turn-again). On the voyage north, they entered Batavia (Wenloch) River, near modern Weipa. There a sailor was killed. No details are known of this fatal encounter, but spears were thrown "by wild, cruel dark barbarians".

About six months later, two vessels commanded by Luis Vaez Torres and Diego de Prado sailed safely through Torres Strait from east to west. These persistent Spaniards began their voyage in Peru and sailed on from Torres Strait to the Philippines. The symbolism of the year 1606 for Australia's contact with seafarers from the world beyond, was increased within a few weeks. While sailing on around West Irian, Torres's ship met "Moors". These Islamic traders

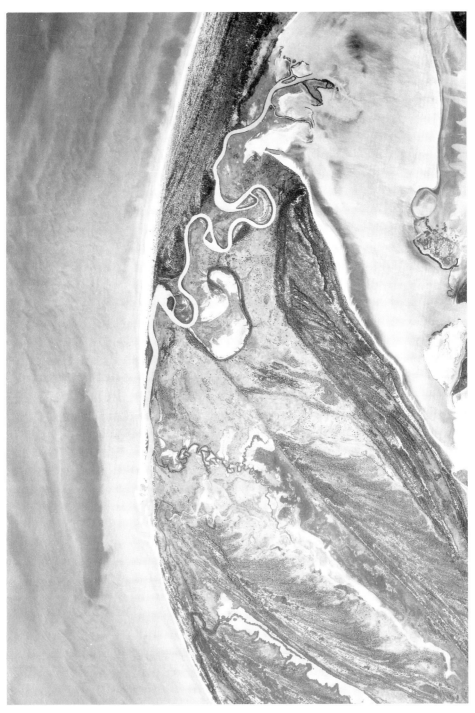

An aerial view of Cape Keerweer (Turn-again), named in 1606 by Willem Jansz. The cape is south of the mouth of the south-flowing Kirke River, where the smaller creek enters the sea. Note the parallel lines of sand dunes and the shallow water, which made this coast unattractive to Dutch explorers. It is probable that the coastline has advanced westward during the intervening 382 years. (D 54/7 Aurukum, Division of National Mapping)

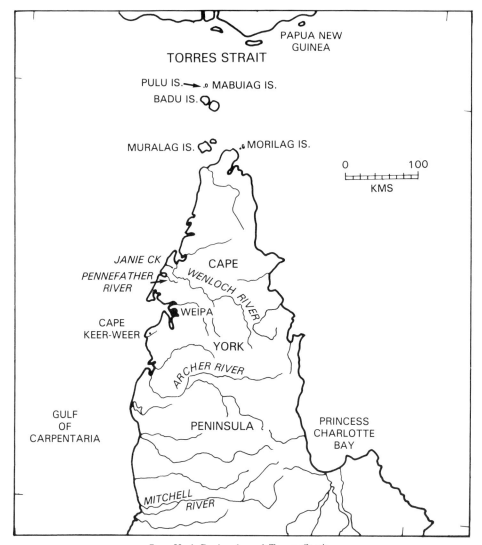

Cape York Peninsula and Torres Strait

probably were Buginese or Macassarese people from eastern Indonesia. If they had not already entered Australian waters by that time, they would do so later. Europeans in the nineteenth century knew them as "Malays" or "Macassans".

Torres probably sailed close enough to Cape York to view it, but his route through Torres Strait is a matter of dispute. More importantly, the crews landed on islands in Torres Strait (so named by later British, not by Torres). During the several weeks when they cautiously worked their vessels through the shoals and reefs, they landed to replenish their water supplies. Prado noted that, when his boat approached an island, "the indians took to the hills". Unfortunately, they were less prudent when Torres landed. Torres later wrote to the Spanish king, describing that part of the voyage which commenced in the Louisiade Archipelago and included Torres Strait. During their various landings, he reported, they kidnapped "twenty persons of different peoples, in order with them to give a better account to Your Majesty . . . although up to now they do not make themselves understood well". Nothing further is known about these sad captives, who evidently reached the Philippines, but they probably included Torres Strait Islanders.

The Aborigines of Cape York also were the first Australians to be described by outsiders. Jan Carstensz focused European attention upon Aboriginal Australians through his experiences there during April and May 1623. His tiny and rather unseaworthy yachts, the *Pera* and the *Arnhem*, traversed over 700 kilometres of Cape York's western shore late in the wet season. Although they failed to probe any entrance to Torres Strait, they extended Dutch knowledge south beyond Cape Keerweer to around the Gilbert River. Fortunately the records of the *Pera* survived. They show that Carstensz was a conscientious leader, who recorded events in fair detail in his journal. He led eight of their seventeen attempts to land on the shore, in order to take on water and to assess local resources and the inhabitants. Aborigines were encountered on nine occasions and his fleeting observations establish that Aboriginal land use and technology in 1623 was as well adjusted then as it was three centuries later.

Carstensz felt depressed by the flatness of the country and its lack of economic potential. He hoped for spices, cloth and precious metals, unaware that the red cliffs of weathered laterite near Weipa consisted of aluminium-rich bauxite, destined to ensure further encounters centuries later. The sandy coastal fringe mostly consisted of a series of ridges, salt flats, swamps and innumerable mangrove-lined tidal creeks. These alluvial flats were far richer in good resources than the Dutch appreciated. Stretching inland for five to twenty or more kilometres, this landscape produced vast supplies of edible tubers and corms, fish, shellfish, crabs, wildfowl, honey, various edible fruits, reptiles, marsupials and plants during both the wet and dry seasons.

Some idea of the richness of food resources, not apparent to Dutch merchants more interested in finding an export economy, is provided incidentally by Carstensz. He estimated that the large groups of people whom they met at intervals along the coast numbered up to 200 individuals, so the coastal zone was well populated. This is emphasised by the probability that, by May, when the country was drying out and becoming accessible, some groups would have moved inland to exploit their clan territories. Another indicator of productivity was recognised only recently. There are many shell mounds on the Love River, north of Cape Keerweer, while there are immense mounds further north, near Weipa, on the Embley and Hay Rivers. It is estimated that these latter mounds contain over 200,000 tonnes of shells (chiefly cockles). Many of these 500 shell dumps, or middens, are little more than a metre high, but some stand out in this flat landscape as hills, up to thirteen metres high. The largest contains over 9,000 cubic metres. Radiocarbon dating proves that all this food was harvested, cooked, and the shells discarded, during the last ten or twelve centuries. They were forming when the Dutch arrived. Most of these mounds are on the Register of the National Estate, constituting some of the world's largest surviving shell middens.

The region retains its importance today for Wik-speaking Aboriginal people. A recent survey of traditional sites within a radius of less than thirty kilometres from Cape Keerweer mapped over 300 places known as clan localities for food resources, camping or ceremonial activities. Of those clan territories stretching from the Archer to the Kendall Rivers, some 800 sites have been mapped, further testimony to the intensity of occupation.

It is interesting that Carstensz described items of material culture which match closely with those of three centuries later. Spears and hooked spear-throwers were universal, as were stone and bone tools. Resin was used as an adhesive and woven fibre containers were common. Body decoration included body painting, feathers and nose-bones. Breakwinds were situated on the beach in order to maximise the breeze. Carstensz mentioned roots as a food source, and at that season tubers and corms were indeed basic resources. Presumably Carstensz witnessed the traditional activity of firing the country, because he twice noted that thick smoke haze made the coast invisible.

Previously, on their voyage to Cape York along the southern coast of New Guinea, disaster had struck the expedition. The *Arnhem's* skipper sent men ashore without informing Carstensz on the *Pera*. Evidently discipline was lax, and ten crew members died when Papuans attacked them. Perhaps understandably, therefore, all landing parties on Cape York were well armed and alert.

The first Aborigines were seen north of the Edward River, but the first close encounter occurred near that river on 18 April. When a wary party landed, they were met by large numbers of inquisitive people, both armed and unarmed. They "showed no fear and were so bold as to touch the muskets of our men . . . while they wanted to have whatever they could make use of". This peaceful and historic meeting between the two races soon ended. The visitors "diverted their attention by showing them iron and beads, and espying vantage, seized one of the blacks by a string which he wore round his neck and carried him off to the pinnace; the blacks . . . set up dreadful howls and made violent gestures". It is evident that the Europeans were the aggressors. Not surprisingly, when a shore party was cutting firewood on the following day, they were attacked. During that exchange, an Aborigine was shot.

Because Carstensz was instructed to capture informants for interrogation by Dutch East India Company officials, he later offered to pay any crewman ten pieces of eight if he kidnapped an Aborigine. As he shrewdly noted, "the men may use greater care and diligence". However, two weeks passed before he paid any reward. By that time they were headed north and were back at the Archer River. When the Dutch landed there amongst the peaceful and curious Aborigines, they distracted them with another display of beads and metal. Two sailors seized an unarmed man and held him round the waist and by a noose around his neck. As he was dragged away to the boat, his people attempted to rescue him, and one of them was shot. Three days later, probably on the Wenloch River, near Mapoon, 200 armed men opposed their landing. When an Aborigine was wounded, he was seized and the unfortunate man died while being rowed out to the *Pera*.

Carstensz felt aggrieved that, although "we have treated the blacks or savages with especial kindness, offering them pieces of iron, strings of beads and pieces of cloth . . . in spite of all our kindness and our fair semblance the blacks received us as enemies everywhere". Despite these protestations and gifts of trinkets, obviously the Dutch were the aggressors. They had been received with interest on their first landfall, but with prudence on several occasions when the Aborigines hid. Although the Aborigines appeared normally armed, they did not resort to force until the Dutch used treachery to capture prisoners. The cost to the inhabitants, according to Carstensz, was three dead and two kidnapped. These latter unfortunates were never heard of again.

When he assessed the potential of this coast for his employers, Carstensz judged the region and its people harshly. The land, he concluded, was "the most arid and barren region that could be found anywhere on earth; the inhabitants, too, are the most wretched and poorest creatures that I have ever seen". "A barren and arid tract", he repeated five days later, "without any fruit-trees, and producing nothing fit for the use of man". Even so, on the day in which he wrote so negatively, he had landed and "gathered excellent vegetables or pot-herbs". His pessimism foreshadowed the famous comment of the first English visitor to Australia. William Dampier's shrill and dismissive words on the Kimberley coast during 1688, have echoed down the centuries — "the miserablest people in the world".

Such findings satisfied single-minded Dutch merchants, who left Australia largely alone as their empire expanded. There is a hint in his journal, however, that Carstensz preferred not to return to this shallow and shoaly coast with its armed spearmen. Like all Dutch explorers, he seldom walked out of sight of his ship. After all, a flat and watery landscape should not have proved unfamiliar to a Dutchman, and he did compare the two lands. The numerical superiority of the population impressed him. As he observed of the Dutch, despite the advantage of their muskets, their powder could become damp during the wet season and sheer numbers might overpower them.

The prompt departure of the Dutch, their adverse reports on this and other expeditions, and a failure to penetrate the coastal fringe, must have been assisted by a fear of Aboriginal attack. Oral tradition amongst Aboriginal people on this coast today claims that the Dutch settled there before abandoning the area. Although their facts are wrong, because the *Duyfken*, *Pera* and *Arnhem* remained no more than two days anywhere, there is a sense in which the threat of Aboriginal attack on their tiny ships and small crews was a deterrent. An Aurukun elder spoke in opposition to an Anglo-Dutch mining venture in 1975. "They had defeated the Dutch before at Cape Keerweer", he asserted, "and they could do it again."

Tasman voyaged along this coast in 1644, but no records survive. Cape York was otherwise avoided by the Dutch until 1756. History then repeated its dismal saga. J.E. Gonzal anchored *de Rijder* in Albatross Bay, later moving south from Weipa to the Archer River. The Dutch were greeted near Weipa by men in canoes, who beckoned them ashore and led them to welcome freshwater wells. The Dutch again initiated aggression. After supplying their hosts liberally with alcohol (arak) and sugar, on both occasions they attempted to take hostages. Having tricked the unsuspecting people, the Dutch kidnapped two men and wounded a third. Only after this gross and cynical violation of the rules of hospitality, did the Aborigines use force in vain attempts to free their kin. At least one of these captives reached Batavia, where he learned to speak a Malay language.

Probably both the captives lived on in Batavia as curiosities to be exhibited to travellers. In 1774, Lord Monboddo (James Burnet) published the first of his studies *Of the Origin and Progress of Language*. In developing his notion that speech was not natural to the human race, but was developed through human intellect, he claimed that groups of primitive people existed (amongst whom he included orangutangs!) who knew no speech. It was eccentric ethnology, but its invalidity is irrelevant here. What matters is that he supported it by citing contemporary "people living in the lowest state of barbarity". Monboddo continued, "And I know a gentleman who saw in Batavia two savages brought from New Holland, that appeared to him to be perfectly stupid and idiotical, though he had no reason to think that they were more so than the other natives of that country." On the basis of Gonzal's sample, therefore, people who were not like the ill-informed and uncomprehending "gentleman", were dismissed as a continent of sub-humans.

Cape York beaches from Mapoon to beyond Cape Keerweer therefore witnessed the first recorded European contacts with Aborigines. The curious but welcoming indigenes first experienced here those twin symbols of white intrusion — guns and alcohol. Their society was judged savage by sailors, whose false sense of racial, moral and cultural superiority justified their treachery and violence. Cape Keerweer was a landmark which played an important role in all early Dutch voyages and featured on charts. Probably because it was mentioned in mission schools along this coast, Cape Keerweer also became identified in Aboriginal oral tradition as the place of the first racial encounter where huts were constructed. It has been listed on the Register of the National Estate as a symbol of that meeting of cultures.

Were these 1606 and 1623 visitors the first foreigners on northern Australian beaches? Papuan canoes surely reached the islands of Torres Strait and Cape York, and this subject is discussed separately. Whatever special pleaders may claim, no certain visits by aliens can be authenticated. This book relates to encounters or places for which positive evidence exists. Substantive evidence is lacking to support those romantic enthusiasts who conjecture earlier Asian or European voyagers. Examination of the unsubstantiated assertions made by lunatic fringe theorists merits a separate book. These include champions of contact from Egypt of the pharoahs, Israel's lost tribe, and beings from outer space. It is necessary to refer to them, because such theories impinge upon popular concepts of Aboriginal society.

There are two candidates for plausible landfalls in Australia, but no matter how convincing the case, archaeological substantiation is lacking. The first concerns the fleets of Chinese junks commanded by eunuch Ch'eng Ho between 1405 and 1433. His junks made the Ming Dynasty known throughout western Indonesia, and they even cruised in Timorese waters. As trade and monsoonal winds blow constantly across the Arafura Sea, it is possible that junks reached Australian shores, either by chance or design. There is no evidence that such voyages took place. A soapstone figurine found under a Darwin banyan tree in the 1870s has too many alternative possibilities to be cited as evidence.

The case for Portuguese contact has been argued forcefully in recent years. The strongest claims for their voyaging in Bass Strait depend upon a re-interpretation of historical events in Sumatra during the 1520s, and a reconstruction of maps of Java la Grande dating from around 1540. The coastline of southeastern Australia appears to be outlined. It has been argued that daring French seamen from

Dieppe visited western Indonesia around 1529. They possibly obtained useful cartographic information from Portuguese seamen, with whom they socialised in Sumatran wharfside bars. Upon their return to Dieppe, masterly cartographers incorporated their information on superbly crafted maps. The Portuguese bureaucracy was so secretive about discoveries, however, that these restricted matters never appeared on Portuguese maps. That such data were recorded in their files is admitted, but these probably (and conveniently!) were destroyed in the great Lisbon earthquake of 1756.

It would be foolish to deny the possibility that Portuguese ships touched Australia. After all, Portugal annexed Timor and the Aru Islands in 1511, both close bases to Australia. The problem is that there is no evidence for northern coastal contacts. The Dauphin map, produced by the Dieppe cartographers, it is claimed, reveals a detailed knowledge of the southeastern coastline, when certain manipulations are made to adjust for projection and other errors. The claim relates to the three ships under the command of Cristovao de Mendonca, which almost may have circumnavigated Australia during the early 1520s. However convincing the comparison of the re-aligned Dauphin map with the southeastern coast, Mendonca seems to have been a maritime prodigy. If he sailed down the eastern coast first, as the reconstruction requires, he voyaged in the face of the prevailing winds along the south coast until his presumed decision to turn back in the vicinity of Warrnambool. As his long voyage was unvictualled in any established port, food for three years had to be collected along the coast. This was a task which sixteenth and seventeenth century captains found difficult to accomplish. More pertinent to this book, there is no evidence for any Portuguese contact with Aborigines, except for some tenuous linguistic evidence which may link Timor with Melville Island, west of Darwin, during the early nineteenth century.

If protagonists of Mendonca's voyage appealed only to the charts, their case might be stronger, for there are remarkable resemblances to the Australian coast. Many supporters also appeal to erroneous archaeological data, and this wishful thinking is unscholarly. Such are the alleged Portuguese cannons found early this century in Napier Broome Bay, on the Kimberley coast. Their origin and age are dubious and even if they were Portuguese, they were probably second-hand possessions, armament on nineteenth century trepanging praus from eastern Indonesia. It is interesting that Europeans living at Napier Broome Bay around 1920, considered that it was hazardous to reside on islands in that bay without arming against Aboriginal attack.

A stone structure at Bettangabee Bay, on the southern coast of New South Wales, has been claimed as a fort constructed by Mendonca's crew. In fact, the ruins date from the whaling era of the 1840s. A pot dredged from the seabed at nearby Gabo Island is attributed to the same source. While its style is Mediterranean, its form is so generalised and ubiquitous that such ceramics could have been tossed from a modern migrant ship or belong to Italian fishermen from Eden.

The trump card of the Portuguese lobby is the "mahogany" ship, long sought amongst the sand dunes west of Warrnambool. A wreck was beached there without doubt. It was first reported in 1836, but it had disappeared by 1880. Perhaps it was buried beneath drifted sand, but it has not been seen again. Its

Portuguese identification is obscure. Its timbers appeared dark and hard and its design seemed antique, so mahogany and Portuguese caravel became the popular identification of wood and craft.

Wood which was claimed to have come from this wreck was identified recently as eucalypt. Its radiocarbon 14 age also is disconcerting. The timber's age is best translated as falling between AD 1660 and 1710. Note that this dates the age of the wood, not the date of the ship's construction. Presumably, also, the softer outer growth zone of the timber would have been trimmed off, so an eighteenth century age is more probable. Perhaps this timber belonged to another wreck, however, so optimists will continue to seek the original wreck. If science has not resolved the problem in the Portuguese favour, neither has the analysis of existing documentary evidence by observers. That it was constructed of unusually hard timber and was of unconventional build seems the most that may be claimed. This surely is an unsubstantial reason for attributing the ship to Mendonca's flotilla and claiming 250 years precedence over Captain Cook.

Even more inconsequential is the evidence of the bunch of keys found at a Geelong waterfront limeworks in 1847. Governor La Trobe chanced to call there the day after their discovery and was stimulated to investigate them. Unfortunately two of the five keys had been given to a child and the three inspected by La Trobe were lost subsequently. Their finder stated that they were fifteen feet below the surface, in a shelly band, and this fact is invoked to urge their age. On the other hand, La Trobe later remarked, that "there could be no question but that they were keys, very little, if any way corroded with rust, very similar to those of the present day". It is remarkable that iron keys could survive in such good condition in a saline environment for over three centuries. It also is relevant that La Trobe described the shelly material as "so little altered as to be scarcely decayed, even preserving their enamel". Not very substantial evidence, it seems, on which to base a voyage into Corio Bay during 1522.

Instead of special pleading involving evidence which no longer survives, it is worth considering other facts. Once Flinders and Bass discovered Bass Strait in 1798, a rush of sealers descended upon its islands. These sealers came from many foreign ports, including east coast America. The period before 1836 therefore witnessed many craft in these stormy waters, constructed from various tree species and manifesting different styles of construction. Chance unrecorded wrecks on the western Victorian coast might be expected. At least, to postulate an early nineteenth century origin for the mahogany ship and the iron keys is a more plausible explanation than is the presumption that the Portuguese strewed the coast with clues three centuries earlier, and that they survived the destructive elements.

The principles of verifiable evidence and the most economical explanation also must apply to the evaluation of other exotic antiquities. These random items include Palaeolithic handaxes near Esperance (from ship ballast?), iron bolts in rock near Point Piper, "Spanish" words engraved at Bondi, an Egyptian coin of Ptolemy IV near Cairns, a Roman coin at Bendigo and Polynesian stone adzes from southeastern Australia. Returning servicemen or curio conscious ship captains were avid collectors. Their treasured souvenirs may be lost or discarded by a later generation, to be refound. Some of the alleged discoveries also may be hoaxes by publicity seekers. Perhaps it should be termed the "Lasseter syndrome''. Like Lasseter's reef of gold, some of these finds have been publicised by extrovert outback characters, unversed in archaeology, anthropology, history or verbal restraint.

Uninformed enthusiasts or cranks on the ''lunatic fringe'' denigrate the individuality of Aboriginal culture, which explains the present discussion. The indigenous inhabitants all too often are the last to be credited with originality. Possibly it all began in 1838, when explorer George Grey located Wandjina paintings in the Kimberleys, and he attributed them to foreign visitors. Ever since that time, much rock art has been attributed to alien artists. Styles and motifs are assigned to Egyptians, Indians, Assyrians, or other fabled peoples from antique lands. Others assert that Aboriginal artists simply copied designs imported from outer space. Von Daniken is amongst those ''experts'' who identify Wandjinas as helmeted spacemen, from the comfort of an overseas armchair.

Not only are such claims unsubstantiated, but they constitute a racist denigration of the creativity of Aboriginal cultures, past and present. They imply that Aborigines lacked imagination or innovation. Their ''methodology'' consists of isolating selected and visually striking designs and images from the total symbolic system in which they functioned. The Cleland Hills engravings in Central Australia are images which delighted the lunatic fringe. Only a few human faces were emphasised, chosen from hundreds of markings, and declared to be influenced from overseas. The explanation differs when these motifs are assessed within the entire corpus of this artistic complex, which stretches westwards to the Pilbara coast. Placed within context, these faces remain enigmatic, but they belong within the symbolism, inter-regional contacts and technology of indigenous art. Such Dreaming encounters took place within regional contexts and between Aboriginal minds, and not because of invaders from outlandish countries, or influences from Mars.

Karrakatta
Bay

CHAPTER
THREE

A Dampierland Tercentennial

William Dampier anticipated Governor Arthur Phillip's Australian landfall by precisely a century. The first Englishman to step ashore in Australia anchored on the western side of King Sound on 5 January 1688. This is the Kimberley territory of the Bardi people today. From Dampier's account of the *Cygnet's* course, they were in the vicinity of Karrakatta Bay, north of the modern Lombadina community settlement. Dunes fringe sandy beaches and mangrove patches, with paperbark swamps behind the dunes.

The crew beached the *Cygnet* at spring-tide, taking advantage of the ten-metre tidal range. They careened the vessel, repaired sails and replenished water supplies. As they camped on the beach and remained in the area until 12 March, Dampier had opportunities to inspect the coastal strip and some of the numerous adjacent islands. He also saw Aboriginal people at close quarters.

When this literate buccaneer published his *New Voyage Round the World*, it became a best-seller of 1697. His account of New Holland amounted to fewer than 2,500 words, but it was more perceptive and accurate than generally has been allowed. Literary acclaim won him respectability at the court of King William III, and he soon was confirmed as captain of HMS *Roebuck*, to explore the South Seas. He returned to Western Australian waters during August 1699, first exploring and naming Shark's Bay. His evident caution, through fear of shoals or of being blown onto the shore, ensured that he became frustrated by waterless fringing islands — Dirk Hartog, Bernier and the Dampier archipelago, west of the Burrup Peninsula. In desperate need of drinking water, he was too far west to find the Gascoyne or other mainland rivers, so he set his course for Timor. Therefore, his *Voyage to New Holland* (1703) only supplemented his original account and did nothing to alter his unfavourable first impression of that arid coast or its people.

South of modern Broome, on the coast of Roebuck Bay, frustration led him to set a precedent followed by many land explorers. After failing to make contact with reluctant men who ran away (not surprisingly, as Dampier's ten men were armed with muskets and cutlasses), "at last I took two men with me . . . purposely to catch one of them, if I could, of whom I might learn where they got their fresh water". At much the same latitude in the 1870s, Colonel Egerton Warbuton chained captives to trees with the object of compelling them to lead his party to water. Dampier only succeeded in provoking a fight in which one of his men was wounded, while he shot and wounded an Aborigine.

Probably because the future of Australian maritime exploration rested with the British navy, Dampier's views on Aborigines proved more influential than those of Dutch explorers. In any case, little differentiated their respective contempt expressed about Aboriginal culture. Later explorers used Dampier as a yardstick for the continent. Off the New South Wales south coast in 1770, Joseph Banks observed of distant figures on the land, that "so far did the prejudices which we had built on Dampier's account influence us that we fancied we could see the colour when we could scarce distinguish whether or not they were men". When Banks recognised differences between Dampier's statements and his own experience, he ignored the possibility that cultural differences or sheer distance explained the contrasts. He blamed the privateers with whom Dampier sailed, because Dampier probably became "a little tainted by their idle examples" and so failed to keep an accurate journal.

The Karrakatta Bay area, southwest of Swan Point, is nominated to the Register of the National Estate, because it witnessed the first British landing in Australia, and because Dampier's stay there proved crucial in forming his opinions about Aboriginal society. In their turn, they became incorporated into philosophical and explanatory models of social systems over the two following centuries. More specifically, however, Dampier referred to stone fish traps which functioned in identical fashion as presently utilised traps in the bay. While Bardi people believe that these traps have "been here since before the Bardi became men", Dampier's evidence establishes that this technology and economy have functioned at least since before white men became Australians.

A stone fish trap in Karrakatta Bay, maintained by Bardi people, where the ten-metre tidal range strands fish. In 1688, William Dampier's ship was beached near here and he described similar fish traps in operation. (Moya Smith)

Dampier was a direct and effective writer, who proved quotable as a travel writer across the centuries. No passage is better known than his striking condemnation of the physical appearance and society of Dampierland people. A part is quoted here.

> The Inhabitants of this Country are the miserablest People in the World. The Hodmadods [Hottentots] . . . though a nasty People, yet for Wealth are Gentlemen to these; who have no Houses, and skin Garments, Sheep, Poultry, and Fruits of the Earth . . . . And setting aside their Humane Shape, they differ but little from Brutes . . . .

Such sentiments doubtless attracted those white colonists who sought "authoritative" opinion for sustaining their right to dispossess the inhabitants. As will be explained later, Dampier believed that these people lived entirely on marine produce, and that there were virtually no exploitable resources on the land. This was certainly incorrect, but he erroneously provided a classic instance of terra nullius, a people who were transients in a wilderness and who made no attempt to wrest a living from the land through their own productive exertions. So his anthropological interpretation denied them any right to occupy that land under that theory. His negative comments found their way into most subsequent accounts of Australian Aborigines.

Dampier may be due for reassessment. His "purple passage" evidently was a popular journalistic summation. A shorter version (the Sloan manuscript) exists, presumably earlier, which implies no more than frustration that the crew was unable to obtain agricultural produce or meat from the inhabitants:

> For wee begun to be scarce of provision, and did not question but these people could relieve us; but after all our search near the sea side and in the country wee found ourselves disappointed, for the people of this country have noe houses . . . neither have they any sorte of grain or pulse; flesh they have not, nor . . . cattle, not soe much as catt or dog . . . noe sort of fowle, neither tame nor wild, for the latter I saw very few in the country, neither did wee see any kind of wilde beast in the country, but the track of one.

This passage reads like unadorned factual reporting. The country cannot have been so barren, yet it must have appeared so to Dampier, for whom even the vegetation was unfamiliar. In light of these conclusions, there was a sense in which the inhabitants were deprived, unfortunate, or "miserable", because in this desert even wild birds and beasts were rare. Omit the oft-quoted diatribe from Dampier's 1697 book and make allowance for some colourful seventeenth century terminology, and Dampier's account of the country is reasonable.

As for his version of Aboriginal society, it represents the most informative account by any visitor before Captain Cook. Dampier's description of stature, pigmentation, facial features and cranial shape, hair form and texture, are all identifiably Australian. So also are his statements that people congregated in bands of from twenty to thirty people, and that tooth avulsion, the absence of the two upper incisors, was general. He noted with interest that people moved between islands by swimming, without using canoes or logs. His much quoted reference to people with half-closed eyelids, "to keep the flies out of their eyes", may seem unflattering, yet it has the ring of cruel experience. His personal exasperation is reflected: flies were "so troublesome here, that no fanning will keep them from coming to one's Face; and without the Assistance of both Hands to keep them off, they will creep into ones Nostrils, and Mouth too . . . ". As the buccaneers camped for weeks on the beach, the flies must have been presented with an unprecedented breeding ground. Unlike the crew which was moored to its ship, Aboriginal people shifted camp when garbage and odour became problems.

Dampier's most immediate ethnographic observation concerned the local fish traps. Apart from three species of shellfish, Dampier believed that Aboriginal diet was exclusively fish. Quite obviously terrestrial plant, reptile, small animal and honey sources would have been exploited, and the fact that Dampier referred to spears and clubs ("swords") indicates equipment for the hunt. However, as this was the wet season, people would have concentrated on coastal resources. They also visited nearby islands, for these would be waterless during the "dry". Dampier claimed:

> Their only Food is a small sort of Fish, which they get by making Wares [weirs] of Stone across little Coves . . . every Tide bringing in the small Fish, and there leaving them a Prey to these People, who constantly attend there to search for them at Low-water . . . . In other Places at Low-water they seek for Cockles, Muscles, and Periwincles: Of these Shellfish there are fewer still; so that their chiefest dependance is upon what the Sea leaves in their Ware . . . they presently broil on the Coals . . . .

This type of trap is maintained there today and is considered the most efficient form of harvesting fish by the local Bardi community. Stone walls were built between rocky outcrops, forty metres or more apart. Many thousands of stones were collected from the vicinity for each retaining wall. The wall of one trap is 1.3 metres high and about one metre wide. Their construction and maintenance represented an important communal activity.

As there is a ten-metre tidal range, fish swim inshore on the tide and become trapped behind the wall as the tide recedes. The water continues to filter through the loosely packed stones, leaving the fish stranded in pools. It is an easy matter to collect them. One of the traps is covered by up to seven metres of water at high tide today, but the pools are exposed for collection for about five hours daily. These functioning traps can amply supply the protein and energy needs of communities, although both dietary preferences and the need for carbohydrate foods make such concentration impossible. When people move from the vicinity of a trap, the custom is to breach the dam wall, thus ensuring that the fish are not wasted. Between this deliberately destructive breaching and the natural movement of stones due to the strong currents, a continuous cycle of reconstruction is necessary. Consequently, although the modern traps may be at the same locations as those seen by Dampier, they are not the same traps. Yet the construction technology and their use are as Dampier saw them three centuries ago.

What is important about Dampier's witness, and that of Carstensz, amongst Dutch navigators of the seventeenth century, is that their descriptions accord well with the material culture practised in the Kimberleys and in Cape York over two centuries later, when European occupation commenced. Aboriginal people transmit their traditional information orally and through different art forms. Here is independent written European testimony that societies of 1688, or 1623, were indeed comparable in their material manifestations to those in 1788, or 1888.

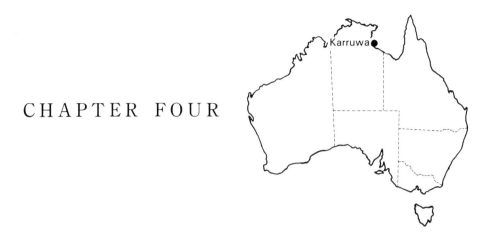

CHAPTER FOUR

Praus to Carpentaria

Karruwa or Garruwa Island (Little Vanderlin) covers only fifty sandy hectares, suitable merely for temporary human visitation. It is in the Register as a well preserved example and symbol of an Indonesian industrial and commercial enterprise, trepanging, which interacted with Aboriginal Australians. Karruwa preserves one of several extensive archaeological relics on the Sir Edward Pellew Island group, in the Gulf of Carpentaria. Dozens of similar places, but mostly less intact, occur behind the beaches of Carpentaria's islands, Arnhem Land and Kimberley. Their beginning dates at least from the mid-eighteenth century until their termination in 1906, when a racially sensitive Australian government ordered this Asian traffic to cease.

The crowded praus sailed out of eastern Indonesian harbours, especially Macassar (Udjung Pandang) in southern Sulawesi. The northwest monsoon blew them to the Cobourg Peninsula in about ten days. After coasting eastwards into Carpentaria, they returned home when the southeast trade winds commenced. Other praus ventured to Kimberley waters, but less intensively. They came to these shallow waters and sheltered, sandy bays, to collect millions of trepang (sea-slug, sea-cucumber). Although crews also bartered with Aboriginal groups for turtle shell and cypress pine timber, it was the trepanging upon which their economy depended. Its dried flesh was marketed in Canton, offering eager Chinese gourmets a combination soup and supposed aphrodisiac.

While Chinese merchants in Macassar owned most praus, they were crewed by Bugis or Macassarese, renowned seamen who became familiar to coastal Aborigines. Their now-fabled exploits are commemorated nostalgically in Arnhem Land song, dance and painting rituals. The term "Macassans" is used to refer to these visitors; the name by which they knew tropical Australia was Marege.

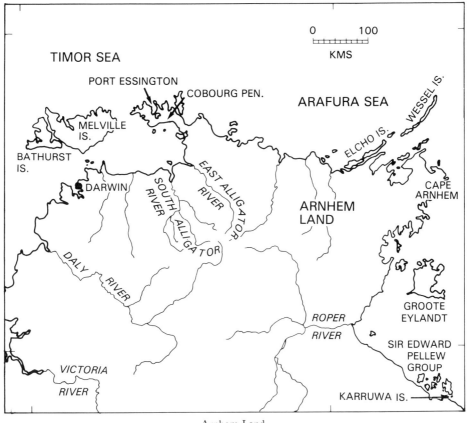

Arnhem Land

This far-flung industry became known to the European explorers during the 1803 wet season. The French commander, Nicholas Baudin, found it "extraordinary" that several praus were on the Kimberley coast during April. He called them "Malays", but likened them to Timorese. Two months earlier, Matthew Flinders encountered six praus off northeastern Arnhem Land, which he promptly named "Malay Road". His fears of piracy turned to curiosity after he met Pobasso, the informative squadron commander. He learned that sixty praus, crewed by over a thousand men, were working the Arnhem Land coast.

Pobasso's story clarified his previous discoveries in the Pellew group. When Flinders charted those islands during December 1802, he avoided Karruwa because there was shallow water in the two kilometres separating it from Vanderlin Island. On nearby Vanderlin and North Islands, however, he was intrigued by "indications of some foreign people", who discarded pottery, bamboo and other items. "But what puzzled me most", Flinders remarked, "was a collection of stones piled together in a line . . . with short lines running perpendicularly at the back, dividing the space . . . into compartments", in each of which lay charcoal. North Island produced thirty-eight such partitions.

Flinders was the first European to describe an Australian trepang processing site, in all particulars similar to the Karruwa relics. Each separate bay in the stone

Karruwa Island (Little Vanderlin), two kilometres southeast of Vanderlin Island. The shallow water and sandy western beaches made this island an ideal trepang processing site. (Department of Lands and Housing, Northern Territory, Darwin)

line was a hearth, which supported an iron cauldron for boiling trepang. Such lines contain five or six hearths, presumably the appropriate number of cauldrons supervised by one attendant. The bamboo fragments scattered about doubtless belonged to the stock of bamboo poles and rattan matting transported on praus as demountable smokehouses, in which trepang was dried. Ashy depressions in the sand mark locations of smokehouses. The necessary quantities of firewood came from adjacent mangrove stands, cut and stacked for drying on the previous visit. Surviving stumps preserve the cut marks of small metal axes. Half a hectare of mangroves had been felled for fuel on North Island, reported the *Investigator's* botanist.

The rapidity with which crews performed their industrial tasks astonished the Port Essington commandant, who visited praus on the beach south of the British settlement, "scarcely an hour after their arrival and thought to find them landing their things; but . . . a little village was formed, the fires were burning with the kettles [cauldrons] on and a party had gone out to fetch trepang, while those in camp were busy in arranging everything necessary for preparing it". One or two weeks passed while the local catch was processed, before the praus moved east to another base. As five or six praus normally collaborated, with about thirty men aboard each boat, these beach encampments must have included up to two hundred men. Not surprisingly, they left witnesses to their stay. The stone

Remains of the stone hearths on Karruwa upon which trepang were boiled. Nearby are tamarind trees which seeded from fruit brought by the Macassans. (Richard Baker)

hearths are the most evident traces. At Anuru Bay, opposite Goulburn Island, twenty-one lines survive, although it is unlikely that the hundred or so hearths were in simultaneous use.

Pottery water jar and cooking pot fragments, bottle glass and other remnants litter these sites, although the cloth and bamboo remarked upon by Flinders have perished. One imported food, tamarind fruit, has seeded. Many Macassan sites are marked by their attractive feathery vegetation, standing tall against the seascape. Karruwa has a stand of tamarinds on the foredune, a prominent feature above the low scrub and sandy heath. Regrettably, fossickers pilfer sites in mindless curiosity. These places merit greater respect, as an important heritage of non-European Australia.

Aboriginal societies were in prolonged contact with these visitors along hundreds of kilometres of coastline. Consider the numbers of Indonesians involved. At its peak early in the nineteenth century, over 1,000 men annually stepped ashore in Arnhem Land. If a conservative average work force of 400 is postulated spanning 150 years, this amounts to 60,000 visitors to Arnhem Land alone. As they frequented the beaches for some twenty weeks, each person is likely to have camped ashore at five or more different localities. The opportunities for cultural encounters were legion. Karruwa was near the end of the trepanging cycle, but even if five praus beached there every third year, over 5,000 men could have camped during 150 years.

Like the Aboriginal economy, the Macassan industry was attuned to a seasonal routine. Praus arrived with the monsoonal wet season and sailed homewards when the dry season began. They appeared around the same date annually and revisited favoured havens so regularly that, during the 1880s, the South Australian customs officer knew where to harass them for taxes. He visited the Pellew Islands in 1885. This fixed routine must have created a sense of anticipation and excitement amongst local communities who awaited their arrival. This is reflected today in traditions about those bygone times. Lazarus Lamilami, a Maung elder on Goulburn Island, recalled that his people "were very friendly with the Macassans. They used to address them by the Aboriginal words for brother or uncle or father. They were happy when the season came for them to come back."

Relations were not always so friendly. Sometimes isolated praus were attacked and plundered, for metal items and canoes provoked covetousness; hostilities also involved disputes over women; savage Macassan reprisals are known. However, peaceful co-existence was mutually beneficial, so friendly relations normally prevailed. In any case, apart from the ubiquitous kris, the Macassans possessed few muskets. As their wet season presence coincided with the maximum Aboriginal dispersal over clan territories, it is relevant that the visitors normally outnumbered the local inhabitants. Even so, the Macassans helped ensure their security by selecting small peninsula or island locations, to minimise opportunities for surprise attack. In this sense, also, Karruwa islet is a classic site witness.

Peaceful interchange permitted the Macassans to process their catch without interruption. They occasionally utilised Aboriginal labour, but chiefly they profited from Aboriginal supplies of turtle shell and, after their European introduction, buffalo horn. Permission to hew long cypress pine logs enabled building projects to be completed in Macassar, some of which still stand. With so many itinerent men, however, perhaps their chief benefit was the solace of Aboriginal women. Some prau captains are known to have formed regular liaisons at different localities, one evidently fathering nine children by three "wives". The possibilities for gene flow from such encounters are evident. As this sexual situation extended throughout possibly two centuries, it also implies that Asian diseases could have been introduced. In the case of smallpox, however, such a time frame favoured the development of immunity along the coastal fringe.

Material advantages flowed to Aboriginal communities in the form of metal hatchets and knives, glass, cloth, some rice, tobacco and alcohol. Lamilami recalled that, if the praus made a good catch, they invited Aborigines to farewell parties "with a lot of food and drinks". By this he meant anidji, alcoholic liquor. Guests were asked to store turtle shell and buffalo horn for the next Macassan visit, in reciprocity.

Each prau carried from two to six dugout canoes, used to collect trepang. Aborigines adapted their economy to these seaworthy craft with sails. Sometimes they obtained them through exchange or by salvage from wrecked praus, for many wrecks occurred. Theft was common. Later, Aborigines constructed their own canoes, using metal tools. An increased efficiency in turtle and dugong hunting resulted, as did social mobility along the coast between affiliated groups, facilitating ceremonial activities. Another social innovation was the adoption of the Macassan form of tobacco pipe. To a society in which ritualised gift exchange was universal, these new products may have enhanced the prestige of coastal people, as valued goods moved inland. A British resident at Port Essington settlement in 1842 remarked, that "all the clothes, iron, axes, etc., that the natives of the coast have taken from us goes into the interior".

Many Aboriginal men voyaged on praus. Those who travelled around the coast may have promoted friendly relations between related groups and Macassans. Others visited Macassar. Lamilami remembered that "our people liked to go there and see these different things". It is not difficult to imagine the prestige which resulted from such adventures, when "they used to come back with stories". Some were unable to obtain passages home, however, and seventeen Aborigines were reported living in Macassar in 1876. As men from all along the coast travelled to Indonesia, it reinforced the acceptance of Macassans. Place names with a Macassan origin are numerous, as are words in Aboriginal vocabularies. Art, mythology and ritual life reflect a distinctive Macassan imprint. Even eighty years after the traffic ended, contemporary song cycles and bark painting motifs are replete with Macassan associations.

In northeastern Arnhem Land, mortuary ceremonies for certain clans include the representation in sand of a prau. A mast and flag are erected within it, probably symbolising the departing spirit. Fifty years ago, another clan had adopted the square-faced glass bottle as a totemic object, while ritual paintings on a carved wooden replica included trepang. Another remarkable reflection of the

A Macassan trepang fishing depot. Harden S. Melville was an artist on HMS *Fly*. He visited Port Essington in 1843 and probably sketched this scene there. When it was published in 1862, he added an exotic mountainous backdrop. The trepang are being boiled in cauldrons standing on stone hearths; demountable smokehouses for curing are in the background; praus are beached. Note the Aborigines at the left of the picture in friendly discourse. (*The Queen*, 8 February 1862, courtesy Weekend Gallery, Canberra)

impact of the Macassan experience exists in this same region. Near Cape Arnhem, on a flat, pebbly surface by the beach, stones have been arranged into pictures covering an area eighty metres by seventy metres. Several patterns depict praus and canoes, others outline features of a trepanging complex, including hearths and smokehouses. Stones portraying buildings in Macassar also survive. On an island in Arnhem Bay, miniature models of hearth lines were constructed by local people.

While many tales recall mutual violence on the trepanging coast, Aboriginal people believe that it was a great period in their history, a golden age, contrasting deeply with European-Aboriginal relations. While time is a softener and source of nostalgia for times past, there were marked differences between the nature of Macassan and European encounters. The very survival of the Karruwa encampment reflects this reality, for it would be deemed "useless" land by Europeans.

The Macassans always were fleeting visitors, not attempting to settle permanently. They assessed a place by its sandy, isolated beachfront, rather than by its fertile hinterland. Never penetrating beyond the coastal fringe, their only explorers were captains who sought new trepanging fields within the limits of the seasonal round. Despite their boats and paraphernalia, the trepanging crews were peasant fishermen, whose material culture, living conditions, diet and social expectations were comparable, often inferior, to those of the Australians. Generally, they benefited from amicable relations, were not economic competitors, and treated Aborigines as equals. Although nominally followers of Islam, the basically animistic beliefs of these eastern Indonesians made no demands upon Aboriginal religious life.

Consequently, economic and social co-existence proved possible during a period longer than the phase of European settlement. The later white occupation involved direct competition for land, resource control and souls, by people equipped with material superiority and imbued with an assumed social superiority and sense of spiritual mission.

The remarkable permeation of Aboriginal culture by Macassan influences should provoke those who maintain that Aboriginal ceremonial life is unchanging, or that conservative elders dominate communities to such an extent that economic or technological innovation proves impossible. That is the most significant lesson of this encounter between Australians and Asians.

Adventure Bay

CHAPTER FIVE

Adventure Bay: "A Convenient and Safe Place"

On 29 November 1642, Abel Janszoon Tasman rounded Fluted Cape, on Bruny Island's southeastern shore. As he was entering Adventure Bay an adverse wind forced him to turn and run with it for two days. Tasman's first Australian landing was made, therefore, well within Blackman Bay, near modern Dunally. A monument there commemorates the occasion. Although the Dutch sailors heard noises in the bush and saw numerous "smokes", the Tasmanians remained hidden throughout their stay. Tree trunks had notches cut into them at considerable distances apart, so Tasman concluded that the people who used them as steps, "without doubt . . . must be men of unusual height". This was a credulous age, when mermaids decorated map margins and the unknown might be populated with monsters. Taking advantage of the vast empty space on contemporary charts of the southern world, the satirist Jonathan Swift later made Gulliver sail to the country of the Houyhnhnms, situated west of Tasmania.

The preconceptions of the first Europeans who actually met Tasmanians were equally fabulous, although pleasantly unreal. Marion du Fresne sailed into Marion Bay in 1772, just north of Tasman's haven. As a Frenchman, Marion was influenced by notions of noble savagery, expounded by Rousseau and apparently confirmed by Bougainville's ecstatic experiences in Tahiti only four years previously. "Everywhere we found hospitality, ease, innocent joy, and every appearance of happiness", Bougainville reported.

Anticipating a comparable state of natural innocence in Tasmania, Marion prepared for this first encounter. He arranged for two crew members to strip naked, so that they emerged from the surf as "natural" men, bearing trinkets and enlightenment for the naked islanders. Given the problems which clothing raised when later explorers landed, there was some point in this device. The pale-skinned visitors were received "evidently with joy for they put down their arms

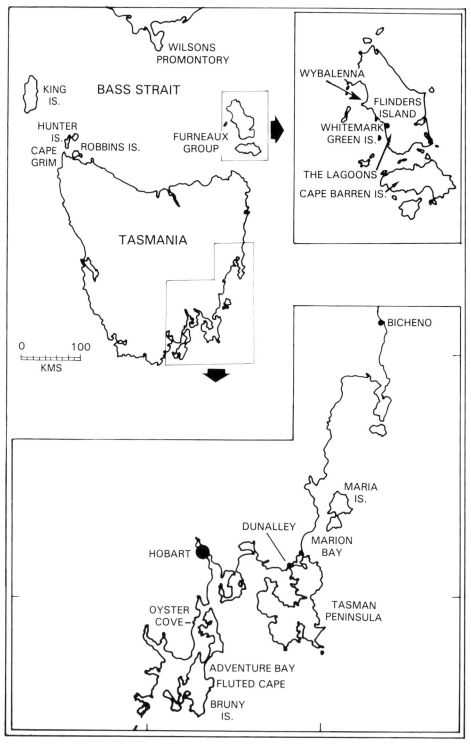

Tasmania

and approached our men". Surprisingly, to the French, "they showed little curiosity for what they had been given", except for their examination of a mirror.

The reception party probably consisted of bands of Pydairrerme or Portmairremener people, part of the Oyster Bay tribe. Following the watery arrival of the two volunteers, the longboat was beached and its crew was welcomed. Marion was presented with a burning brand in some solemn ceremony. Possibly it was a friendly gesture to warm him. In any case, he evidently erred in assuming that he was meant to thrust the firestick into an adjacent unlit bonfire pile. The main cause of deterioration in relations, however, was the approach of a second longboat. Alarm spread and it was evident that the crew should not land. Stones and spears were hurled eventually, slightly wounding Marion and another officer. The longboats backed off, but attempted another landing further along the beach. When the warriors threatened them, Marion ordered his men to fire. The age of the noble savage ended abruptly on the beach of Marion Bay. The volley "drew from them horrible cries, several being killed and several wounded".

This meeting obviously produced responses on both sides, but they were marked by mutual misunderstanding. Although further French expeditions under D'Entrecasteux and Baudin brought scientists and artists whose vision of the newly discovered people was tinged with sympathy for the independence, simplicity and nobility of a "primitive", uncluttered, lifeway, the age of scientific observation prevailed.

Having gained a beachhead in the traditional European manner of force, Marion was unaware that the "enemy" probably was following its own traditional and structured means of emphasising its rights during a meeting with visitors to its territory. Future explorers tended to treat the Tasmanians, along with the flora and fauna, as natural history specimens. N.J.B. Plomley aptly concluded that "it was scientific curiosity, in fact, that did all the damage, because it condemned the various native races to be thought of as strange species rather than as people with lives of their own".

Marion's visit, once the tranquillity of innocence was shattered by muskets, conformed to Plomley's pattern. Curious about their dark pigmentation, the body of a dead man was measured. "On washing him we found that his natural colour was reddish, and that it was only smoke and dirt that made him look so dark." (On the mainland, only two years earlier, Joseph Banks was intrigued by the same problem. He chose a living specimen: "I tried indeed by spitting upon my finger and rubbing, but altered the colour very little".) Marion's team also noted middens and identified shell species present. They observed widespread burning of the landscape, which they correctly attributed to human action. It is interesting that they found one tree unaffected by flames, which must have been deliberately protected, possibly because "the savages gained something useful from it". Mainland Aborigines in recent times certainly manipulated the flora in this manner.

Adventure Bay became the focus for much subsequent visitation. British navigators particularly found it to be a convenient anchorage for watering and wooding on voyages of Pacific exploration. It was on the sandy shore of Adventure Bay that the Nuenonne people of Bruny Island first met British seamen. For ships heading into the Pacific, the spectacular dolerite cliffs of Fluted

The black bulk of the Fluted Cape dolerite cliffs proved a landmark for early mariners reaching Bruny Island (D.J. Mulvaney)

Adventure Bay, Bruny Island, a haven sheltered by Fluted Cape. The *Bounty* anchored here in 1788. (D.J. Mulvaney)

Cape proved a landmark, for they rise to a height of 270 metres. The Fluted Cape State Reserve is in the Register, although the shore where seamen cut firewood and filled casks with water from two or three small streams is not included. Passing the northern end of these scenic cliffs and Penguin Island, vessels entered a curving bay with deep water and sandy beaches. Small freshwater streams provided water within 50 to 300 metres of the beach near its sheltered western end. William Bligh found it "a convenient and safe place for any number of ships to take in wood or water".

The bay was named by Tobias Furneaux, after his ship, which anchored for five days during 1773. His enthusiasm for the place impressed naval commanders. Cook arrived there on 26 January 1777, during his last voyage and eleven years to the day before the first Australia Day. On board was Omai, the celebrated Tahitian "type specimen" of a noble savage, then on his way back from England to Tahiti. At Adventure Bay, Omai "proved to be by far the best fisherman". On this voyage, Bligh was master of HMS *Resolution*, the ship which gave its name to the creek where they watered. Bligh returned there in 1788. He had harnessed the prevailing westerly winds by sailing east from Cape Horn, an epoch-making innovation in navigation. His voyage became celebrated for other reasons, however, for HMS *Bounty* was bound for Tahiti and filmic immortality. Bligh returned in 1792 with HMS *Providence* and HMS *Assistant*. His officers included Matthew Flinders and George Tobin, the latter a competent watercolourist. Later that year, the French expedition led by Bruny d'Entrecasteaux established that this was an island, and not part of Tasmania, as believed hitherto. In 1793, they also used the resources of Adventure Bay. On their 1798 voyage of Tasmanian circumnavigation, Flinders and Bass attempted to sail HMS *Norfolk* into the bay, but the winds proved contrary.

These British visits between 1773 and 1792 provided the first British reaction to those Tasmanians who were soon to be swept aside by British colonists. The English speaking world got to know the Tasmanians largely from fleeting accounts of the eighty or so Nuenonne inhabitants of Bruny Island. The best known of all those unfortunate people, Truganini, was born there within a few years of British settlement. The association of these factors with such luminary figures in British maritime history means that the environs of Fluted Cape assume a significance beyond that of their geological formation and natural grandeur. It is to be regretted that beachfront development and vegetation clearance conflict with these historical associations involved in a meeting of cultures.

Nuenonne-British relations during this initial period proved excellent. Nuenonne prudence in fact resulted in the failure of the Furneaux expedition to sight even a single person. They reported smoke from camp fires, burned scrub, abandoned shelters, discarded baskets and extensive shell dumps. As a parting gesture, the visitors left "medals, gun flints and a few nails" and hoop iron tied to trees or placed in shelters. These gifts possibly facilitated Cook's warm reception in 1777.

When Cook dropped anchor, however, two days passed before any people appeared, although smoke betrayed their presence. While crew members were cutting wood, they were startled when nine or ten men suddenly strode out of the bush. They were relieved to see that only one man was armed and he soon dropped his spear. They approached confidently and watched the woodsmen at work, even attempting to handle a saw. Not only were they fearless in this meeting, but Surgeon Anderson observed that they "did not express that surprize which one might have expected from their seeing men so much unlike themselves". The British were treated neither as gods nor feared aliens.

On the following morning Captain Cook and Omai landed and gifts were presented. Relations were mutually agreeable, with laughing women and children mingling. The happy occasion was terminated abruptly by the intrusion of Omai the Polynesian, the man from the third culture. The peaceful spearman had been encouraged to throw at a target. He proved so ineffective that the scornful Omai fired his fowling piece at the same point, presumably to show his superiority, and "to shew his new acquired Tricks". The stunned Nuenonne were transfixed momentarily before disappearing into the bush.

The officers feared that friendly contact was lost, so they were pleased, on the following morning, to see about twenty people waiting on the beach. Cook repeated his previous performance and loaded them with gifts. A precious sketch was made at the time. Cook appeared in full dress, a detail which may have

Cook's journal for 29 January 1777 describes meeting about twenty Tasmanian men on Adventure Bay beach. One man "was much deformed, being hump-backed, he was not less distinguishable by his wit and humour". He must be the figure in the right foreground of this picture, *Captain Cook's interview with the natives in Adventure Bay, Van Diemen's Land*. Bligh was present, and when he returned on the *Bounty* in 1788, he identified this man "for his humour and deformity". Note the parallel scars on some men, a characteristic Tasmanian ritual marking. (In the P.A. Fannin collection, Naval Historical Library, British Ministry of Defence, London. Artist J. Webber. Photographer Clare Bassett)

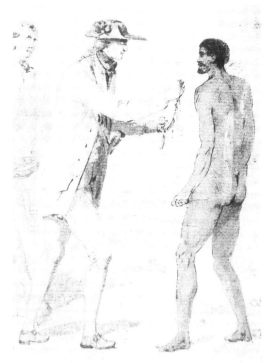

A detail of the historic encounter in Adventure Bay. "I gave each of them a string of Beads and a Medal", Cook reported. He had purchased 240 yards of ribbon for medals. One of these medals was found on northern Bruny Island in 1914. Medals also had been left previously by Captain Furneaux, who named Adventure Bay in 1773, after his ship. (Photographer Clare Bassett)

impressed the Nuenonne with the solemnity of the ceremony. Their impassive bearing may have constituted traditional etiquette, for Surgeon Samwell was interested that "they did not take so much notice as might have been expected". In their eyes, however, this shower of ribboned medals may have represented formal reciprocity for their wood, water and the excellent grass which was cut on Penguin Island for the livestock. In 1914, one of Cook's bronze medals was discovered at Killora, at the northern end of Bruny Island. The medal was struck to commemorate Cook's second voyage, so he carried a store with him, as a suitable personalised trinket. Cook had an ample store of medals, because the Navy Board had 2,000 struck in 1772, "to be distributed to the Natives".

The bronze *Resolution* and *Adventure* medal, struck in 1772 to commemorate Cook's second voyage, but also carried on his third voyage. The image of George III is on the obverse and *Resolution* and *Adventure* on the reverse; it is about forty-three millimetres in diameter. The specimen shown is in New Zealand, where at least five medals have been found. (Whakatane and District Museum, New Zealand)

These experiences can have done little to prepare the Aborigines for future racial contact and they did not further British comprehension of Aboriginal culture to any extent. However, this mutually agreeable contact did contribute to a more charitable view of the Tasmanians. In reflecting on these people, Anderson remarked with some surprise, that "these indians have little of that fierce or wild appearance . . . but on the contrary seem mild and chearfull without reserve or jealousy of strangers". "Their features are not at all disagreeable", he added, only a century after William Dampier had found Aboriginal features so repugnant.

The *Bounty* spent about two weeks at Adventure Bay during August 1788. Fletcher Christian took an armed guard when the shore party went for food and water, but there was no need to fear attack. Almost eleven days passed before Aborigines were sighted, and that was at the northern end of the bay. Bligh set off to meet with them, but a heavy surf was running and he could not land. Bligh therefore stood in the boat some twenty metres out and threw presents wrapped in paper. The Nuenonne "would not untie the paper till I made an appearance of leaving them. They then opened the parcels and . . . placed them on their heads. On seeing this, I returned towards them, when they instantly put everything out of their hands, and would not appear to take notice." No other communication between them proved possible.

Amongst the group on the beach Bligh recognised a familiar figure. He had seen him previously during Cook's 1777 visit. He was distinctive because he was deformed, and his outgoing and cheerful character made him memorable. Surgeon Samwell noticed him as a "most curious, inquisitive and busy man". Despite his hump-back "he expressed great joy by laughing shouting & jumping". Either the master of arms on *Resolution*, or as seems more probable from the style, John Webber, was sufficiently impressed to include him in his sketch of Cook presenting medals. This Nuenonne man must be the first original Australian who can be identified as an individual, with historic continuity between alien visits. He is a true Bicentennial Australian. In Arnhem Land at this same period, however, Indonesian (Macassan) trepangers were returning annually to that coast, where they must have recognised, and been welcomed, by individual men and women.

Bligh is renowned for his dedication to the propagation of Tahitian breadfruit. White Australians should honour him for his other horticultural proclivities. The *Bounty* had accumulated plants and fruits in Cape Town. It also was well stocked with gardeners, so Bligh urged them to introduce cultivated plant species to Tasmania. At selected places around Adventure Bay, therefore, they planted vegetables (onions, potatoes, pumpkins, cabbages, corn) and various stone fruit seeds, vines and "three fine young apple trees".

As the potential father of Tasmania's apple industry, however, Bligh was realistic about the chances for successful propagation. "A circumstance much against anything succeeding here", he admitted, "is, that in the dry season, the fires made by the natives are apt to communicate to the dried grass and underwood."

Bligh was a persistent man with broad scientific interests. He returned for the third time to Adventure Bay during February 1792 for two weeks. Winds and surf were so strong that the Aborigines probably exploited the lee side of the island. At least the crew encountered them briefly once only. These twenty Nuenonne accepted some biscuit as a present, but rejected other trinkets, including rings. Their "wigwams" were visible in various places and inspection established the wide variety of shellfish and crabs in their diet; "but it is remarkable we never saw any fish bones". This percipient observation by Bligh has been borne out by archaeological research. Aboriginal ancestors consumed many fish several thousand years ago, but centuries before Europeans arrived it had become a taboo food source, for reasons unknown.

Poor farmer Bligh found that his horticultural experiment had failed, but optimistically he made the best of the situation. "It was a peculiar satisfaction to me, to find one of the apple trees I planted here in 1788 — only one remained, and this altho [sic] alive and healthy had not made a shoot exceeding 12 or 13 inches." Undaunted, he planted figs, quinces, pomegranates, strawberries and nine oak seedlings. Before Bligh sailed, "as the last service I could offer this country I sent a cock . . . and two hens loose . . . on Penguin Island". Like the sow and the boar released there by Cook in 1777, there is no evidence that they bred. Presumably they were eaten by Nuennone.

Twelve months later, the D'Entrecasteaux expedition in search of La Perouse anchored in Adventure Bay. Labillardière reported seeing a notice on a tree, that "near this tree Captain William Bligh planted seven fruit trees, 1792: Messrs S. and W. botanists". Labillardière made sarcastic comment about the undue deference paid to Bligh by anonymous botanists, but recorded that all but one of the trees which they planted "had thriven very well". Despite Labillardière's disparaging sentiments, however, the initiative and optimism were Bligh's. Evidently, however, these plants failed to propagate.

Bligh's attempt to introduce the neolithic revolution to Adventure Bay failed. For another decade the Nuenonne bands continued their seasonal round as hunters, foragers and marine food collectors. Then, in 1803, a handful of Europeans landed at Risdon Cove, on the Derwent River, sixty kilometres distant.

Point Possession,
King George Sound

CHAPTER SIX

British Ceremonial at King George Sound

Captain George Vancouver was rewarded with a superb view when he climbed a steep granite rock in King George Sound, on 29 September 1791. On the bare summit of Point Possession, "the British colours were displayed, and having drunk His Majesty's health, we took possession of the country". Although the British government never recognised Vancouver's resourceful full-dress imperial action in annexing the coastal territories of the southern Nyungar people from Walpole to Esperance, his favourable description of King George Sound ensured the end of Nyungar isolation. Total annexation soon followed.

Point Possession is unaltered today. It defines the entrance to Princess Royal Harbour, across the strait from Albany. The stone cairn which tops it is a replacement for Vancouver's original stone marker. It is in the Register, symbolising Britain's first involvement in the southwest, foreshadowing positive interaction between Nyungar and early maritime explorers and the strategic settlement at Albany in 1826. Behind Point Possession, the Vancouver peninsula shelters another registered place. The Quarunup complex of buildings was a quarantine station established in 1875 to safeguard the health of new Australians.

Archaeological evidence at Upper Swan proves that the southwest was inhabited around 38,000 years ago, while around King George Sound a minimum occupation of 19,000 years is established. In 1791, Mineng dialect clans of the Nyungar language group owned the area.

During a two-week stay, Vancouver's crew failed to see any Aborigines. They visited and sketched clusters of deserted semi-circular huts, while in his ignorance of local Nyungar place names, Vancouver studded King George Sound with its present English derivatives. It was late in the wet season, when most people lived inland. However, bewilderment also may explain Nyungar concealment. Boats were unknown to them. Later observers were surprised that coastal Nyungar

The bare rock (middle ground) is Possession Point, where Vancouver claimed the region for the Crown in 1791. The view is from near the former quarantine station on the Vancouver Peninsula. The channel from King George Sound into Princess Royal Harbour (foreground) is visible behind Possession Point. Flinders staged his ceremonial farewell to the Nyungar on the Albany shore, left rear. (D.J. Mulvaney)

Nyungar territory in southwestern Australia

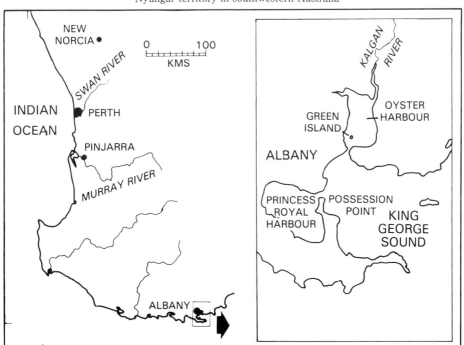

used no watercraft, and they did not swim. The sight of HMS *Discovery* and its unusual passengers may have proved a challenging experience. Presumed cultural taboos also meant that they did not gather shellfish, so Vancouver's men feasted upon immense oyster beds in Oyster Harbour.

Aborigines caught abundant fish, however, in coastal and riverine traps. Vancouver noticed stone traps on Oyster Harbour's northern shore, but he greatly underestimated their potential productivity. The remains of eight structures survive (eleven were counted there in 1818). They are in the Register. The two best preserved traps combine to extend one hundred and nine metres along the shore and almost thirty metres seaward. Vancouver also travelled up the Kalgan River, noting various fish weirs, some using wooden stakes. Remnants of stone structures still extend across the stream.

Ten years later Matthew Flinders spent December charting King George Sound. The Nyungar were exploiting their coastal resources and by now they possibly were accustomed to sea-borne visitors. Flinders soon climbed Point Possession for the view, but he based his shore camp on the site of future Albany. They maintained friendly relations with the co-operative Nyungar. Flinders found that others had visited King George Sound, and opposite Point Possession they found a "garden". It probably was the grave of the captain of the *Elligood*, who died in 1800, the first of many whalers and sealers to use the harbour, once news of Vancouver's discovery spread.

These ruffians impacted fiercely upon Nyungar society for the quarter century before the Albany settlement established more honourable racial relations. The sealers were hustlers, and they needed women. It is significant that an American brig arrived there in 1803, "on the strength of the information given by Vancouver". Although its captain had no maps of the Australian coast and had killed few seals en route, he sought 20,000 skins.

On the last day of his survey Flinders made the happy decision to honour their Aboriginal friends by staging a ceremonial parade. Probably no action by the visitors appeared more solemn or meaningful than this act of pomp and circumstance. As a spontaneous act of goodwill, this ceremony contrasts with Vancouver's imperial flag waving on Point Possession. Let Flinders recall his thoughtful gesture:

> Our friends, the natives, being at the tents this morning, I ordered the party of marines on shore, to be exercised in their presence. The red coats and white crossed belts were greatly admired, having some resemblance to their own manner of ornamenting themselves; and the drum, but particularly the fife, excited their astonishment; but when they saw these beautiful red-and-white men, with their bright muskets, drawn up in a line, they absolutely screamed with delight; nor were their wild gestures and vociferation to be silenced, but by commencing the exercise, to which they paid the most earnest and silent attention. Several of them moved their hands, involuntarily, according to the motions; and the old man placed himself at the end of the rank, with a short staff in his hand, which he shouldered, presented, grounded, as did the marines their muskets, without, I believe, knowing what he did. Before firing, the Indians were made acquainted with what was going to take place; so that the vollies did not excite much terror.

The crew's immediate embarkation probably confirmed the significance of the occasion for the witnesses. Like their traditional Aboriginal activities, therefore, this encounter was ritualised and transmitted across a century. With their outstanding flair for mimicry and parody, the happening was perpetuated in dance and song.

When Daisy Bates visited King George Sound in 1908, she was told about Koorannup, the place of the dead spirits across the sea. She identified with Flinders, a Koorannup ceremony which involved the *Investigator* crew returning from the home of dead spirits.

> They made a dance of the visit and parade . . . . I got all this from the only old man left, a grandson born about 1830 or 40. He saw the dance as a boy and taught it as a man. He covered his torso with red and put white pipeclay across the red and did with his club what he had seen his fathers and grandfathers do as the bayonets were exercised. Nebinyan died in 1908 [sic] a very old man and he could tell me all the history of the visit — its importance made it a sacred dance and memory . . . .

This episode indicates the extent to which unexpected European interventions impinged upon the belief systems of Aboriginal societies. Few Europeans comprehended the spiritual underpinning of such early encounters. This Aboriginal application of ritual exchange, of formal ceremonial involving hierarchy, persons with special functions, particular dress, and display of regalia, has application to later developments. The popularity of enlistment in the Victorian Native Police corps, in particular, is relevant. So also is the enthusiastic participation in organised European sport during the nineteenth century, especially cricket.

Sydney

The House That Phillip Built by Sydney Cove

Governor Arthur Phillip laid the copper foundation plate of his Sydney home on 15 May 1788. As the first substantial dwelling built in European Australia and the official residence of its first nine governors, its surviving foundations are in the Register. The architectural simplicity of its initial six rooms reflected the feeble hold which the commander-in-chief of the invasion fleet had upon these shores. Aboriginal shell-middens provided the lime for the mortar used. Its embellishment by successive governors mirrored increasing confidence and sense of prestige. The early addition of a verandah was an environmental concession, but Francis Greenway's major additions for Lachlan Macquarie were adaptations to the requirements of rank and European picturesque taste. Even the 1845-46 transfer to the present Government House, Gothic in design and grander in proportion, and the demolition of the original place, testify to increased security, prosperity and changing aesthetic perceptions of the colonists.

The numerous paintings of the externals of that first Government House foster a sense of historic consciousness in reliving the struggles and developments of the first half century of European Australia. This place was home and office to the most powerful individual in Australasia, and focus for much of Sydney's political and social life.

Its symbolism also for Aboriginal Australians is obvious. Here resided the power controlling this continent's occupation. Changing official policies, often ambiguous both in their intention and in their implementation, issued from here. They merit brief mention.

A British administration imbued with the perfectionist beliefs of the Enlightenment instructed Phillip, to "endeavour by every means in his power to open an intercouse with the natives . . . requiring all to live in amity and kindness with them; and if any of our subjects should wantonly destroy them or give them

This painting in the Watling Collection must date from around 1792, when Governor Phillip left the colony. It is titled *A View of Governor Phillip's House, Sydney Cove, Port Jackson, taken from the N.N.W.* Bridge Street today covers the garden and the front of the house, while Phillip Street runs to the left. The footings of the rear of the house and of some outbuildings survive. After Arabanoo died from smallpox, he was buried in the garden. (Reproduced with the Trustee's permission from a painting in the Watling Collection, British Museum (Natural History), and courtesy Friends of the First Government House Site)

unnecessary interruption in the exercise of their several occupations, it is our will and pleasure that you do cause such offenders to be brought to punishment''.

Comparable statements underpinned instructions to all incumbents of the first Government House. Moral uplift, intended to induce Aborigines to act like the British, was a policy warmly endorsed by Lachlan Macquarie, who instituted a school for Aboriginal children and an annual charitable feast and gift day for clans assembled at Parramatta. ''It seems only to require the fostering Hand of Time, gentle Means and Conciliatory Manners'', he optimistically told Lord Bathurst in 1814, ''to bring these poor Un-enlightened People into an important Degree of Civilization, and to Instil into their Minds, as they Gradually open to Reason and Reflection, A Sense of the Duties they owe . . . Society in General (to Which they Will then become United).''

Macquarie's ethnocentric assimilationist theory possibly was the Australian climax of Enlightenment thinking based upon Natural Reason. Ironically, popular opinion would align with that of his future senior judge, Barron Field. Field proclaimed that Aborigines were incapable of civilisation, because they lacked the faculties of ''reflection, judgement or foresight''.

When Governor Darling was briefed in 1825, evangelical sentiments overlay the rationalistic humanitarianism. To Darling's duties was added the instruction, to "promote Religion and Education among the Native Inhabitants . . . by all lawful means prevent and restrain all violence and injustice . . . and . . . take such measures . . . with the advice of . . . [the] Archdeacon, to be necessary for their conversion to the Christian Faith and for their advancement in Civilization".

Darling supported Macquarie's Native Institution, which had been transferred from populous Parramatta to more remote Blacktown in 1823. He involved the Church of England in the project, designed to educate and christianise sixty children. Never prospering, however, it closed in 1829. The site of this first abortive educational and missionary venture is in the Register.

Governor Gipps adhered to Colonial Office principles in 1838, when he executed seven white men involved in the slaughter of twenty-eight Aborigines at Myall Creek (another registered place). So much for justice in racial relations, but the contradictions inherent in official policy had been firmly stated three years earlier by Governor Bourke. Bourke acted promptly (and correctly, according to customary interpretations of the law) to disallow John Batman's agreements with the Yarra and Geelong Aborigines. Any Aboriginal title to land was denied: "every such treaty . . . and contract with the Aboriginal Natives . . . for the possession, title or claim to any Lands . . . is void and of no effect against the rights of the Crown".

All governors in Phillip's house reacted to Aboriginal resistance or violence. Their administrative actions reflect the contrast between Colonial Office theory and colonial reality. W.E.H. Stanner analysed the fumbling errors and misunderstandings during Phillip's regime. Beginning with ethnocentric optimism, it witnessed "romanticism turned into violence, the realism into indifference and the sardonicism into contempt".

It was Governor King, however, who confronted the dispossession issue. His 1802 proclamation outwardly deferred to administrative policy, but it offered a legal loophole for land-hungry colonists, self-defence.

> I do hereby strictly forbid any of His Majesty's subjects . . . from using any act of injustice or wanton cruelty to the natives, on pain of being dealt with in the same manner as if such act of injustice . . . should be committed against . . . any of His Majesty's subjects; but at the same time that His Majesty forbids any act of injustice . . . yet the settler is not to suffer his property to be invaded, or his existence endangered by them, in preserving which he is to use effectual, but at the same time the most humane, means of resisting such attacks.

"Effectual" defence took various forms, for which the euphemism, "dispersion", concealed the violence involved in ensuring settler land tenure. Within a few years, troops and police were hunting down Aborigines who plundered farms or who killed settlers. Naturally some positive action was required, but it frequently took the form of indiscriminate killing, often for minor offences. Like King, even Macquarie empowered angry settlers to use force, if they considered that Aborigines had broken the law. This open authority to act as accuser, judge and executioner received added sanction in 1824, when Governor Brisbane declared martial law in the Bathurst region. The missionary, L.E. Threlkeld, reported outright atrocities committed there by settlers and police.

Apart from the general symbolism of Government House for Aboriginal history, it also provided the setting for more personal encounters. The place has direct associations with the Sydney area clans of the Dharug and Kuringgai people.

Interpersonal relations at the highest level commenced on the last day of 1788, when Arabanoo was kidnapped at Manly, on Phillip's orders. By that time, frustrated and disillusioned Aborigines were attacking people and property, or avoiding settlements. Phillip held a simplistic notion of the situation. By learning the language, he hoped to end skirmishes and establish closer ties, while also finding out more about the country and its exploitable resources. He expected to impress the sullen tribespeople by demonstrating kindness and goodwill towards captives, hardly an orthodox manner of winning friends and influencing people.

Consequently Arabanoo (known initially as Manly), became the first named Aboriginal Australian to experience an extended close encounter with the invaders. A man of dignity, good humour and sturdy spirit, Arabanoo soon accepted his captivity and made no attempt to escape after his chains were released. He was interested in his unfamiliar environment, proving popular with the officers. He shared Phillip's company so comprehensively that he was described as "quite one of the Governor's family". He slept in a hut near the guardhouse, which had been built before his capture, but ate his meals with the governor. After Captain Hunter sailed the *Sirius* into harbour, Arabanoo and Phillip dined aboard.

Gentle Arabanoo "displayed . . . symptoms of disgust and terror", when he was compelled to witness a convict flogging. It was intended to demonstrate the "cause and necessity" of punishment, it being calculated that he later would expound the principles of British justice to his people. It is ironic that this arbitrary barbarity was more painful and degrading than any Aboriginal ritual practices for which the colonists denigrated "savage" society. Arabanoo was the first of his race, also, to sample systematically the curious habits of the newcomers. He drank tea "with avidity", "began to relish" bread, but treated alcohol "with disgust and abhorence".

Arabanoo therefore is a metaphor for the later history of his race. He was treated with studied paternalism, condescension or contempt, always within a harsh penal code. He was provided with the future staples — flour, tea and sugar, while the attractions of urban life and handouts bound him as securely as chains. Unlike many of his people, however, he did not seek the solace of alcohol. He succumbed within eighteen weeks to another alien disease, smallpox.

The metaphor was completed by Bennelong, his immediate successor as captive counsellor to the governor. Bennelong immediately became addicted to grog. Phillip so patronised him that he had freedom of entry into Government House, eating and drinking with Phillip, while his entourage camped in the yard. Phillip later provided him with a square brick hut on Bennelong Point. Foreshadowing the failure of so many government Aboriginal housing projects, the design was unsuited to Aboriginal needs. While it must have been superior to most Sydney housing in 1790, a contemporary noted that "neither he nor his family will live in it; they will sometimes stay in the place for a day, then make a fire on the outside of it. In short, they prefer living in the woods . . .".

By the time that Phillip departed, there were fringe-dwelling mendicants throughout the settlement. He sailed for England in 1792, taking Bennelong to meet King George III. Around that time, the convict-artist, Thomas Watling, arrived. In yet another preview of the future, Watling voiced a grievance which has many unfortunate echoes today. The preferential treatment which Phillip offered the displaced clan elders caused bitterness amongst the convicts. Venting convict spleen, Watling denounced such differentials between idle and naked savages and the convict "wretches, who are at least denominated christians". "This may be philosophy, according to the calculation of our rigid dictators", he wrote, "but I think it is the falsest species of it that I have ever known . . .". Disgruntled and prejudiced persons continue today to denounce concessions to Aborigines as unjust.

Smallpox proved lethal to Aborigines, who lacked an immunity to it. An epidemic devastated the Sydney region from April 1789. It is disputed whether it originated with the Europeans, or whether it spread from northern coasts through contact with Macassan trepangers. Its cause is less relevant here than its consequences. A massive population decline occurred around Sydney. Possibly the infection fanned across the interior along rivers, either at that time or during another outbreak in 1829, lowering the population density even before Europeans arrived to settle.

Arabanoo helped to care for his stricken people, thereby increasing his risk of infection. After an illness lasting six days, he died on 18 May 1789. William Tench, paying tribute to Arabanoo, recorded that "the governor, who particularly regarded him, caused him to be buried in his own garden, and attended the funeral in person".

First Government House site assumes great symbolic importance in the light of all these considerations. The first Aborigine to have prolonged contact with the first governor lived and died there. As he died from the most lethal affliction brought by aliens to this continent, the place also serves as a memorial to that disease.

The extensive grounds of Government House are built over today, but Arabanoo's grave is unlikely even to have survived Governor Bligh's residence. Always an energetic gardener, Bligh, who arrived in 1806, remodelled the garden. Almost a hundred convicts laboured to remove rocks and smooth the landscape, to plant clumps of trees and to lay out paths. The place soon conformed to the dictates of fashionable English landscaping. As a European tomb was demolished in the process, it is unlikely that Arabanoo's grave escaped the improving leveller's attention.

The foundations of the rear of Phillip's house and of some outbuildings survive. The New South Wales government proposes to erect a building appropriate to conserving and exhibiting the evidence at this historic place. The plans also need to take account of the symbolism of this place for Aboriginal society.

Cape Grim

CHAPTER EIGHT

Terror at Cape Grim

December 9, 1798, was an eventful day in the tragically brief career of Matthew Flinders, when Bass Strait was added to the world's shipping lanes and the route to Britain was thereby substantially reduced. Early that morning he and George Bass headed west in the waters north of Three Hummock Island. Later, when "a long swell was perceived to come from the south-west . . . Mr Bass and myself hailed it with joy and mutual congratulation, as announcing the completion of our long-wished-for discovery of a passage into the Southern . . . Ocean".

They already had been amazed by the flight overhead of a stream of mutton birds (shearwaters). It continued unabated for an hour and a half, Flinders estimating that over one hundred million birds were packed into the rapidly moving stream.

Turning into the swell, they swung the *Norfolk* south along the western side of Hunter Island, seeking the Tasmanian coast. It came into sight near dusk. Flinders noted in his journal that this northwestern cape of Tasmania was terminated by high, "dismal-looking cliffs, which appear as if they had not had a respite from the dashing of a heavy sea almost up to their summits for this thousand years". It was a symbolic place for the two explorers, as Flinders later explained in his *Voyage to Terra Australis*. "The north-west cape of Van Diemen's Land, or island, as it might be now termed", he wrote proudly, "is a steep, black head, which, from its appearance, I call Cape Grim".

It was a prophetic name, for the place witnessed grim and shocking events. Savagery occurred here around 1827, but it was virtually ignored at the time, when Aboriginal depredations and resistance had made their society public enemy one. These deeds became widely known only in 1966, when N.J.B. Plomley's meticulously edited *Friendly Mission* was published. These are the journals of George Augustus Robinson, "the conciliator", who induced most

Tasmanian Aborigines to leave the bush and go to a central "welfare" settlement in Bass Strait. Robinson twice visited the Cape Grim region, during 1830 and 1832. As he talked with Aboriginal people and with settlers about the incidents and interviewed two of the four persons directly concerned in the massacre, his testimony is significant. Modern Aboriginal Tasmanians have so identified with the sufferings of their ancestors, that they have lodged a land claim for Cape Grim.

Cape Grim is in the Register not only because of these Aboriginal associations, however, but because of its symbolic importance in the Bass and Flinders identification of Bass Strait. It forms its western bastion. It also is a striking natural feature steeply rising to a maximum height of ninety-four metres. The cliffs at Cape Grim consist of massive layers of black volcanic rocks — lavas and tuffs — of Tertiary age, resting upon Precambrian quartzites. At contact surfaces between bands of hard basalt and the softer tuff, ocean pounding and chemical weathering have produced some large caves. In places, the cliffs rise sharply to over seventy metres above the ceaseless surf, rolling in unimpeded across the southern ocean.

It is such a focus for driven winds that an important meteorological station has been established near its treeless grassy summit. Its chief function is to monitor air quality, one of a small international series of air pollution sampling stations. There are few areas where purer air might be measured more easily. It is accessibly situated at almost 41°S latitude, so the gales of the roaring forties power in. Unfortunately for the original Tasmanians, human morality at this dark place has not always matched the natural purity of its atmosphere.

Across the shallow sea at Hunter Island, archaeological excavations at Cave Bay Cave (a place in the Register) established that human visits extended back beyond twenty thousand years ago. This was a period of low sea level during the ice age, when Hunter Island and Cape Grim stood out as hills on the dry plains which connected them. Because of this proven antiquity for people in northwest Tasmania, the sea caves at Cape Grim possess potential for systematic excavation. Their unfolding archaeology could produce evidence about life there before the Europeans. Robinson visited one of them in 1830, which he described in terms which indicate that it was an important seasonal base. There is midden debris there, but as it is close to the sea, the deposit has been disturbed by storms. Even so, it has scientific and cultural potential, as well as being the scene of a major tragedy, presumably early in 1828.

At the time of contact, the coastal fringe belonged to people of the so-called North West tribe. Two other "tribes" were affiliated in some social and economic manner — the South West and the Big River people. Robinson knew the band whose territory included Cape Grim as the MIME. ME. KIN. NER or the MINE. KIN. NER. The land around the Cape may have been called MINE. DIM. MER. One resource of this area was ochre and another was seals, but its outstanding attraction was the mutton bird. Many of those millions seen in flight by Flinders nested on the northwestern offshore islands. The Doughboys provided an accessible supply within swimming distance of Cape Grim, on calm days during the summer breeding season. These birds evidently provided a dynamic mechanism for a little known system of band movements across northwestern

Tasmania, presumably involving some reciprocal economic or social exchange benefits.

People did not live by birds alone. Rich marine and coastal fringe food sources existed. The many middens in this area testify to abundant shellfish species. An enormous oyster shell and seal bone midden, further south at West Point, accumulated over two thousand years. It is in the Register. West Point midden also is important for some circular depressions on its summit. These were round huts, sunk into the mound for protection against the wind. One of the largest known clusters of these circular hollows is at windswept Cape Grim. There are at least nine of them in the area Europeans called Victory Hill. If people occupied these huts simultaneously, it constituted a village. Presumably it housed an entire band. Such a hut cluster merits inclusion in the Register, even without the other attributes of Cape Grim. Future excavations here may provide considerable insight into life before European times. At present, the Cape Grim area is known only by the descriptions of Robinson, made at a time when the traditional society had been decimated.

Following the voyage of Flinders and Bass, the people of the northwest suffered under two onslaughts. The first was an immediate influx of sealers to the islands and their capture of Aboriginal women, a matter discussed elsewhere. The landtakers proved equally brutal. It is relevant that most of the men who supplied the labour force for both developments were former convicts or escaped convicts, at that time living beyond the effective reach of the law.

From 1826 the Van Diemen's Land Company was granted over 100,000 hectares of northwestern and offshore island land, intended for grazing sheep. When Robinson first visited Cape Grim in June 1830, the VDL Company maintained four sheep runs there. Two years later, 3,000 sheep and about thirty employees were in the area.

Although the London directors instructed their field superintendents to live amicably with the Aborigines, violent actions by their work force virtually were ignored. Even the VDL Company's senior officer, Edward Curr, was equivocal. In his dealings with the governor, he minimised racial violence, while he turned a blind eye to most actions. Aware that government officials in Tasmania or London might prove critical, he wanted justification for all actions, so his files were in order. Minor pilfering therefore should be tolerated, but the killing of a sheep or other indications of "hostile intent constitute good grounds for retaliation". In contemporary Tasmania, retaliation was a euphemism for execution. At a period when laws in Britain were being applied in less draconian fashion, Curr clearly held that any attack on property, such as sheep spearing or hut burning, merited death. Whereas British law prosecuted the offender, frontier conditions left discretion in the hands of those holding the rifles. It is surely a significant indicator of prevailing attitudes that, although records document the killing of only three Europeans by Aborigines in northwestern districts, at least sixty-nine Aborigines were shot.

The sequence of events at Cape Grim may be reconstructed from Robinson's journal, although there are options, depending upon whose version is accepted. According to the shepherds questioned by Robinson, it all began around late 1827 with an unprovoked attack by warriors. A hut was raided and a shepherd was speared in the thigh; meanwhile "several blacks" were shot. Later, and presumably in retaliation, thirty sheep were driven over the cliff. (The number of sheep destroyed may have been greater.) So the situation built up to a flash-point and four shepherds planned massive retribution. Robinson talked with two of these men during his 1830 visit, William Gunshanan and Charles Chamberlain.

Robinson was told a different version by Aboriginal women living with sealers within twenty kilometres of Cape Grim. Trouble began, they said, when these shepherds "got the native women into their hut and wanted to take liberties with them, that the men resented it and speared one man in the thigh; that they then shot one man dead, supposed the chief". Sheep were later driven off the cliff top. The accounts are similar, but the shepherds omitted the first step in the saga, and one which is plausible given the relations between settlers and women at this period.

Innocent people now moved into the tragedy. What probably was a band of northwestern tribe people arrived for their seasonal mutton birding activities. The able bodied men and women swam over to the Doughboys for the birds, leaving their children in the care of the old people at a cave at the base of the cliff. At this spot it was possible to descend the sixty metres or more from the cliff top, along a steep path. It made an excellent camping place. There still is a spring of good drinking water today near the bottom of the path, close by the cave. It is a spacious cavern, according to Robinson measuring "forty by seventy and forty feet high".

It was fine weather and the sea was calm, so the expedition was successful in taking mutton birds, which were tied in bundles in grass and towed back to the cliff. The band was sitting round the fire sampling their newly won delicacies when the four shepherds rushed in with guns firing at "those unprotected and unoffending people". Thirty people died, according to Robinson. This was equal to an entire clan's membership, or as many people as occupied the "village" of hut circles on the hillside above. Some died where they sat at the hearth; others dashed into the sea; those who ran up the pathway were chased and forced over the cliff; some gained the clifftop, but were shot and were hurled over the cliff, alive or dead; an old man who hid in a cleft was shot in the head. Robinson saw human bones at the base of the cliff over two years later.

When Chamberlain recounted the incident to Robinson, he "related this atrocious act with such perfect indifference my blood chilled". Two months later he met the unrepentant Gunshanan, who "seemed to glory in the act and said he would shoot them whenever he met them".

By that time, however, two or three years had elapsed since the Cape Grim massacre. Robinson found that this continued hatred of Aborigines was shared by A. Goldie, the company supervisor for the Hampshire-Surrey Hills district. A few months after Robinson's visit, Goldie's brutality proved too much even for Curr, who forced his resignation. Goldie shot a woman walking with her child on Emu Bay beach. Curr condemned the killing as "revolting" and "murder in the moral sense". As martial law had been proclaimed before the murder, the solicitor-general ruled that Goldie could not be committed for the crime.

Curr had justified a previous killing by Goldie and others, during the interval between the Cape Grim and Emu Bay murders. Aborigines had attacked shepherds and wounded four of them, including Gunshanan. The resulting European retaliation killed several Aborigines. Surely though, the attack on the shepherds was itself a retaliation for the Cape Grim events, in which Gunshanan took part. The interpretation of law favoured violent settlers.

In Europe around this period, Gothic romances and Pharaohs' tombs excited a morbid interest in violent death and the macabre. *Frankenstein* was a creature of

Cape Grim cliffs above the site of the Aboriginal massacre. There are caves in the basalt near beach level. It was here that G.A. Robinson reported, "those poor creatures who had sought shelter in the cleft of the rock they forced to the brink of an awful precipice, massacred them all and threw their bodies down". (J. Stockton)

this time. Robinson echoed the ethos of his day, but his reflections were based upon stark reality: "Whilst I stood gazing on this bloody cliff, methought I heard the shrieks of the mothers, the cries of the children and the agony of the husband who saw his wife, his children torn forever from his fond embrace . . . I hastened from this Golgotha."

The hill above this sad place is known as Mount Victory. It was a victory for terrorism and a Pyrrhic victory for European colonists. It is small wonder that contemporary Aboriginal Tasmanians recall the past with horror and anger, and claim something special about the spirit of Cape Grim. Regrettably, George Augustus Robinson's sanctimonious and misguided approach was destined to destroy those people with disease and spiritless morale, just as surely as those armed thugs whom he condemned.

On Robinson's second visit to Cape Grim during 1832, however, he was prophetic: "Their country has been torn from them, their wives and daughters violated and carried into captivity, the men have been murdered for sport and cruelties at which the mind revolts have been practised upon them, but though slow to enrage they never forget an injury."

CHAPTER NINE

Wybalenna
Oyster Cove

"Civilized off the face of the earth" at Wybalenna and Oyster Cove

Before Europeans arrived, the Bass Strait islands were uninhabited. They rapidly became bases for sealers, who captured Tasmanian and mainland Aboriginal women for solace and to work for them. These hardy groups were widely dispersed by 1830. It was in November 1830 that George Augustus Robinson took the first batch of his trusting, voluntary Tasmanian followers into exile in those waters. Their first temporary refuge was just offshore, on Swan Island. Within the next four years Robinson conducted virtually all surviving Tasmanians into protective custody in Bass Strait.

Robinson made a series of epic journeys around Tasmania, which rank as major colonial explorations. He befriended the Aborigines, recording his daily activities in his journal. Their remarkable detail and immediacy make them a vital source of information both for the nature of Aboriginal society and the fatal impact of white settlement. Initially, people felt secure to follow the "conciliator", expecting to escape the horrors of repression and the passions of white men. Martial law had been proclaimed in 1828, and events such as the Cape Grim massacre, and the Black Line military operation then in progress, made Tasmania unsafe for the original Tasmanians.

Sadly, their future condition proved little better than their present state. In advance of their evacuation, little attempt was made to locate and prepare a haven suitable for their needs. Yet their well-being depended upon finding an environment sheltered from stormy Bass Strait, which offered opportunities to resume traditional food getting activities, ample fresh water, and soil suitable for vegetables and crops to sustain their artificially concentrated population. Vain, and now famous, Robinson was more concerned to round up all Tasmanians, than to plan an appropriate new home. Few of the Europeans placed in command were suited temperamentally, while many lesser officials and convicts assigned to assist were unsympathetic, unskilled, or unstable. Robinson delivered his lambs for slaughter by neglect, ignorance and disease.

After about eighteen weeks on Swan Island, the small group spent a week on Preservation Island. Increasing numbers of deportees then lived on Gun Carriage (Vansittart) Island for seven months. When the Tasmanians moved again, in November 1831, their destination was The Lagoons location on Flinders Island; they numbered about seventy-five. These voyages across rough seas wider than any traversed by Tasmanian watercraft, must have proved traumatic experiences. It added to the shock felt by the shattered groups from diverse regions, speaking different languages, adjusting to life together. Now, these disoriented survivors were evacuated to lands unknown to them. Being uninhabited, no clan owned them, so they had no traditional points of reference. If their own estates had benign Dreaming origins, these unfamiliar island prisons were the stuff of nightmares.

The population at The Lagoons soon exceeded 100, as more people were ferried from Tasmania. It was a bleak place, delimited by parallel natural features. The long windswept beach was backed by some ten kilometres of unbroken sand dune, behind which lay a band of swamp. Three kilometres across the sea was Green Island, long and low, providing the only boat anchorage for this ill-chosen settlement. People huddled by the beach, where drinking water was of poor quality; yet the lagoons were sodden places in winter. It is remarkable that only three persons died during their residence there, partly to the credit of W.J. Darling, the imaginative commandant during later months.

Wybalenna in 1845, as seen by Skinner Prout in *Residence of the Aborigines, Flinders Island*. The hospital and the surgeon's residence are the nearest buildings (centre right). To their left is the chapel and behind it is the L-shaped terrace of twenty cottages. The commandant's house is in the centre distance. (National Library of Australia)

Wybalenna

Darling moved the settlement twenty kilometres north in February 1833. Settlement Point, later Wybalenna ("Black Man's houses"), impressed James Backhouse, a humanitarian visitor, shortly before the place was occupied. His description in October 1832 is applicable even today: "There is considerable extent of grassy land about this point. A great part of it is level and with but little wood upon it. Northward . . . rises a ridge of grassy hills, also thinly wooded."

Exactly three years later, Robinson arrived as commandant. He walked the kilometre from the beach, "along a valley studded with trees of evergreens . . . and as the day was remarkably fine had a delightful effect . . . . The different cottages, which skirt a plain . . . had a village-like appearance."

In 1892 Bishop H.H. Montgomery of Hobart (father of the field marshal) visited Wybalenna and took four photographs. This view shows the Aboriginal terrace standing to roof height. The chapel is on the left and the commandant's house, rear right. The bushes, right foreground, may mark the site of the surgeon's residence. (Mitchell Library, State Library of New South Wales)

Wybalenna in 1986, viewed from virtually the same vantage point as that used by Skinner Prout (p.54). Only the restored chapel and the altered commandant's residence survive. The L-shaped terrace is now a grassy mound behind the chapel. To the left of the trees (extreme left centre) is the cemetery. (D.J. Mulvaney)

Viewed from the slopes above Wybalenna today, the setting is picturesque, with the sea and islands in the distance. At the time, it attracted the artists, Skinner Prout and Simpkinson De Wesselow. Its advantages surpassed earlier settlements, but this was no idyllic retreat. Even Backhouse had noted the poor water supply, which remained a problem because nothing was done to improve the supply. Most of the settlement area is in the Register as a place of great significance to Aboriginal people. Yet it is the cemetery, rather than the occupation complex, which is their symbol. The Tasmanian population in 1800 possibly totalled 5,000. Almost all survivors were transported here by 1834, numbering only 170. Thirty-two died at Wybalenna in 1833, and only 123 greeted Robinson on his arrival as commandant in 1835; fewer than 90 farewelled him three years later. When Wybalenna was abandoned in 1847, only 46 people were living.

Robinson controlled Wybalenna for about one-fifth of its existence, but his hand marked the landscape as it exists today. Remnants of his building program are the chapel (poorly restored) and parts of his residence (his privy is a gem). The central focus was an L-shaped line of twenty thatched brick cottages, mercifully backed against prevailing winds and facing onto an open communal area. Regrettably, the close proximity of all Aborigines within this terrace facilitated the spread of infection, contrasting with traditional dispersed settlement pattern. As the community lacked immunity to chest ailments, colds, pneumonia and tuberculosis, amongst other diseases, took a cruel toll, probably accelerated by low morale.

Despite everything, the people clung to their homeland's traditions. A clue was provided by Darling, the first commandant, who told Backhouse about a wallaby food taboo, some persons eating only males and other females. ''They do not give any reason for this, but so strict is their attention to it, that W.J. Darling says he does not think they would deviate from it if they were starving.'' On occasions they also performed ceremonial dances, wore ochre in traditional ways and incised symbolic patterns on their bodies, despite the disapproval of Robinson for ''uncivilised'' habits.

Robinson's concern with formalities and with brick manufacture and building obscured matters of deeper importance. One was the total mismanagement of livestock, although fresh meat could have been plentiful, replacing salt meat which the Aborigines disliked. Others foreshadowed or provided the prototype of the paternalistic government welfare settlement of a century later. As the Aboriginal population dwindled, so their minders increased, thereby diverting funds away from those for whom the system was devised, while denying them any positive role in it.

In addition to the ever-necessary hospital and (often useless) surgeon, a troop was stationed in military barracks. Another small army of civil officials required housing. Many were unsuitable convicts, putting at risk Aboriginal women. Under Robinson, staff included the storekeeper, catechist, brickmakers, sawyers, carpenters, agriculturalists and stockmen, a plasterer, gardener and blacksmith, and the coxswain and crew. They numbered over forty people, almost a ratio of one to two Aborigines. It is evident that, at Wybalenna, only the white population and the Aboriginal burial ground expanded.

Another foretaste was the window-dressing accompanying VIP visitation.

During the summer of 1838, Tasmania's Lieutenant-Governor Sir John Franklin and Lady Franklin stepped ashore. Robinson proudly recorded, that "the Governor expressed himself highly gratified with the native cottages, their manner of construction . . . [was] . . . highly creditable to my judgement". Feverish activity, however, preceded this visit: "The natives' cottages were cleaned, the grounds in front were cleared, instructions issued to the military, domestic arrangements attended to and in fact the greatest possible anxiety was evinced . . . "

The people themselves had no input into such misguided and disastrous efforts to "civilise" them by converting them into docile Christian peasants. Wybalenna remains the symbol of well-meaning attempts to save a few Tasmanians, but conveniently out of Tasmania, during a period ignorant of medical and anthropological understanding. Concealed beneath the grass lies a time-capsule of social history. Systematic research here in the future could recover the foundations of more than thirty structures and associated gardens, fields and tracks. The central core of Aboriginal dwellings offers remarkable prospects for systematic excavation. Wybalenna's successive building phases could be determined, the social stratification within the settlement, and the material conditions of Aborigines and staff might be reconstructed. It is a most extensive area, unencumbered by later occupation. There is an obligation to preserve it without any unsystematic disturbance. Future generations of Aboriginal people, in particular, will use it as a source of information to supplement written records. As the burial ground is set away from the habitation zones, investigations may be undertaken safely without any disturbance of those who died here in exile.

Oyster Bay

The former convict probation station at Oyster Cove, thirty-three kilometres south of Hobart, was abandoned because it failed to meet health standards for convicts. It became the new Aboriginal settlement on 18 October 1847. Robinson visited there four years later, on a nostalgic tour before retiring to England in

The site of the Oyster Cove station from across the harbour, visible as the open area, 1986. (D.J. Mulvaney)

C.E. Stanley's watercolour of Oyster Cove station, c. 1849, early in its Aboriginal occupation. The prominent feature is simply a bell post. (By Charles Edward Stanley [c. 1849]. Watercolour, 26.2 cm x 36.5 cm, National Library of Australia)

financial comfort. Thirteen of the Wybalenna evacuees had died and the dispirited survivors wanted to return to the more congenial conditions on Flinders Island. This wish is surely the index to the anticlimax of their homecoming. It had not proved joyous.

Oyster Cove was cold, damp and unhealthy. In its two sections, the reserve covered almost a hundred hectares, but the huts sat on a low-lying flat area facing the sea, with steep wooded slopes on other sides and a rivulet and mud flats nearby. It was a situation ensuring sodden ground, shade and mist for much of the year. For people susceptible to respiratory ailments, the selection of the site could not have proved worse, but it was accentuated by the accommodation. The shoddy range of slab and shingle construction wooden huts was only a few years old, yet already they were dilapidated. No repairs were attempted until weeks after the Aborigines arrived, and these were minimal. They had fallen into disrepair again by 1852, when only five pounds were expended on their maintenance. The habitual dampness and draughts must have been worsened by outside appearances. As only some structures in the complex were occupied, others collapsed. During a storm in 1864, many were blown down, so rubble lay in piles.

Nothing was ever done to improve housing conditions by building new huts or moving elsewhere. The only brick building housed the superintendent. Food supplies were characterised by their poor quality and frugality. Some of the officers proved incompetent drunkards. Access by local settlers to the women, or by Aborigines to grog, accelerated physical decline. There was no resident doctor to assist.

Mary Ann died in 1873, leaving Truganini the sole survivor of all Robinson's deportees. She was cared for in Hobart, where she died on 8 May 1876. The Aboriginal reserve already had been revoked, in 1874. Early this century, Aboriginal remains were removed illegally from the station's burial ground, on a

Aboriginal residents at Oyster Cove, photographed by Bishop Nixon in 1858. This photograph shows the roughly hewn timber building, with shingles and draughty gaps between planks. N.B. Plomley's identification of the individuals is Tippoo Saib (left standing) and Patty; centre, Mary Ann; sitting from left, Wapperty, Trugernanner (Truganini), Caroline and Sarah. (Photograph by Bishop Nixon, in the J.W. Beattie Album, courtesy the W.L. Crowther Library, State Library of Tasmania)

slope some distance away. At that time the graves were unmarked, and it was unfenced and overgrown.

Not surprisingly, there are no historic structures standing at Oyster Cove today. Amongst the tangled blackberries traces of building foundations are visible. As with the sub-surface remains at Wybalenna, systematic archaeological excavations could recover much evidence. Details of the social, technological and dietary conditions of these neglected people might be reconstructed. One subject of interest is the extent to which they adopted and modified European materials, such as glass, to traditional use.

An Historic Site of 30.3 hectares was proclaimed in 1981. Aboriginal custodians have erected a building and keep some of the grass mown. Their central concern is an area in the middle of the former settlement, where in 1985, those human bones from the cemetery were returned and cremated. Regrettably, due to an insensitive government decision taken without consultation, a large rock was transported intended to seal the cremation. Instead, it was dumped nearby, a symbol to the reality that Aboriginal people were never permitted to determine their own actions.

The Melbourne *Age* newspaper featured an enlightened editorial on Aboriginal welfare problems on 28 October 1858. At that time the Oyster Cove population numbered fifteen. Criticising the institutionalised life of the Tasmanians, the paper reflected: "They were, in the most literal sense, 'civilized off the face of the earth'." It is ironic that while all Robinson's people passed away during their encounter with "protection", elsewhere others survived. Out in Bass Strait, away from colonial control and diet, the descendants of Tasmanian and mainland women and sealers developed a new society.

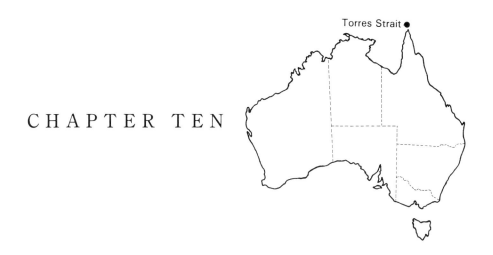

Torres Strait •

CHAPTER TEN

Across Torres Strait

During most of their human history, Australia and New Guinea formed a single land mass. Rising oceans finally submerged Torres Strait, between 6,000 and 7,000 years ago. Only 150 kilometres separate Papua from Cape York, while a string of western islands facilitate inter-island contact to mid-strait, from Cape York to Mabuiag. The antiquity and nature of island settlement remain ambiguous. Facile explanations assume that either the original land bridge, or later island-hopping, provided key routes to or from Australia. Archaeologists cannot prove this. Except for conflicting dates from a site on Sabai, near Papua (2540 ± 60 or 1080 ± 60 Before Present), none of the five other dated sites within Torres Strait may exceed one thousand years.

Historical records demonstrate that many islands were inhabited by Melanesian people at the time Europeans arrived there in the late eighteenth century. Although there are marked differences in the geological origin, resources, and subsistence patterns between islands, an integrated series of trading systems enlarged their resource bases. Superimposed upon some common biological and cultural features, however, are dissimilarities, including language. Eastern Islanders speak a Papuan language called Miriam, while western, central and even northern Islanders speak Mabuiag, a basically Aboriginal language, but distinct from those spoken on Cape York. The analysis of the region is complicated by the lateness of recorded traditions. The key source is the Cambridge expedition to Torres Strait in 1898, about thirty years after missionaries arrived and attempted to suppress traditional practices. These included head-hunting, in the western sector. Such written sources, therefore, date from up to a century or more after British ships regularly passed through Torres Strait.

Although no Torres Strait Islander places are in the Register, consultation with communities progresses. This discussion anticipates an outcome and features four significant places which exemplify different cultural and economic encounters within the region, involving Torres Strait Islanders, Papuans and Aboriginal people. The first, Morilag (Mt Adolphus), typifies the important interplay of trading systems. The others signify cultural interchange, involving the movements of cult-heroes and ritual activities. Mabuiag and adjacent Pulu islands preserve places where Kwoiam, a hero of Australian origin, performed legendary feats and died. Janie Creek, on Cape York near Mapoon, symbolises Papuan and Torres Strait Islander influences on mainland society.

Morilag is a crescent-shaped island of volcanic origin rising to one hundred and fifty metres, five kilometres long and covered with dense bush. It was once rich in food resources, ranging from mud oysters in its mangrove fringe to yams on the ridges; turtles abounded. Although uninhabited, it belonged to the mainland Gudang people, only fourteen kilometres distant on the tip of Cape York. Morilag first attracted European attention in 1791, when survivors from the wreck of HMS *Pandora* attempted to land there. They filled their casks with water, but quickly withdrew when people armed with bows and arrows attacked them.

In 1844 Barbara Thompson was the sole survivor of a shipwreck. She lived with the people of Muralag (Prince of Wales Island), forty kilometres west of Morilag, until rescued by HMS *Rattlesnake* in 1848. She provided valuable information on the role which Morilag played in regional economy. It was visited both by eastern and western Islanders, in addition to its mainland owners. It functioned as a "neutral" clearing-house within a far-flung trading exchange network. Evidently eastern Islanders called there from as far distant as Massid (Yorke Island) in the Murray group, while others also came from Sabai and Papua. It was eastern Islander dry season visitors who attacked the *Pandora's* crew. Thompson reported wet season voyages there from the west, by Kaurareg people from Muralag, who loaded fish, turtle eggs and yams for the return trip.

This complex exchange pattern was reconstructed by David Moore. He infers that uninhabited Morilag supplied food and water for all comers, while mutual obligations ensured peaceful commerce at this agreed market place. Goods exchanged there may have passed along the route in stages, from various owners. These included Papuan canoe hulls, valued conus shell, turtle shell artefacts, a wide variety of ceremonial regalia, and human heads, a precious commodity for western Islanders.

The contribution of Cape York Aborigines to this trade cycle consisted of ochre, spears and spear-throwers. These latter circulated widely, presumably because of the superiority of mainland wood. Morilag's Gudang owners evidently contributed goodwill and permission for all to utilise the venue and to harvest its varied provisions. Morilag is proposed for the Register as testimony to a complex series of contacts which transmitted goods and ideas, particularly within the eastern islands. The existence of Morilag affected the quality of life of communities over a major region, while it exemplifies an entire non-European economic system.

Throughout the western islands and beyond, Kwoiam was an heroic figure. Whether he was an actual person or a legendary amalgam is uncertain. Islanders believe the former, and many traditions have been collected this century about his activities. There are many contradictions, but there is a basic agreement on some matters. Just as the *Iliad* of the Greeks reflected the Bronze Age, these traditions must reflect social and cultural aspects of Islander life before the colonial era.

Kwoiam's father's identity is unknown, but his maternal grandmother's territory was Morilag, so her people were mainland Gudang. Amongst the variant accounts of Kwoiam's prowess, one central agreed detail is his Aboriginality. His kin, when given, were mainlanders. His physique, skull shape, hair form, voice and bearing all connect him with Cape York or Muralag (Prince of Wales Island). Significantly, his weapons were Australian. He invariably used a spear and spear-thrower, never a bow, against his puny enemies.

His magical totemic emblems were different. They were crescent pendants cut from turtle shell, possibly from Maurura, near Thursday Island. These emblems glowed brightly at times when he was on the war-path, and had carved eyes. One was worn as a chest ornament (giribu) and the other hung on his back (kutibu), so he saw in both directions. These symbols remained important in initiation and burial rituals.

Kwoiam's impact was felt following his arrival with his family on Mabuiag. His kinship structure was matrilineal, contrasting with Mabuiag's patrilineal clan structure. Significantly, Kwoiam killed his mother in a fit of rage. He embarked upon a fearsome (non-Aboriginal) head-hunting canoe saga with his nephew. He massacred widely, taking many heads on Boigu and along the Papuan coast. Even those whom he called friends, such as Saibi and Dauan Islanders, he terrorised. He later battled warriors from Badu and Moa, with terrifying success. Finally, he succumbed to their assault after his spear-thrower broke in combat. He died upon the summit of his Mabuiag lookout.

Whatever Kwoiam's historicity, this hero-cult surely symbolises the ideological and cultural conflicts between Aboriginal and Melanesian traditions, in which a distinctive Torres Strait Islander society was forged in these western islands. Incidents after his death are suggestive of the Australian-Papuan dichotomy. His spear and spear-thrower were hurled south towards Australia, and a warrior who began to decapitate Kwoiam was ordered to leave his body intact.

Mabuiag and Pulu abound with monuments related to Kwoiam's career. This roughly trapezoidal island extends about two kilometres along each coast; tiny uninhabited Pulu islet is near its western shore. They both bear the scars of Kwoiam's actions. He lived at Gumu, in the island's southeastern sector. Behind the small coastal flat rises the hill to his lookout. The track up the slope is marked by stones which represent the heads of his victims. His unfortunate mother's head stands prominently elsewhere, though now a boulder. On this hill a spring gushes from rocks. It was formed when the thirsty Kwoiam struck the rock with his spear. As in Biblical tradition, water flowed out. When the warrior slit Kwoiam's throat, his blood spurted over a clump of bushes, whose leaves are spattered red to this day. He was buried on the hill under a cairn of stones and conch shells. Alfred Haddon photographed them in 1899. Later, a missionary disturbed them, but found nothing beneath the surface.

Over on rocky Pulu, Kwoiam's fighting prowess is evident. Numerous parallel slabs of rock represent the headless slain Badu warriors. A nearby cave was used to store actual human heads, until the place was destroyed by missionaries. A prominent rock which stands on the shore, with a protruding tip, is Kwoiam's spear-thrower. Other rocks bear his foot imprint, as he planted it firmly before

One of the features on Mabuiag associated with Kwoiam is this spring. On the rock to the right of the hole Kwoiam sat down to drink from this new water source. The grooves on this sloping rock were made when he straightened his spears. (A.C. Haddon Library, Cambridge, courtesy AIAS)

Kwoiam's tomb, or possibly his memorial cairn, on the hill above Gumu, photographed in 1899 by A.C. Haddon. Pulu Island appears in the centre, behind the hill. (A.C. Haddon Library, Cambridge, courtesy AIAS)

Slain and beheaded Badu warriors in a row after Kwoiam defeated them on Pulu Island. (A.C. Haddon
Library, Cambridge, courtesy AIAS)

The projection on the prominent vertical rock is the tip of Kwoiam's Australian spear-thrower. (A.C.
Haddon Library, Cambridge, courtesy AIAS)

hurling his spear. At the time of Haddon's visit, rock paintings and other
ceremonial places relating to Kwoiam were shown to him.

On Haddon's previous visit to Mabuiag, in 1888, an elder told him of Kwoiam's
fame. It "caused the name of Mabuiag to be feared . . . although the island was
rocky and comparatively infertile, Kwoaim covered it with honour and glory, thus
showing how the deeds of a single man can glorify a place in itself of little worth".

Just as the Mediterranean wanderings of Odysseus are celebrated today, and localities referred to are preserved, so the Register should include these monuments to a legendary Aboriginal hero who travelled far beyond his own territory.

More than 200 kilometres down Cape York's western coast is Port Musgrave, former location of the Mapoon mission. Several kilometres further south is Janie Creek, in the country of the Tyongadyi people. Tyongadyi traditions and rituals tell of clan heroes whose adventures took them from Janie Creek into Torres Strait and Papua. Dances and material objects recalling these wanderings also reflect distinctive Papuan cultural traits. During the early 1930s two anthropologists, Donald Thomson and Ursula McConnel, worked here independently and recorded traditions which are remembered still by some Tyongadyi people.

Around Janie Creek, the sandbanks are a favoured dry season haunt of seagulls, which migrate to Torres Strait during the monsoonal flooding. It may be relevant that the birds flock to sands around Mabuiag. Torres Strait pigeons inhabit the scrub on the higher ground south of Janie Creek, where they spend the wet season. They fly north to Papua during the dry season.

The social life of the Tyongadyi revolved around the contrasting seasonal habits of these two bird species. The clan whose totem was Sivirri the seagull occupied the sandy northern side of Janie Creek. On the southern side lay the clan territory of Nyunggu, the Torres Strait pigeon. In Tyongadyi traditions, Sivirri became a Torres Strait warrior hero, where he died, while Nyunggu went to Papua. Given the nature of the evidence, however, these encounters evidently were two-way because of the marked Papuan and Islander influences on this Carpentaria coast.

Sivirri was the personification of the seagull, a creative innovator in technology and the arts. Sivirri was an inveterate dancer, who seldom stopped dancing and singing. He made a drum to assist the rhythm. He also constructed a special dancing enclosure for the performance of initiation rites. It was rectangular, with forked stakes supporting horizontal sticks with bulrush screens hanging on them. Although similar screened enclosures were used on this coast, their prototype must be with sacred dancing enclosures in Papua and western Torres Strait Islands. The drum has similar links.

Sivirri also was armed with a Papuan bow and arrow. It was he who first produced a wooden dugout canoe with outrigger. In fact, the distribution of outriggers only extended a few kilometres south of Janie Creek, although they were used by people to the north. The origin of the outrigger also may be attributed to Papua, as it was an important item in the trade exchange system. Another remarkable Papuan influence on both sides of northern Cape York, but not attributed to Sivirri's initiative, were the elaborate masks and dress worn by dancers, one of the most elaborate and distinctive art forms of Aboriginal Australia. Tyongadyi dancers wore such masks.

Sivirri took his dances to Mabuiag during the course of his heroic wanderings. Donald Thomson concluded that Sivirri and Kwoiam were the same cult-hero, but this is a questionable matter. The relevant point here is that both versions emphasise the connections between the mainland, Mabuiag, and even Papua. As for Nyunggu, of the Torres Strait pigeon clan, he went on to Papua and never returned.

The area around lower Janie Creek is proposed for the Register because monuments survive to the activities of Sivirri and Nyunggu. After Sivirri built his canoe, it capsized, or became stranded, on a sandbank near the creek's mouth. There it remains, turned to stone, where some rocks resemble a canoe. After Sivirri constructed another canoe he eloped with two daughters of Nyunggu from across the creek. He pushed off from that clan's land with his paddle so strongly that the canoe shot out of the creek mouth. The hole made by his paddle is a well today, adjacent to Nyunggu's original dancing enclosure near the mangroves. As for Sivirri's dancing ground, a clump of trees grew upon it, and they mark its position still.

There is another reason why this area should be in the Register. Although there are custodians of Tyongadyi lore and custom today, it is many years since major ceremonies have taken place. The records of Thomson and McConnel from more than fifty years ago represent an important heritage of Aboriginal culture. In addition to the oral traditions which they were told, Thomson took a series of photographs of Tyongadyi people and their magnificent masks and costumes. He also was given many of these items by the people and they have been preserved in excellent condition. Aboriginal art on bark has become fashionable today amongst non-Aboriginal Australians. At Janie Creek, superb examples of a totally different art form were collected, which demonstrate the richness, variety and complexity of Aboriginal art, which resulted from a mingling of cultures.

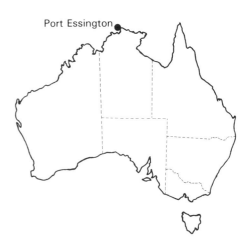

Port Essington

CHAPTER
ELEVEN

Port Essington: A Friendly Frontier

Ludwig Leichhardt tramped into Victoria settlement, Port Essington, in time for Christmas, 1845. "Victoria is indeed a lonely solitary place", he remarked, "no communication with the mainland . . . and rare communication from the sea side." He had reached the third abortive British military settlement in tropical Australia. Port Essington (1838–49) was preceded by Fort Dundas, on Melville Island (1824–29), and Fort Wellington, in Raffles Bay (1827–29). These three places are in the Register as forlorn material testimony to false optimism bred of geographic ignorance, and monuments to the trials of inhabitants of isolated and ill-prepared tropical outposts on an imperial frontier. Their significance is enhanced by the archaeological evidence for social history concealed within these little-investigated time-capsules.

Their importance for documenting the first encounters between British settlers and indigenous people has been less emphasised. In fact, the statements of significance, particularly for Raffles Bay and Port Essington, serve as a metaphor for what might have been in later northern racial relations.

These outposts incurred enormous human cost without ever achieving their chief purpose of creating an Australian Singapore. Indeed, the only trading vessels to pay fleeting calls to Raffles Bay and Victoria were trepanging praus, already familiar visitors to those harbours. Nobody visited Fort Dundas. Port Essington attained temporary importance as a base for naval surveying expeditions and, incidentally, as the elusive goal for Leichhardt's weary party.

"Barren, uninteresting and intensely hot", complained one naval visitor. Another departing critic, naturalist John McGillivray, from the deck of HMS *Rattlesnake*, pitied the residents their discomfort and boredom. "There is probably no vessel in Her Majesty's navy, no matter where serving", he concluded, "the men of which are not better supplied with all the necessaries and comforts of life." In addition, there were a few unfortunate women and children stationed at Port Essington. Low morale and tedium were not the worst features, however, for death and debilitating diseases, particularly malaria, were rife. More than forty per cent of persons stationed there either died or were invalided out. This aura of decay also extended to buildings, for the ravages of white ants rendered them temporary. Victoria was described in 1848 as "ruinous", when even the roof of the stoutest building, the hospital, leaked upon patients and the doctor wisely slept beneath a canopy. While the settlement's abandonment must have proved a relief, the hardships and irritations make the friendly relations maintained with the Aborigines all the more noteworthy.

By 1849, the Iwaidga people of the Cobourg Peninsula had adapted positively to the British occupation. This contrasted with the situation on Melville Island, or during the first year at Raffles Bay. At both forts, mutual distrust prevailed under unsympathetic and uncomprehending commandants, who ruled by discipline and the gun. It culminated in bloodshed within a few months at Raffles Bay. Commandant Smyth hated the place and despised the Aborigines. Exasperated by habitual pilfering, followed by the wounding of a soldier, Smyth responded by ordering an indiscriminate attack on the encampment. In this senseless massacre, possibly thirty men, women and children died. The northern frontier was initiating a sadly familiar settlement pattern.

The arrival of Captain Collet Barker, an energetic new commandant, changed the regional pattern of race relations. A fearless and humane man, he managed to convey a sense of harmony to the local people simply through pantomime. Some form of verbal communication soon followed and, by treating some prominent elders as social equals, he established rapport. He ate and slept alone with them in their camp and reciprocated by entertaining them in Fort Wellington, where Aboriginal dances and hornpipes were staged for mutual entertainment. Trust had replaced angry missiles. While Barker's leadership proved crucial, the role of these elders, especially Mariac, also ensured peaceful co-existence, based upon respect and good humour.

Barker revived settlement morale. The place received refreshing winds and, as productive gardens developed, health improved. When over 1,000 Macassan trepangers entered port, Barker promised them that trade goods would be available upon their next visit. He felt optimistic for the future. The British Colonial Office judged otherwise. Always over a year behind in news of these outposts, the government ordered its abandonment, acting upon Smyth's jaundiced advice.

Barker despondently evacuated Raffles Bay, after offering his Aboriginal friends the gardens. His actions established an harmonious reciprocity which assisted the Port Essington venture, unfortunately a place with fewer environmental advantages than Fort Wellington. When the tiny British fleet sailed into Port Essington nine years later, the Iwaidga people initially believed that Barker had returned. Because of his influence, and probably also because people were accustomed to the annual arrival of Macassan fleets, the British arrival created no traumas and friendly relations resumed. Port Essington proved a remarkable frontier of peaceful co-existence.

John McArthur, marine commandant throughout Victoria's occupation, lacked Barker's warm, informal spontaneity. Although legalistic, he proved a just and stable administrator, who treated the Aborigines as individuals under British law. During eleven trying years, only one Aboriginal death occurred from settler violence. This followed the arrest and subsequent escape of two men in 1847, for pilfering. Called upon by the sergeant, in fine imperial manner, to "halt in the name of the Queen", he then shot one escapee. McArthur charged his sergeant with murder and shipped him off to Sydney for trial, where he was acquitted. Although the offender had left, Aboriginal law required that his victim's death be avenged. In this pay-back killing situation, it is significant that the avengers did not wish to kill a European. They chose Neinmal, an acculturated Aborigine who had become popular with Europeans.

When the overbearing captain of a visiting naval vessel flogged an Aborigine for theft, McArthur protested, although more in defence of his authority than of humanity. Even so, under his control the lash seldom was used, although pilfering was habitual. (Visitors made a standard complaint about Aboriginal petty theft; McArthur knew that it also was a pastime of the marines.) McArthur believed that a night spent in a solitary confinement cell proved a better punishment, because it was feared by the Aborigines.

Contemporary accounts and sketches indicate that Aborigines moved freely around Victoria. Leichhardt noted that the children "are allmost constantly" present. Some residents accept their company willingly. Evidently these included the doctor, because H.S. Melville, a naval artist, felt amused that "young men preferred to allow him to extract their incisors, instead of . . . knocking them out with a stone, on their initiation . . .". Melville actually sketched a group of men beside the hospital.

Archaeological excavations support the case for a more sedentary life by the Iwaidga. Although shell middens along the western margin of the settlement had been accumulating for centuries, they now grew rapidly. Excavation recovered quantities of glass from the upper layers, much of it showing fractures from

Harden Melville visited Port Essington in 1843 and sketched Victoria Square. Note the Aboriginal group sitting by their fire in the "square", while a man carries water from the well. That well survives, together with some of the windlass timbers; the stone footings of the house on the right also survive amongst thick vegetation. (National Library of Australia, Rex Nan Kivell Collection, NK 1890)

The chimney of one of the five houses in the married quarters area. It is semicircular, following the model of Cornish chimney building. A niche supported a vertical beam related to the roof. Excavation alongside one of these cottages showed that Aborigines camped by a wall. (D.J. Mulvaney)

The Port Essington hospital, c. 1843, sketched by H.S. Melville, in *Sketches in Australia*. His chief concern was to depict the Aborigines. Note the ceremonial body scars and traditional equipment, combined with European clothes. Jack White, a crewman on a vessel which visited Sydney, is believed to be one of these men. (National Library of Australia, Rex Nan Kivell Collection, NK 942 [XIII])

The foundations of the hospital photographed in 1966 from much the same angle as Melville's sketch. These ironstone blocks supported a wooden structure, with a projecting enclosed verandah. (D.J. Mulvaney)

utilisation as tools. As stone suitable for artefacts was scarce, the glass proved a boon.

Excavations in and around the houses of married marines produced further Aboriginal artefacts from within Victoria. Over fifty per cent of the glass fragments recovered had been utilised, although most dated from the period after the settlement's evacuation. Stratigraphic analysis established, however, that Aboriginal activities had begun along the exterior of the wall of one house, while it was occupied. The hut's interior had been swept clean, for there were few finds within the earthen floor. It is interesting, therefore, that the tidy housewife evidently tolerated people camping just outside.

John Sweatman, a naval clerk who twice stayed at Victoria, offers illuminating insight into social relations. For some time he was stationed across the harbour at Point Record, where some forty Aborigines camped nearby. Sweatman preferred their "animated" evening life, with songs and dancing, and he often slept in their camp, because the smoke of many fires kept mosquitoes at bay. A group of white men played with the women and children. They rigged swings and the children's pranks so relieved the monotony, that Sweatman appreciatively remarked, "I do not know what we should have done without them". They also swam with the women and children, mainly "for the fun" involved, but also because the splashing and noise would deter sharks and crocodiles (and there was a belief that sharks preferred black people).

The enthusiasm suggests group pleasure in these informal meetings. A cynic might claim that sexual encounters played a prime role in this well-being. As only a few wives lived there, from seventy to over three hundred white men were present, depending upon shipping movements. The demand for sexual favours from Aboriginal women must have been a major economic transaction, in addition to its social aspects. If so, this was a silent service which diarists prudently ignored.

McGillivray dryly observed, however, that "the last importation of the whites was syphilis, and by it they will probably be remembered for years to come". This may have affected Aboriginal fertility. It should be noted, however, that the European death rate probably exceeded the Aboriginal at this time. Smallpox was already known on the Cobourg Peninsula in 1838, presumably via the Macassans, and it was a smallpox epidemic some thirty years later which reduced an estimated two hundred people to twenty-eight.

As Sweatman commented in the context above, that the people "were constantly encamped about us for the sake of what they could get", it could be concluded that this was a classic example of A.P. Elkin's much cited "intelligent parasitism". To agree, however, would be to adopt a cynical ethnocentric viewpoint. The racial encounters at Port Essington were reciprocal, for the relationship was symbiotic. Sweatman acknowledged this, when he immediately followed his remark with the statement, that "by their means we had a pretty constant supply of maroin [cabbage palm shoots], oysters and honey, and were also furnished with plenty of amusement". Other visitors referred to similar food supplies and the relatively good diet enjoyed by Aborigines. A Sydney newspaper report six years previously credited Aborigines with supplying Victoria with palm "cabbage", crabs, oysters, fish and cockles.

That Aborigines avoided work was a claim already common at Port Essington. That the duties involved were of European selection is overlooked. It is evident, for example, that the quantity of traditional food supplied was considerable. The number of men who chose to crew vessels also was large. Several visited Sydney on merchant ships, including five men aboard the *Heroine* on one voyage. They proved able sailors; Jack White "was so active and well behaved" that the skipper intended appointing him boatswain's mate, but the *Heroine* was wrecked. Neinmal assisted McGillivray, the naturalist, who took him to Java and Singapore on HMS *Fly*, then around southern Australia to Sydney. He returned home aboard HMS *Bramble*, accomplished in European ways and with some knowledge of reading and writing.

Port Essington was evacuated in 1849, after eleven years of frontier peace. If violence was avoidable here, could peaceful relations have been maintained elsewhere? It would have helped if Aborigines had been respected as individuals, as they were by those at Victoria. Understanding was a product of adversity. Sweatman praised them as "a merry light hearted people and although an European would think their mode of living the very extreme of wretchedness, they are far happier than many who enjoy every comfort".

On the other hand, the rights of these "noble savages" to exploit their land remained virtually unchallenged. Like the Macassans, residents of this garrison never ventured into the hinterland. Their subsistence gardens and rudimentary pastoralism posed no threat for indigenous economy, or to the freedom of people to follow their seasonal territorial movements and ceremonial obligations.

Neither were the invaders seeking to convert the indigenes to their faith. Established religion played little part at Victoria. A prefabricated church travelled on the fleet, but no clergyman accompanied it. To the surprise of McArthur, a missionary arrived in 1846, but he was Catholic. Angelo Confaloneiri, an Italian Benedictine priest, was the first missionary to the Northern Territory. He arrived destitute, but fortunate to arrive at all, for he survived the *Heroine* shipwreck. McArthur assisted him to settle near the harbour entrance. Though an impractical man, Confaloneiri astonished the garrison by rapidly becoming fluent in the local language. He travelled around the peninsula with the Aborigines, preparing a map of tribal areas, a vocabulary and translations of simple prayers. He made no converts, but his pioneering anthropological work is of interest.

Confaloneiri died from fever in 1848, respected by people of both races, none of whom shared his faith. He is buried in the cemetery, in a sadly vandalised tomb.

There is another consequence of these encounters on the Cobourg Peninsula, which is sufficient to justify Register listing. Domesticated animals from Indonesia were introduced at Raffles Bay and Port Essington. At the latter landed water buffalo, pig and banteng (Bali) cattle; Timor ponies also were released. The later spread of feral buffalo into the Arnhem Land wetlands added a variant to the Aboriginal diet, and employment in the buffalo processing industry. However the impact of buffalo and pig changed the environment in which Aborigines lived. These beasts upset the delicately balanced wetlands ecology. They caused massive erosion and drying because they stripped protective vegetation, uprooted swamp plants, churned waters muddy and impacted marshy soils. Decreased waterfowl and other swamp life resulted. While traditional economy suffered, so also did ceremonial places. Innumerable painted shelters were rubbed and made dusty by pig and buffalo, while the dust attracted wasps to nest on painted surfaces. The control of these destructive agents before the priceless heritage of rock art is obliterated, is one of the most urgent tasks in cultural conservation.

CHAPTER
TWELVE

Moorundie: "Tranquillity Everywhere Prevails"

Moorundie, on the Murray River south of Blanchetown, is a place of great natural beauty, which has changed little since Aboriginal times. The broad river is confined on the east by colourful creamy and orange limestone cliffs, while it flows lazily past its low western bank with fringing ancient white-trunked gums. The Moorundie settlement was made on these channelled alluvial flats during 1841. Although it was abandoned within fifteen years, it is in the Register because of its significance for both black and white Australians.

The Murray River at Moorundie, looking east. The footings of a building are in the right foreground. Before the construction of the barrage at the river mouth, the river level was lower and more distant. (D.J. Mulvaney)

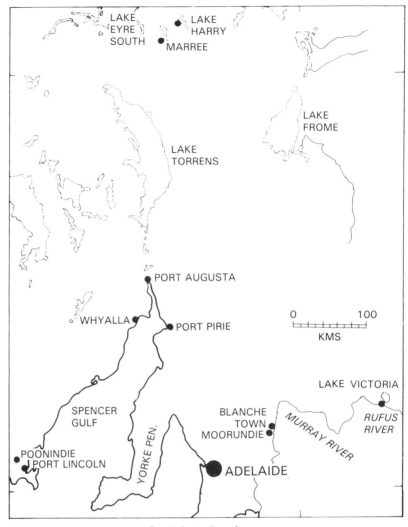

South Australian places

Ngaiawong people inhabited this resource-rich valley for thousands of years. These reedy flats were rich in plant foods and reptiles; in the river were fish, mussels and crustaceans, while its placid surface attracted myriad wildfowl; the tall gums were home to possums and bees. On the cliffs above stretched the mallee scrub, with its arid country resources. Sheltered, sunny places along the valley attracted visitors, who left traces of these varied food remains in the ashes of their fires. Sites at Devon Downs and Fromm's Landing are in the Register, because archaeological excavations demonstrated human occupation of shelters through 5,000 years. Because the settlement pattern was so river-oriented, population along the valley was relatively dense. Inevitably, therefore, early pastoralists droving stock near the water encountered concentrations of people.

Charles Sturt was the first European to pass Moorundie, on his 1829 river voyage. He came there again by land in 1844, laboriously transporting a boat to sail on the non-existent inland sea of his dreams. Sturt's party included John McDouall Stuart, later destined to traverse Australia from south to north. Their Moorundie host was Edward John Eyre, who had crossed the continent from east to west. Eyre was appointed the resident magistrate and Protector of Aborigines by George Grey, explorer turned governor. Grey also visited Moorundie, as did several artists including E. von Guerard, S.T. Gill and G. French Angas. Aboriginal people may find no purpose in recording explorers who "discovered" lands for white settlers. Except for Stuart, however, these talented men were more sympathetic to Aboriginal society than most contemporaries and recorded it in words or pictures. It is provoking to speculate about the Aboriginal topics discussed by such men as they shared meals in Eyre's hut. Moorundie's association with these men, the number of their references to the place and its original inhabitants, and its temporary importance as a nodal point in overland communications, justifies its registration as a European place.

Moorundie also symbolises a turning point in the region's history of racial encounters. Within two years of Adelaide's foundation in 1836, the first cattle herd driven overland arrived there; Eyre drove the first sheep flock there early in 1839. For several years, incoming thousands of stock travelled a route which brought them between the Murray River and Lake Victoria. The short Rufus River which connected the lake and the river became notorious during 1841 for scenes of racial violence.

Roughly dressed limestone blocks, probably the foundations of the right-hand building in the picture on page 79. (D.J. Mulvaney)

The original track from Adelaide to Moorundie descends into the Murray Valley at this point. Moorundie was situated beside the river below, about one kilometre distant. (D.J. Mulvaney)

A pioneer tradition incorrectly attributes the name "Rufus" to waters tinted with Aboriginal blood. Even before any bloodshed, however, Eyre travelled that route and commented upon the muddy waters of the Rufus flowing into the Murray. He already had crossed the Rufus in June 1838, and observed of that resource-rich area, that its population "had increased to many hundreds". Because this narrow, fertile habitat was traversed lengthways by mobs of stock and nervous drovers, the chances of confrontation were maximised.

Eyre's 1839 diary entries of his droving venture are penetrating. Once they passed beyond settlements along the Murrumbidgee River, his men "talked or thought of little else" but encountering Aboriginal attack. When a West Indian negro drover was speared soon afterwards, however, Eyre refused to retaliate. After enterprising bush surgery to extract the spear, Eyre entered sympathetic, rational explanations for the incident. His reflections, only published in 1984, were prophetic:

> But the only idea of the men was retaliation — to shoot every native they saw. No doubt this principle has been very often acted upon and thus the innocent punished for the guilty. Occasionally, too, I believe the natives have been shot at without provocation, merely because the white men were afraid of them and it was easier to shoot them at a distance . . . than . . . to allow them to come near and have to watch them with vigilance . . . . The party who commits such an aggression may perhaps pass safely in consequence, but the chances are that the next Europeans coming that way, ignorant of what has taken place and unsuspicious . . . may be waylaid . . . .

Three overlanding parties were attacked at the Rufus River during mid-1841, with loss of life on both sides. It culminated in a fourth encounter, involving troopers, settlers and, embarrassingly, the chief Protector of Aborigines. Official accounts blamed the Aborigines, but admitted about thirty Aboriginal deaths. A settler was informed by Aborigines later that the number was "much larger". As parties had been unmolested at the Rufus during the previous three years, it seems likely that provocation came from overlanders, as Eyre predicted.

The actions of Alexander Buchanan are relevant. During 1839, he fired across the river near modern Wentworth, killing "five or six"; two more were shot in later separate sightings. Nearer the Rufus, they "saw a good many blacks opposite bank . . . fired . . . and killed one". Buchanan met Governor Gawler and Sturt two days later, sailing upstream. They asked Buchanan whether "the blacks had been troublesome". His reply was "pretty quiet", although his diary admits, "did not say we had shot any".

Grey appointed Eyre to Moorundie in October 1841. When Eyre resigned three years later, he claimed that "not a single case of serious injury or aggression ever took place on the part of the natives against Europeans", along its entire disputed course. His small detachment of police troopers, housed in stone and brick barracks, was never required. Within a few weeks, Eyre visited the disaffected Rufus country to conciliate and to urge "that the white man wished to live with them upon terms of amity".

Governor Grey and Eyre both wished to save lives on humanitarian grounds and were well intentioned, even though expediency also featured. Eyre was trusted because he treated Aborigines simply as human beings. He also acknowledged that as settlement developed along the Murray, Aboriginal society increasingly

Looking west across the Murray River in the early 1840s to Moorundie. The artist of *Soldier barracks Moorundie on the River Murray, S.A.* is unknown. The larger building may have been the barracks or the courthouse. Note the low freeboard bark canoe on the river. (The Mortlock Library of South Australiana, from Miss L.M. Eyre, Gloucestershire)

The same large stone building, with brick chimney, as shown on page 79; date unknown. (The Mortlock Library of South Australiana, negative 6017)

had "a just right" to recompense for their loss of access to natural resources. However, even he saw the solution as one of Aboriginal adaptation to European ways. At the end of his Australian career, he concluded, "that the most important point, in fact . . . essential . . . is to gain such an influence or authority over the Aborigines as may be sufficient to . . . induce them to adopt, or submit to any regulations that we make for their improvement . . .".

Eyre's dictum represented the birth of paternalism in South Australia. Moorundie symbolises those frontier posts to which people "came in" to receive the benefits of the pax Australiana. Moorundie offered a firm inducement for population concentration, beyond natural curiosity about the strange customs and impedimenta of the newcomers. Monthly handouts of flour and related commodities were the bait, with annual blankets as a bonus. People were suspicious initially. Only 25 attended Eyre's first muster, but there were 76 next time and 124 at the third monthly muster; the average monthly attendance in 1844 was 171. Occasionally, 500 people assembled, confirming a neighbour's claim that "great mobs of blacks . . . even from near the Darling" were drawn there. Ironically, this social mobility was facilitated by the traditional kinship and ceremonial gift exchange network operating along the river.

Eyre's policy allowed people to retain some dignity. Except for the prescribed government rations, he gave goods only as payment for labour services as barter in return for fish or game. Yet few officials were as understanding as Eyre, and even he witnessed the loss of self-respect and social disintegration resulting from introduced diseases. Infections were spread, Eyre believed, through the social virtues of exchanging infected clothing and by "spending their time in the dwellings of the sick". Overcrowding in the camp and numerous Aboriginal visits to Adelaide must have worsened problems. Although Eyre's English readers needed a classical education before comprehending his discreet Latin footnote, he judged that venereal disease was "the most common and dangerous" factor. He found little trace of disease in 1841, but within three years "very many were in a dying condition".

Distribution of flour at Moorundie. The artist, George Hamilton, overlanded sheep from Melbourne in 1839. The event depicted occurred during Eyre's first year at Moorundie, 1841. It illustrates the concentration of population caused by ration handouts. In addition to dietary deficiencies resulting from unsuitable food, this mingling of people encouraged the spread of introduced diseases. (Frontispiece to E.J. Eyre, *Journals of Expeditions*, vol. 2; photographer Robert Edwards)

The outpost survived until 1856, although the garrison had been withdrawn previously. The projected township of Sturt never developed, and communication routes evolved elsewhere. Eyre's wooden house was dismantled upon his departure. Traces of the foundations of the barracks survive, and dressed limestone blocks of another building indicate the optimism of Eyre's period. They are closer to the river today because its level rose when the barrage was constructed at the Murray mouth. In a silted channel there are posts and other remnants of a dam constructed by Eyre, from whose water he irrigated paddocks of lucerne, maize and wheat. It was the first irrigation property on the Murray, half a century before the Chaffey brothers.

This important place merits systematic archaeological investigation. In addition to identifying buildings and industrial activities, the location of Aboriginal encampments requires recovery. Where the former Adelaide track climbs the valley wall, erosion reveals shell middens. Are they prehistoric, or are they related to Moorundie times?

Eyre published an account of his explorations after he reached London in 1845. It included 365 pages on the "Manners and Customs of the Aborigines of Australia", the greater part drawing upon his Moorundie experience. It provides a heritage resource for modern Aboriginal people. Eyre should be respected by all Australians for his interest in, and his honourable dealings with, the people of the valley whom he "pacified". Yet his very success facilitated colonial settlement. Five years after Eyre's departure, Sturt praised his achievement. In a sense, it was a requiem for the people of the Murray: " . . . instead of the Murray being the scene of conflict and slaughter, its whole line is now occupied by stock-stations, and tranquillity everywhere prevails".

Molong

CHAPTER
THIRTEEN

A Wiradjuri Memorial near Molong

Yuranigh, a Wiradjuri from the Molong area, guided Sir Thomas Mitchell's Queensland expedition of 1845-46, from nearby Boree to 150 kilometres west of Mackay. He died in 1850 and was buried on a hillslope amongst yellow box gums (*Eucalyptus melliodora*), on old Gamboola Station, three kilometres southeast of Molong. The place is on the Register. It is unique as a memorial dedicated by mourners from two cultures, exhibiting signs of respect from both.

Major Mitchell made a pilgrimage there on a bitterly cold August day in 1851; his diary betrays his deep emotion. With numb fingers he sketched the scene, including designs carved on trees by Yuranigh's people, "The place for the tomb was selected as usual in a sweet retired spot", Mitchell observed approvingly, "and the cuttings on adjacent trees were deep and permanent looking. No sculptured marble ever told so plainly the regard and affection of the living for the dead."

Mitchell was prophetic. Almost 150 years later, some carvings survive. According to a plan drawn for him in 1854, five trees had been marked. The bark was removed the side of each trunk facing the grave and geometric patterns were cut deeply into the living heartwood. One tree must have perished early, regrowth obscures the design on a second, but two living trees bear visible signs. The fifth tree died and toppled over early this century. The carved section of its trunk was sawn off and insensitively re-erected in a concrete-based shelter. Its designs are the most prominent of all. National Estate funding has assisted the New South Wales Parks and Wildlife Service to complete a survey of existing carved trees. Conservation measures are in hand for this place.

This celebrated group of carved trees may be the latest surviving occurrence of the traditional burial custom for important Wiradjuri and Kamileroi people of inland New South Wales and southern Queensland. Probably over 1,000 carved

Yuranigh's memorial, Molong. His grave is right centre, while the fenced trees and the roofed trunk were carved by his clansmen in his honour. (D.J. Mulvaney)

Yuranigh's tomb, with Mitchell's original headstone horizontal. His inscribed tribute was reproduced on the new headstone. (D.J. Mulvaney)

One of the carved trees which face Yuranigh's grave. As the tree has grown since 1850, it has grown over the original surface. (D.J. Mulvaney)

trees survived into this century, but fires, vandalism and natural decay took a heavy toll. Others were sawn down and transported elsewhere. Recent surveys indicate that fewer than 300 survive, but of these, only 78 trees are standing in place in New South Wales, 33 of which are dead. This meagre total emphasises the significance of the Yuranigh group. The meaning of these attractive patterns is obscure, but probably they encapsulate symbols of clan and other territorial affiliations. Their inner meaning would have been understood only by appropriately initiated persons.

If the surrounding Aboriginal memorials bear mute testimony to respect, the honorific, traditionally British inscription on the gravestone, is intended for all comers. It resulted from Mitchell's initiative after he visited Yuranigh's grave. He arranged for a stout post and rail fence to surround the entire complex (now disappeared), and for a headstone and fenced grave. Some government funds were used, but Mitchell paid most costs himself. The perimeter fence was in place by 1852, but the finely engraved tribute was erected two years later. The grave fence was renewed in 1900, when the fallen headstone was duplicated and re-erected on a base of Molong marble.

Yuranigh was a man with the rare distinction of status and honour in two worlds. His grave is one of the few memorials erected freely by nineteenth century whites to honour black achievements. At his graveside, Mitchell called him "my faithful native ancilliary". It evidently took some time for his virtues to impress themselves upon Mitchell. In the published *Journal of an Expedition into the Interior of Tropical Australia* (1848), the three Aboriginal guides were not listed amongst the 29 Europeans, 80 bullocks, 17 horses, 250 sheep, 8 drays and 2 boats which left Boree, sixteen kilometres from Molong. One Aborigine soon quit the expedition and Yuranigh is mentioned only three weeks after they left Boree. Thereafter, however, Yuranigh received over ninety references, always appreciative.

Yuranigh was dependable and companionable. He retrieved straying beasts, located lost party members, unerringly found water, climbed hills and trees to scan distant prospects. More importantly, he acted as interpreter or mediator with each new Aboriginal group, frequently turning hostile receptions into helpful welcomes and his prudent advice avoided violence. He reciprocated Mitchell's interest in natural history. He collected plants, explained bush lore, commented upon Aboriginal artefacts and drew attention to regional variations in shells, bees and birds, amongst many subjects. He accompanied Mitchell on almost every excursion ahead of the main party. Near the future Isisford, on the future Barcoo River, Mitchell named a lagoon, "Yuranigh's ponds"; a Queensland county also now bears his name. Upon their return to Sydney, Mitchell secured a "small gratuity" from the governor for Yuranigh and found him paid employment as a stockman.

Yuranigh was one of a large, but little acknowledged, group of Aborigines who accepted European domination, and worked positively within those confines. He seems to have enjoyed his work and expedition members benefited. So did Yuranigh's people, because his sensible advice probably saved their lives on many occasions.

Major Mitchell has been criticised for his bloodstained past, because he "dispersed" Aborigines on the Murray River in 1836 by shooting them. Just as Yuranigh's co-operation with him should not be likened to a pliable Wiradjuri "Uncle Tom", meekly doing Mitchell's bidding, Aboriginal critics should not judge Mitchell only by those harsh actions. Ten years later, and perhaps through Yuranigh's influence, Mitchell was wiser and more tolerant. Like many other white Australians, prolonged encounter with Aborigines achieved a greater understanding. It is regrettable that earlier crimes or policies are emphasised, rather than crediting those who changed their attitude. In Mitchell's case, the concluding section of the published account of his 1846 expedition provides one of the most perceptive assessments about the plight of Aboriginal society written during the first century of European Australia.

Mitchell was an incipient ecologist. Consider his conclusion, that "fire, grass, kangaroos and human inhabitants, seem all dependent on each other for existence in Australia". He understood why Aborigines retaliated against settlers, because it "must be obvious to the natives, with their usual acuteness, as soon as cattle enter on their territory".

While preparing his journal for publication, Mitchell reflected, that "it would ill become me to disparage the character of the aborigines, for one of that unfortunate race has been my 'guide, companion, councillor, and friend' ". This public tribute related that Yuranigh's "intelligence and his judgement rendered him so necessary to me, that he was ever at my elbow . . . . Confidence in him was never misplaced. He well knew the character of all the white men of the party. Nothing escaped his penetrating eye and quick ear."

As a person, Mitchell admitted that Yuranigh "was small and slender . . . but he was of most determined courage and resolution". Writing privately to seek news of him in 1850, Mitchell regretted that Yuranigh "was of a very weakly frame — his stomach diseased". In fact, he already lay in his secluded grave. Later, when the melancholy Mitchell visited the place, he became "so benumbed that I could scarcely mount my horse — 'Old Jack' who was well known to the deceased — we three had travelled together beyond the line of Capricorn . . .".

CHAPTER
FOURTEEN

Two Innovative Missions: New Norcia and Poonindie

New Norcia

Travellers come suddenly upon New Norcia. As the northern highway crests a rise in the bush, the startling complex is seen on the Moore River plains. It is unique in Australia. Vernacular architectural forms of solid merit jostle with Classical, Byzantine and Gothic styles, given added variety by a Latin church tower and a red brick Edwardian octagonal beehouse. Painted with the colourful flamboyance of Mediterranean taste, this exotic Spanish Benedictine monastic complex merits its place in the Register for its architectural exuberance alone. The heritage began in 1846, with its foundation as an Aboriginal mission, and that role warrants its chief Register status.

At that time, the Victoria Plains formed the frontier of settlement in the thinly populated colony. It also was prime land, unlike the sites of many later missions which were marginalised into establishing upon unsuitable remnants unwanted by settlers. Particularly from around 1857, this mission took an independent course, under Dom Rosendo Salvado. The early Benedictines were zealous men, willing to endure hardship, but they also were practical and industrious. Many later missions aimed to shelter urban fringe dwellers, already socially disoriented. Salvado's recruiting area was less disturbed and, by gradually increasing the area of the estate and by ensuring that the railway was laid many kilometres west of New Norcia, he attempted to minimise European impact.

Inspired by the desire to raise an independent Christian community of peasant farmers and artisans, the monks taught by example. Moral and religious instruction were linked to useful training, based upon the ethic of private property. Their mix of tuition, work and socialised leisure better suited Aboriginal concepts of time and motion, than the routine at many other missions.

Because land ownership and education formed the basis of Salvado's view of Christian formation, married men were given a plot of land and a cottage. Perhaps because the monks laboured enthusiastically beside the Aborigines, the latter proved willing learners during the early years of the estate. Salvado praised their adeptness with sickles, for "they became such experts . . . that they very soon surpassed the white people". Listen to Salvado address them after the harvest, as they gathered round the wagon holding each man's yield:

> Each one of you now has his own wheat, and this will be divided into two lots: the first will be for your own food and seed for next year; the second is for sale . . . to Perth. You will put aside the money you get for it to buy clothes, sheep, pigs . . . and these will belong entirely to you; but you will not be allowed to slaughter or sell for the time being without my permission.

Optimistic paternalism, obviously. Even so, although the spiritual success of New Norcia seems moderate, its achievements in the material world surpassed most other missionary endeavours. The people enjoyed a dignified and self-reliant communal life over the following half century, which witnessed social disintegration around the continent. By the 1880s Aboriginal residents numbered one hundred. The 117 occupants of 1887 rose to 132 in 1898, while 163 lived there in 1904. The mission village of twenty-one cottages in the sixties more than doubled that number later in the century.

New Norcia Mission from across the Moore River, c. 1869. Father Martinez musters the boys on the near bank. In the left, rear, are Aboriginal cottages; the church and monastery are to the right. (Courtesy Battye Library, 73632P)

The initial government grant of eight hectares was increased largely by purchase, to about 400,000 hectares during the eighties. Salvado has been criticised for establishing this capitalistic pastoral empire, chiefly based upon Aboriginal labour. Charles Rowley adopted a more positive approach in his sad chronicle of *The Destruction of Aboriginal Society*. As a virtually self-supporting institution he observed, it "was pioneering the technical and commercial education of the Aboriginal; and Aborigines from here held skills which are still rare among part-Aborigines".

A comparable viewpoint in 1986, across the tree-fringed Moore River, with the much enlarged monastery prominent. (D.J. Mulvaney)

The combination of Aboriginal and Benedictine skills indeed established a major wool industry, harvested extensive cereal crops, bred quality horses for Britain's Indian army, and produced olive oil and wine, together with butter, macaroni and soap. The large commercial flour mill which opened in 1879 is operating still. Girls also learned practical domestic arts. Across the estates, improvements provided public facilities, such as roads and over one hundred wells. Salvado revealed the secret of his success when he described his practical and considerate approach to track construction. In order to lay out seventy kilometres of the Perth road, he recruited fourteen Aborigines. He rostered them for duty: four took turns at clearing the track, two hunted game for their meals, while eight rested. This personal, thoughtful contact must have done much to sustain Aboriginal morale.

While New Norcia achieved fame as a centre of agricultural innovation and productivity, it also became renowned in the eighties for its social accomplishments. As a fine musician himself, Salvado encouraged music. A twenty-member string band was formed, while a brass band was directed by Paul Piramino, an Aborigine, who also played the organ for the boys' choir. Their repertoire was varied. These groups all entertained in Perth's Town Hall.

Salvado, in 1879, encouraged H.B. Lefroy, a pastoralist neighbour and a future premier, to form an Aboriginal cricket team. They wore eye-catching uniforms and fashionable band-box hats trimmed with ribbon. The team performed so well in Perth and other centres, that it was termed The Invincibles. New Norcia fielded a team for the next twenty-five years. These accomplishments impressed visiting governors and other dignitaries, including Sydney's Cardinal Moran in 1887.

During this period of Australia-wide Aboriginal neglect and social disintegration, New Norcia proved an oasis of human dignity and caring. Its inhabitants drew praise from the press and the public, from the governor down, even though frequently patronising in tone. Nothing could protect the community, however, from European diseases. Amongst these inroads, a measles epidemic during the early eighties proved a killer.

With the advent of the new century, Western Australia's population multiplied during those golden years. New Norcia ceased to be a remote bush settlement, and some of the skilled Aborigines obtained work elsewhere. The frontier had shifted to the Kimberleys. When, in 1907, the Benedictine Order undertook to maintain a mission at Kalumburu, it diverted energies and resources. Aboriginal people remained at New Norcia, and a community lives there today, but they were no longer the central focus.

Salvado's successor, Abbot Torres, gave the monastery a new orientation towards the education of white children. Torres was a builder with eclectic tastes, and ornate boarding colleges arose. New Norcia entered an important phase as a European educational and cultural centre. The vernacular estate buildings remained, but many of the Aboriginal cottages were demolished during the 1920s, the remainder being levelled during the fifties. The present Aboriginal community lives in houses north of the monastery.

In 1986, 140 years after New Norcia began, happily a Heritage Trail was established, with informative signposts. Although the tourist views the accumulated buildings, the twentieth century structures are the most prominent. With the museum and tourist guide book, however, it is possible to visualise the place of a century ago. Aboriginal New Norcia resulted from a positive and fruitful encounter between Spaniards and several hundred Aboriginal people.

Poonindie

The Poonindie Native Institution, twenty kilometres north of Port Lincoln, suffered both from its own success and envious neighbours. From its foundation in 1850 its growth paralleled New Norcia, as it became economically viable and socially relevant to Aboriginal needs. It existed independently of government grants or benefactions throughout its last thirty years, even contributing to the support of other missions. The 1876 donation to the Aborigines' Friends Association was £ 50. Its unjustifiable closure in 1894 resulted from a cynical government and trustees manipulated to ensure the land's transfer to greedy local farmers. St Matthew's Anglican Mission Church is in the Register, although other structures also merit inclusion.

Unlike New Norcia's rural population, Poonindie's first residents were transferred from the Adelaide School for Aborigines, located near North Terrace. They had received European education and religious instruction, but city life proved vicious. Remote Poonindie was intended to foster a segregated community, transplanted from corrupting urban influences. Within a few years, however, it served mainly to shelter Port Lincoln and Eyre Peninsula people.

Poonindie's philanthropic sponsor and superintendent until 1855 was Adelaide's Anglican archdeacon, M.B. Hale. Hale backed his idealism with self-sacrifice and his own capital. Like Salvado, Hale identified with the welfare of his flock, and like him, he became a bishop, successively of Perth and Brisbane. Hale obtained a government grant of 1,200 hectares on the Tod River, whose waters provided "a never-failing source of pleasure and occupation to the natives". Nobody had taken up this vacant land previously, and Hale acquired a sheep run of thirty-one square kilometres to extend it to commercial proportions. The Aboriginal reserve was surveyed by John McDouall Stuart, the explorer. Because it proved suitable sheep and wheat country, it became coveted. That was in the

St Matthew's Anglican Church, Poonindie, focus of the Poonindie Native Institution 1850–94. Completed in 1855, it served variously as a school, residence, store and church. (D.J. Mulvaney)

A surviving Aboriginal stone and brick cottage, Poonindie. (D.J. Mulvaney)

future, however, when Hale stocked it, using two thousand pounds from his own pocket; he also expended other personal capital.

As with Salvado, Hale envisaged an independent peasantry, so he encouraged married couples to come by providing them with huts and plots of their own. It began with four couples, but there were eleven by 1853. The New Norcia parallel continues, because Aborigines performed most tasks. Hale worked alongside the men. His thumb provided his rule. "I had to be a learner myself", he recalled, "I had to get what information I required from books, and I then had to reduce it to practice in order to become a teacher." His improvisation extended to a home-made wool press. After 1852, Aborigines performed most ploughing and shearing tasks. Eleven bales of wool increased to 100 bales in 1872; they ran 10,000 sheep during the eighties. The 700 bushels of wheat harvested in 1855 sufficed to feed the community and to provide future seed.

Hale adopted a work schedule appropriate to Aboriginal stamina and interest. After Hale's departure for Perth, a government inspector criticised Aboriginal notions of a day's work. They were "treated too indulgently" by Hale, he found. Further, Hale "had done much harm in his farewell address by telling the natives that he left the property . . . for them and extorting them to look after it". As a consequence, they "acquired false ideas of independence".

As these erroneous ways included making the place pay, and successfully competing against local labour, it is evident that the inspector's implicit accusations of laziness were unfounded.

During the 1870s, the benefits of Hale's approach and the quality of the soil became apparent. The men on the estate were paid wages, and in 1875 this amounted to about £ 700; it reached £ 720 in 1877. In addition, when not needed on the estate, they took contract jobs shearing or grubbing roots for district farmers. Some men earned up to £ 70 by such efforts, employing "bush" Aborigines themselves. The largest pastoralist in the district told Hale in 1872, that "he habitually employed the Poonindie shearers, and bore testimony to their useful and good conduct". One of them, Tom Adams, was acknowledged to be the region's best shearer. At the 1879 district ploughing contest, "the natives succeeded in obtaining all the best prizes, much to the surprise of . . . the competitors, who were farmers of long standing". Such achievements probably aroused resentment amongst the white labour force.

The resident population rose to around a hundred as a result of inflow from the region, because only sixty-seven came from Adelaide. In 1883, J.W. Bull, a settler-historian, described the community as "leading a respectable, useful, and happy life . . . in a model village, occupying neat cottages". Adelaide's Bishop Short judged the village choir and flute players, "a delight to themselves and all who heard them".

As at New Norcia, social graces extended to the cricket field. Even in 1853 cricket was played vigorously, as a contemporary sketch of a team in the field shows. In that year, young Nannultera was painted with his bat by Michael Crossland, and the portrait is now in the Australian National Gallery. These clues provide some of the earliest evidence for systematic Aboriginal cricket. The team later played at Port Lincoln. During the seventies members voyaged to Adelaide to challenge the St Peter's College eleven.

A terrible flaw marred the quality of life of this self-reliant community, because chest ailments took a heavy toll. During the fifties, when population numbers averaged sixty, twenty-nine deaths occurred, and ten died in 1860; only three live births were recorded. The death rate amongst Eyre Peninsula Aborigines also was high; an estimate reduced it from two hundred to thirty or forty people during this period. Special factors at Poonindie, however, may have accentuated pulmonary infections during its first decade. Couples occupied tiny wooden one-room huts, with shingle roof and clay floor. As they leaked, floors muddied and people preferred to sleep outside by fires. They ate communally in a large stone kitchen, which may have facilitated the spread of germs.

More substantial dwellings followed, health improved and babies were born. Eight two-roomed brick cottages with fireplaces were occupied by 1859. At least one of these still stands and an archaeological survey of the mission area is required. The extent of building is further evidence for gainful Aboriginal employment. Brick manufacture began in 1852, the clay pit situated within a few hundred metres. In that year, 20,000 bricks were produced, with Aborigines assisting the process. The largest structure, the church, was begun by Hale in 1854 and completed the following year. Originally, it was the school, while the missionary occupied the first floor. When it became the church, the upper space served as the school.

St Matthew's is in an excellent state of preservation and is an unusual structure. It is built of stone with brick quoins, the walls being forty-five centimetres thick. The inside measures about eleven metres by five metres, the upper floor being supported on massive eucalypt beams. The side walls rise to above five metres, but the gabled ends reach to almost nine metres. The most unorthodox external feature results from a fireplace on each floor, with separate flues. The massive chimney towers above, nine metres tall. Two attractive indoor features are the pews, presumably mission products, and a large bay window with four lights.

While Christian fellowship and harmony continued within St Matthew's, groups in Port Lincoln agitated from around 1870 for the resumption of Poonindie's land. The appeal was for democratic working-men's blocks, but it was a democracy only for whites. Complaints levelled at the mission were contradictory and largely specious. The main grievance, simply stated, was that the Aborigines occupied good land and they should be transferred to less productive soil.

Throughout the next twenty years the clamour continued, although official investigators always supported the Aboriginal enterprise. In J.W. Bull's opinion, "it is almost past credence" that the local parliamentary member could act for "greedy constituents", to evict these "civilised and Christianised natives". Within ten years and without just cause, regrettably, the trustees capitulated to pressure. The mission closed in 1894, although the grudging government established a Poonindie Trust of £1,000 to compensate the trustees. Some of the dispossessed had lived at Poonindie all their lives; for others it was their second loss of land through European action. No satisfactory provision was made for the unfortunate people. Many were sent to overcrowded Point Pearce mission on Yorke Peninsula. Two families had homes built at Raukkan, on Lake Alexandrina, from Poonindie Trust funds. So it was that an integrated self-sufficient community was dispersed and made destitute.

Cullinlaringo

CHAPTER
FIFTEEN

Massacre and Dispersion at Cullinlaringo

The Cullinlaringo attack occurred silently and with tragic efficiency on the warm afternoon of 17 October 1861. Horatio Spencer Wills, the only armed man in the camp, emerged from his tent with a revolver. He fired once and was struck down. Swiftly, Kairi warriors armed with clubs, axes and spears moved in. The unsuspecting party died within a few moments. Women still held their sewing and the bullock-driver, his whip. A shepherd, who was minding his flock some distance away, escaped to break the terrible news. Nineteen people died — eleven men, three women and five children — in the largest massacre of white people by Aborigines in Australian history. Even so, that total was dwarfed by those shot in retribution over the following weeks.

The party from Victoria had depastured its flocks on the rolling plains northwest of the future Springsure only two weeks previously. In the mountains, eighty kilometres south, was Kenniff Cave, which the ancestors of the Aborigines had been visiting throughout 19,000 years. Despite this tenurial disparity in length of occupancy, following the anthropological notions of the day, most people denied the Aborigines any title to the land. An economy based upon hunting and gathering activities was judged to be an unproductive use of the soil. When the Queensland governor, Sir George Bowen, wrote to the colonial secretary a few weeks later, to inform him of the Wills disaster, he expressed the notion succinctly: "the territory over which these *few* Aboriginal tribes *wandered* for it would be incorrect to state that they ever in any strict sense *occupied* it" (italics inserted).

The implication of Bowen's remarks was that Australia was sparsely populated by a nomadic people whose parasitic economy depended absolutely upon what nature provided unaided. He expressed the Eurocentric notion of terra nullius, that land uncultivated by human hands was waste land, virgin soil placed there by

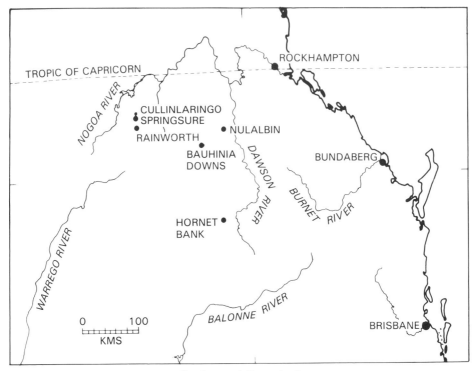

TROPIC OF CAPRICORN

ROCKHAMPTON

NOGOA RIVER

CULLINLARINGO
SPRINGSURE
RAINWORTH
BAUHINIA
DOWNS

NULALBIN

DAWSON RIVER

BURNET RIVER

BUNDABERG

HORNET
BANK

WARREGO RIVER

0   100
KMS

BALONNE RIVER

BRISBANE

South-central Queensland

God for plough or pasture. Bowen was blissfully unaware that the needs which he saw for settlers were identical to those of Aborigines. He told the colonial secretary in 1862: "Grass and water — these are the two requisites for pastoral occupation. Let these be furnished and Australian colonization can enter upon its first phase."

Therefore, while control and exploitation of grass and water for pastoral or agricultural purposes conveyed upon the European invaders a title to the land and a right to defend it by force, rights to the same resources were effectively denied to Aborigines. An exposition of this doctrine was literally carved in stone, over the forlorn grave of William Newbold, in the Rockhampton cemetery. Before he died from tomahawk head wounds, Newbold shot his Aboriginal assailant. The inscription tells the rest:

> Died March 2nd 1868, aged 21 years,
> From the effects of wounds
> received in pioneer warfare.
> Pity him, stranger, thus cut off in
> early youth whilst in the discharge
> of his duty and in obedience to that
> earliest of God's commandments,
> "Go forth and subdue the earth".

Research over the last quarter century has demonstrated the errors of the notion that there was no input of Aboriginal intelligence or labour. Aboriginal men and women actually manipulated the varied environments within the boundaries of their territories; their movements were closely regulated by seasonal, technological and ceremonial considerations; and they were never random. Productivity of plants and animals was maximised by many means, while ceremonial systems which exchanged economically valued goods were complex and far-reaching. Archaeologists and historians also argue that population numbers have been underestimated and that a drastic revision upwards is necessary. The conventional number of 300,000 for the continent may be doubled, at least. In any case, the Nogoa and Dawson River regions were thickly populated areas.

The grave of Horatio Wills, with a fence around its finely engraved headstone, is set on rising land above Garden Creek, a tributary of the Nogoa River. Less than fifty metres west is the unmarked, but fenced, mass grave of other casualties, hurriedly buried two days after they died. A few kilometres across the grassy plain towards the southwest are the prominent hills named Spencer and Wills; Mt Horatio is to the northwest, across Garden Creek.

The site of the 1861 Cullinlaringo massacre, with the mass grave. The grave of Wills and Garden Creek are outside this image, to the left. (D.J. Mulvaney)

The grave of Horatio Spencer Wills, 1861. (D.J. Mulvaney)

This incident, with its high number of violent deaths of Europeans is notorious, but there were numerous other bloody encounters in which Aboriginal warriors took the offensive. The killings began in 1788, with the spearing of a convict. Although many attacks on Europeans were unprovoked by the victims, as was the case at Cullinlaringo, many were direct responses to European violence, especially the abduction of Aboriginal women. In Queensland during the second half of the nineteenth century, it is estimated that at least 850 Europeans, Chinese, or other aliens, were killed. The Australian total since 1788 may number from 2,000 to 2,500, but even this formidable number probably is less than one-tenth of the Aboriginal deaths from European bullets.

The Wills massacre site is listed in the Register as an exemplar of this Aboriginal resistance to dispossession. Its importance is magnified for Aboriginal Australians because of its appalling consequences. The place also has meaning for European Australians, because it testifies to the very real hazards which faced colonists and the hardships endured by pioneer women and children. Horatio Wills also was a person of some importance in Victorian pastoral and political history. He had proved an extremely successful pastoralist at Lexington, near Ararat, and he served a term in the Victorian Legislative Council. Added piquancy stems from the presence of his eldest son, Thomas Wentworth Wills, who escaped death because he left with a wagon a few days before the attack to collect stores from another station. His activities in Melbourne already ensured his immortality in sporting history. He was one of three enthusiastic innovators who inaugurated Australian Rules football. After his return to Melbourne in 1864 he became Victoria's leading intercolonial cricketer and captain of the colonial team. He also was the first captain and coach of the 1866–68 Aboriginal cricket team, discussed in chapter 16.

Horatio was the second (but unrelated) Wills to achieve a pathetic and sentimental popular notoriety during 1861. W.J. Wills perished on Cooper's Creek only three months before this massacre, with his impetuous leader, Burke. It could be claimed that both H.S. and W.J. Wills were needless sacrifices to the failure of colonists to come to terms with the realities of Aboriginal social and economic organisation. Horatio had an excellent record of friendliness to the Victorian Aborigines around his Lexington station, while Tom learned to speak something of their language. Guns never were necessary. In this different Queensland situation, he treated the Aborigines in a similar relaxed manner. Yet he and his massive flocks may have been judged by these Aborigines whom he tried to befriend, as yet another destroyer of their lands. Possibly he violated traditional rules or unintentionally occupied sacred places. Certainly, he typified those settlers who seriously underestimated Aboriginal abilities to communicate widely amongst themselves, and their powers of co-ordinated opposition. William John Wills, on the other hand, perished from starvation and exhaustion, amongst people who would have nourished him willingly, if ignorance had not led the explorers to fear them as treacherous savages and to hold their society in contempt.

The four blocks of country covering 250 square kilometres for which the lease was transferred to Wills, had been selected by Peter MacDonald. He called the property Cullinlaringo, a Spanish derived term, meaning "sought and found". In fact, its inhabitants were Kairi people. Wills decided to settle there during a visit in 1860, when he saw eager men moving in to select land in this recently explored region. It took his party eight months during the next year to travel his stock and equipment from Brisbane and Rockhampton. The hardy wives of two of the men in the party, while travelling on bullock wagons and drays with their families, bore babies. It must have proved a relief to arrive at Garden Creek and undertake the exhausting but positive labour of establishing a base. Within a fortnight some shelters and fencing were completed and gardens commenced.

  These doomed people may have paid the penalty for crimes committed by others before their arrival. Even so, the presence of several thousand sheep, and cattle, horses and unusually lavish equipment, made their own impact upon the environment and its inhabitants. It increased pressure on resources, excluded Aborigines from watering places and the wagon loads stacked with material proved a visual temptation.

  Contemporaries referred to Horatio as "old Wills". In fact, he only turned forty-nine on the day they reached Cullinlaringo. In this frontier society of resilient youth, however, he must have seemed aged. A relevant factor in the tragic saga of frontier conflict was the youth of the protagonists. William Newbold was twenty-one; Jesse Gregson, at Mount Rainworth, the nearest neighbour to Wills, was aged twenty-four. Most of the police officers commanding native police were young and inexperienced. Lieutenant A.M. Patrick, who was a prime factor on the Nogoa in providing the Aborigines with grievances, complained to a squatter that although most officers bagged their first Aborigine soon after they went on field service, he had yet to kill one after some months. To such gun-toting potential firebrands, "old Wills" who stockpiled his arsenal without arming his men, who was "prepared to civilise and make use of the Aborigines, and he had made good friends with them from the start", must have seemed a crank. In his old age, Gregson recalled that, when he warned Wills never to trust Aborigines or to let them approach his camp, he retorted, "I don't think so and I knew all about blacks before you were born".

  Horatio Wills, who had little eduction in his Sydney youth, had expectations of amply providing for his children. Three sons were currently at school in Germany, while Tom had been educated at Rugby. His correspondence with his boys overseas shows him as a devoted parent with a sense of fun. Evidently he was an easy-going leader, expecting good, not the worst, from the despised Aborigines.

  The brutality of this massacre, when even babies were hacked or clubbed to death, becomes even more tragic in the light of this knowledge. In this sense, the wrong people suffered. This group was led by a humane man, who preferred a mature approach to threats, as the way to accept Aborigines. Such families unfortunately were rare in central Queensland. The occasion provided less balanced settlers with a ready excuse for tough policies. They felt justified in their mistrust of and belligerence to Aborigines, because Wills had failed to heed their warnings. It set back the cause of those who favoured humane approaches. Three men in the area who opposed the majority line, Frederick Walker of Nulalbin and Charles and Henry Dutton of Bauhinia Downs, were ridiculed, and their advice was ignored by government officials.

  More typical was the reaction of the squatter, Oscar de Satgé. "The feeling in the outside country became deeply aroused by this terrible massacre, which no doubt acted as a warning to many not to trust or admit the blacks . . . I carried away this lesson . . . with me, and vowed I never would have the blacks in on any station I managed, and I kept to this rule for over ten years, until the Peak Downs blacks became absolutely civilised.'' The repercussions spread. A few months later, when Landsborough was searching for Burke and Wills, some Aborigines gathered near his camp at night. He was south of Longreach, over 450 kilometres from Cullinlaringo. The party fired at the Aborigines, killing one and wounding others. ''Perhaps these blacks'', Landsborough remarked, ''as they said they had visited the settled country, may have had a part in the massacre of the Wills family.'' It was an an improbable assumption, but a most convenient excuse for murder.

The seeds of Aboriginal discontent were sown long before the Wills station was sited on Garden Creek. As the tide of pastoral expansion surged westward along the Dawson and Nogoa River systems during the fifties, pressure on Aboriginal resources mounted. Jiman, Wadja and Kairi people were ''dispersed'' and Aboriginal women were taken by Europeans. This latter factor appears to have been involved in several major incidents. The first multiple casualties suffered by settlers in the region occurred in 1855. In an attack on Fraser's Hornet Bank Station, southwest of Taroom, in 1857, eleven men, women and children were killed. The pay-back symbolism of the brutal rape of Martha Fraser and her two eldest daughters before their death is evident; but the settlers ignored it. An orgy of retaliation was visited upon the Aborigines of the region. One member of a posse which went ''hunting'' for six weeks, recalled that ''some we found at one place and some at another . . . upon the whole they got their deserts at our hands, so far as it was in our power to deal out rough justice''.

In events such as these, it is important to note how colonists used language to emotive effect. In outback Australia, the murder of Europeans by Aborigines was termed a ''massacre'', which of course it was. However, when settlers used arms against Aborigines, or when native police under European command shot their people, the term used was ''dispersed''. Dispersal suggests a non-violent moving on, whereas the reverse was normal. Like ''rough justice'', it sounded less brutal than massacre or execution, although the consequences were similar and the number who died was far greater. Most frequently, ''dispersal'' followed the spearing of cattle and sheep, not humans. As this cycle of massacre and dispersion often involved attacks upon innocent Aboriginal groups (and this assertion can be documented), it hardly is surprising that settlers who were innocent of killing Aborigines also suffered. In the sense that all settlers dispossessed Aborigines without any arrangements for compensation, however, nobody was blameless.

It is important to remember, also, that many members of the European community were aware of the frontier violence and opposed it. It is easy to portray misleadingly a society overcome with racist hysteria. Listen to the editor of the Brisbane *Courier*, as early as 8 November 1861, deploring the white backlash following the Wills massacre:

> Nothing in the way of compensation or precaution will be gained by counselling an indiscriminate slaughter . . . although it is easy to conceive that the complete extermination of the offending tribe would be a labor of love to some persons . . . . There is no doubt that the Aborigines acted in much the same manner as any of us would act towards those whom we could not but regard as intruders and invaders. The system which sanctions our appropriation of the native territory, and which assumes the right of dispossessing the Aborigines of their hunting and fishing grounds, without making the

slightest provision for their physical well-being, is one of very doubtful morality . . . every one of these savages is a British subject.

"The Native Police Force", the editorial continued, "is a sham and a delusion. They never do anything with the blacks but shoot them." This comment relates partly to events close to the scene of the Wills massacre, where matters took a serious turn weeks before the party arrived. Criticisms of the ruthless conduct of the native police ("a force who hunt blacks for their amusement", as one squatter concluded), but particularly of the callous attitude of its European officers, resulted in the appointment of a Select Committee of the Queensland Legislative Assembly. This pastoralist-oriented committee presented its report in July 1861. It admitted the validity of many criticisms and some staff changes in the police resulted, but it recommended the retention of the native police system. It emphasised that to ensure efficiency (and fear or hatred), native troopers who served in one district must be recruited from far distant places, so as to have no local affiliations. With unrealistic optimism, it concluded that "the destruction of property and loss of life on either side has considerably diminished".

That committee received two highly critical submissions from a former police officer, Frederick Walker of Nulalbin, shortly to depart in search of Burke and Wills, and from C.B. Dutton, of Bauhinia Downs, both places being well east of Cullinlaringo. Their complaints about the actions of native police officers were ignored and they were not called to give evidence. Their chief concern was the overbearing and officious conduct of inexperienced Lieutenant Patrick, whose series of actions contributed directly to the flashpoint situation created by the arrival of Wills.

Dutton wrote in March detailing a series of incidents when Patrick used his troopers on Bauhinia Downs, against Dutton's advice, to force his Aboriginal employees to move from his homestead area, and then destroyed their weapons. Patrick then established a police camp five kilometres away, an action provocative both to the Aborigines and to Dutton. As Dutton predicted, such bullying and provocation would foster a "deep implacable revenge for unprovoked injury", that was "fearfully dangerous to all".

Walker complained that around this period, Patrick also provoked trouble on Albinia Downs, in the Springsure area, which resulted in a needless incident in which several Aborigines were shot. In an extraordinary procedure, Patrick was cleared by his superior officer in Rockhampton, Lieutenant W. Bligh. Bligh sent copies of these accusations to Patrick, who denied them. Bligh therefore simply informed the authorities and the Select Committee in Brisbane, that the criticisms were groundless.

Patrick's probable motive was to goad those squatters who defended Aboriginal interests. Oscar de Satgé, no supporter of "soft" policies, conceded that the Dutton brothers were "warm protectors from anything like cruelty or injustice". It is relevant that, in November, Patrick resumed his harassment under the guise of the massacre emergency. He terrorised Dutton's employees and ordered them to leave, along with females whom Walker had left there under Dutton's protection while their menfolk accompanied Walker out west in the search for Burke and Wills. Patrick was acting under orders from Lieutenant Bligh, who ruled that no Aborigines could enter any station homestead area. "Anticipate considerable opposition from Messrs Dutton and F. Walker,'' he advised cynically.

After Dutton had read the Select Committee report and realised that his complaints had been ignored, he wrote indignantly to the government. His letter was dated 14 October, only three days before the massacre. He sought "to secure to the Blacks . . . a recognition of their rights as human beings, which the whole conduct of the Native Police has ignored".

In July, Patrick shifted his operations to Rainworth, neighbouring Cullinlaringo. It was to Rainworth that a surviving shepherd later brought news of the massacre and subsequent operations were planned. Jesse Gregson, the manager, adopted the firm policy from his arrival at Rainworth in June 1861, that no Aborigines could mix with his men or enter camps. "We agreed that . . . we did not wish to interfere with the blacks as long as they did not molest us." Even on the day of his arrival, however, his stern rule impinged upon the lifeways of these people. They were following their traditional practice of firing the grass, a form of "firestick farming", which cleared the brush and improved productivity. Gregson ordered them to beat out the flames and to move away, probably unaware that, on his first encounter, he had interfered drastically in their economic life.

Two weeks later, Patrick's troop arrived to check on the state of the peace, and immediately was involved in a confrontation. Gregson noticed that some sheep were missing and on the following morning they set out to trace them. They soon came upon a group of Aborigines with the sheep, in the process of cooking one. If they had been European cattle duffers, the penalty would have been arrest, a trial and imprisonment. Conditions were different for Aborigines. The police rode out of the bush, surprised the thieves and fired at close quarters, wounding at least four of them. In the scrimmage which followed on the rocky ridge, Gregson shot Patrick in the leg by accident, so the engagement suddenly ended. This mishap probably saved Aboriginal lives, because those who escaped would have been pursued. Even so, some of the wounded Aborigines later died.

According to a Wills family tradition, Tom Wills later was told by an Aboriginal stockman that these deaths were a critical event. As they had to be revenged, "they sent runners all over the country and were collecting at Separation Creek", hidden by the hills only about ten kilometres from the site which Wills selected for his homestead, but which soon became his grave.

A further possible factor in the worsening situation was the reported abduction of one or two Aboriginal boys from this region. It was reported in the Sydney press that they were taken to Sydney. The matter aroused anger amongst their people and ensured retaliation.

Immediately news of the Wills massacre broke, Daniel Cameron wrote urgently to the Brisbane authorities. As a settler at Planet Downs, he explained that in his twenty months occupancy he had experienced no Aboriginal problems. On the contrary, he detailed the considerable work completed by his dozen Aboriginal employees. He warned that, as few squatters shared his optimistic opinion, "retaliation and revenge will be quick and sharp". He predicted that "the advocates of treating them little better than inferior animals will exult in their extermination while those holding different views will be anomalously placed — the innocent and guilty alike will disappear and individuals of both sexes . . . will not scruple to condemn those who afford the natives an asylum or any tolerance".

And so it came to pass. A detachment of eight native troopers under Lieutenant Cave set out on 26 October. They shot five men in the scrub two days later. At dusk on the same day, Cave reported, they cornered a group on a rocky hilltop. "They made no stand — their loss was heavy — and . . . many were killed from falling over the cliffs." Commandant Bligh proved more reticent. He informed Brisbane authorities that three other police parties were on separate patrol in the region, but provided no details of their activities. He also proved vague in reporting his own patrol, when he raided a camp and destroyed weapons. His laconic comment, "I am sure that, that party will not collect again" has overtones of "dispersion". De Satgé approvingly commented, that the Aborigines were "thoroughly punished for their misdeeds".

These casualties followed upon the initial posse formed by Gregson, MacDonald and other squatters after they had buried the Wills party. Governor Bowen reported that about thirty Aborigines were shot by that party, whose "uncontrollable desire for vengeance took possession of every heart". Although a humanitarian, Bowen obviously approved of their action. It is likely, however, that the governor was provided with a minimum estimate of the mayhem.

Support for the assumption that the death roll was larger is provided by Wills family correspondence. Tom Wills wrote to his sister, presumably around the end of October, reporting that sixty Aborigines had died up to that time. His mother wrote to her sons in Germany on 21 December, that "the horrible wretches have payed dearly for it — for the settlers that went after them said they had shot 300 — and some seventy more that were killed by the black police".

In the aftermath to the disaster, but at a time when the danger to European settlement from Aboriginal resistance must have declined, settlers prudently prepared for law and order. Despite opposition from Charles and Henry Dutton, late in 1862 a Native Mounted Police Barracks was established at Spring Creek government reserve, in the Springsure area. That same year, Jesse Gregson employed a carpenter at Rainworth. His achievements included "a large stone store", which stands there today. As Rainworth Fort, it is listed in the Register. Its thick walls and concealed upper storey horizontal window slots,

Rainworth Fort constructed in 1862 as a store, but also possibly as a defence against an Aboriginal attack which never came. (D.J. Mulvaney)

do suggest fortress-like qualities. Possibly its secondary role was a potential refuge in case of attack.

By the time it was constructed, this function was superfluous. Landholders were in more danger from bushrangers than from Aborigines. It was to Springsure, around the turn of the century, that the fabled Kenniff brothers drove their stolen herds. Kenniff cave, a site of importance to Aboriginal people throughout nineteen millennia, eighty kilometres to the south, also is listed in the Register. It is ironic that such an important Aboriginal place is named for the lawless activities of these over-rated louts, but within their generation, cattle and sheep had inherited the land.

CHAPTER
SIXTEEN

Harrow

A Madimadi Cricketer at Lord's

Muarrinim (or Unaarimin), known to Europeans as Johnny Mullagh, was one of Australia's first cricketing celebrities. This quiet, unassuming all-rounder was born into a Madimadi clan around 1841. His people were displaced almost immediately by flocks of sheep which occupied Madimadi country, in the Harrow-Edenhope region of western Victoria. Muarrinim passed most of his life on two pastoral holdings, Pine Hills and Mullagh, whose combined 40,000 hectares presumably included his clan territory. Both station homesteads survive as examples of pioneer vernacular architecture, and are in the Register. "Mullagh Johnny", as he was called originally, took his name from Mullagh Station.

A capable horseman, Mullagh lived a solitary bush life, variously working as a groom, shearer and rabbiter. He never married. Yet this gentle recluse achieved greatness on the cricket field and, when assessed within the playing conditions and standards of his time, his feats of batting, bowling, and sheer endurance, bear comparison with the achievements of the greatest modern all-rounders.

Mullagh was the star member of the 1868 Aboriginal cricket tour of England, during which they won 14 and lost 14 of the 47 matches played. This was the first overseas team from any country to tour England, a decade before the first white Australian Test team. At Lord's, Mullagh's first innings score of 75 was the highest total in either team, while he took 8 wickets for 101 runs from 61 four-ball overs. His victims included past MCC president, the Earl of Coventry. (His Balmoral team-mate, Cuzens, captured 10 wickets for 117 runs, including a future MCC president, Viscount Downe.) Regrettably, the Aboriginal fixtures were not included in English statistics as first class matches, although a number should have been so classed. Most sports historians overlook Mullagh's prodigious tour analysis. He played in 45 of the 47 matches during the 1868 tour, scoring well over one-fifth of the team's runs (1,698) and taking over one-third of the wickets (257).

The Mullagh memorial, Harrow oval, erected in 1891 by
public subscription. (D.J. Mulvaney)

Mullagh's tomb in the Harrow
cemetery, which is inscribed "world
famed cricketer". (D.J. Mulvaney)

His 1877 overs included 831 maidens. When he was not bowling, he was the
team's most successful wicketkeeper. Even after play ceased there was no
relaxation, because it was customary at that period in commercial cricket to hold
associated athletic events. The Aborigines did so, but also added exhibitions of
Aboriginal traditional skills. Mullagh was a fine sprinter, the team's best high
jumper and a boomerang thrower of repute. Mullagh obviously combined
versatility with quality performance.

Mullagh became a Western District hero. Upon his death in 1891, a public appeal was launched by the *Hamilton Spectator*. It provided his tomb with an engraved headstone and iron railings, and also perpetuated his memory at the Harrow cricket oval, with a pink granite obelisk surmounted by a white urn, in High Victorian taste. Both these Mullagh memorials are in the Register. They symbolise the 1868 tour, while commemorating a sportsman who beat white Australians at their archetypal game.

From the middle of last century, cricket developed into an important socialising sport on large stations and rural centres, and other Aboriginal people participated in white cricket teams before the 1868 tour. These Western District men were the first to play as a full team which challenged European clubs; nobody else received such highly professional coaching. The Madimadi and Wutjubaluk men involved first received rudimentary instruction around 1864. Cricket was popular because of the publicity surrounding two lucrative Victorian tours by English professional teams in 1861–62 and 1863–64. Knowledge of the latest rules, which included overarm bowling, was brought home on vacation by the Scotch College schoolboy son of David Edgar, of Pine Hills. Consequently, Mullagh was an early initiate. William Hayman, an enthusiast at Lake Wallace South Station and who later travelled with the team to England, founded the Edenhope cricket club. Forty kilometres northeast, on Mount Talbot Station, C.W. Officer coached Aborigines on level ground near the homestead.

The initial prime mover was Tom Hamilton, of Bringalbert Station. He arranged challenge matches between station teams, which included Aborigines. As a novelty, he arranged an all-black team to challenge white teams. By 1866 the blacks were victorious. In March 1866, he daringly challenged the more select Hamilton club, and the Aborigines won easily. Having shaped their course, Hamilton's energies were directed elsewhere. He drove a mob of horses to Darwin in 1872, while the Overland Telegraph Line was under construction.

Late in 1866, local supporters brought to Edenhope T.W. Wills, Victoria's best cricketer, where he coached the Aborigines at a camp beside Lake Wallace. It was Tom Wills who escaped death at Cullinlaringo in 1861 (see chapter 15). Wills led his team onto the Melbourne Cricket Ground on Boxing Day 1866, but they lost the match. A disastrous tour to New South Wales followed under Wills. The team returned home dispirited and in poor health, but Mullagh already had shown great promise.

The team reformed around September 1867, and its morale revived, with the arrival in Edenhope of Charles Lawrence. Lawrence, a capable Surrey all-rounder, came to Australia with the first English tour and remained to become an influential coach. He saw the Aborigines play in Sydney and, together with two Sydney businessmen, decided to promote an English tour as an investment. In the event, finances broke about even.

After a series of trial matches, thirteen Aborigines under Lawrence's captaincy sailed for England, arriving there in May 1868. One of them, King Cole (Brippoki) died in London and two others returned early. This placed a burden on the remaining team, two of whom played in all forty-seven matches. Mullagh, Cuzens and Lawrence carried the team, in all departments of the game.

Back in Victoria early in 1869, both Mullagh and Cuzens were engaged by the Melbourne Cricket Club for the 1869–70 season, but neither of them was happy in

Melbourne and they departed for home territory within a few weeks. Mullagh's eight innings averaged 34.5, the second highest that season for the MCC team.

Over the following twenty years, Mullagh played for the Harrow Club, with legendary success. Evidently, he emerged from the bush to play without any practice. Yet he scored a century in 1871. He headed his club's batting averages (21) in 1878–79, while his bowling average of 3.5 surpassed all others. He scored 92 in an innings during the next season, and his 1881–82 scores were 110, 61, 10, 3, 6, 47 and 97.

His achievements were known in Melbourne, so when Lord Harris captained the All-England Eleven during 1879, Mullagh was included in the Victorian team. Facing the slow bowling of England's star bowler, Emmett, Mullagh held the side together in the second innings, with a patient 36 out of 156 scored by Victoria. The *Australasian* praised his "graceful forward play and strong defence". Writing forty years later, Lord Harris described Mullagh as "a very elegant bat".

Mullagh was selected as the sole club representative during the 1884–85 season in a team from the Western District–Mt Gambier region which played in an Adelaide competition. Mullagh opened the batting in each of the five matches played. His total of 104 runs, average 26, topped his team. Facing the young Test bowler, Geroge Giffen, he batted through the innings of 116 at Norwood, to be 43 not out. His 25 against North Adelaide was the highest score.

Mullagh faced occasions of racial discrimination or insult with sturdy dignity. On the English tour, when his team was excluded from the York refreshment tent, he refused to take the field again. In the Western District, when called a "nigger" by an opposing captain, he deliberately hit a catch. Assigned a bed in the stable instead of the pub, as being adequate for a "nigger", Mullagh slept elsewhere in the open.

Mullagh was characteristically alone in his bush camp, in August 1891, when he died. His well attended funeral in the cemetery above Harrow provided a remarkable testimony to the respect in which he was held by Europeans. Four members of the Harrow cricket club carried his coffin to the grave from the cemetery gate. His own bat and a set of stumps were placed on his coffin, on which all the club members tossed sprigs of yellow flowers and black berries, to symbolise the club colours. Until a recent fire destroyed it, Mullagh's portrait was displayed thereafter in the Harrow Mechanics' Institute.

Harrow today is a decayed rural village and Mullagh's memorial stands forlornly in the former oval where he achieved so much. This ornate column and his well preserved tomb deserve greater public attention. During a period when Aborigines were credited with little aptitude, intelligence or application, this Madimadi man achieved a dignified distinction, which led to his acceptance by Western District pastoralists and the Marylebone Cricket Club, amongst other Establishment bodies. His achievements should have given them cause to question their prejudices. Aboriginal people today should feel proud of this native son.

CHAPTER SEVENTEEN

Anthropology Along the Overland Telegraph Line

A continuous black ribbon of tarmac has linked Adelaide and Darwin since February 1987. As an engineering landmark, these 3,000 kilometres of road cannot compare in importance with the completion of the Overland Telegraph Line, in August 1872. This probably was Australia's most considerable engineering achievement during the nineteenth century, when a single iron wire carried on wooden poles joined these same centres, and bound Australia to world affairs.

It was an exceptional feat, stimulating pride in the infant South Australian colony, founded only thirty-six years previously. It produced a rash of exploration, as Europeans criss-crossed arid central lands, while pastoralists and prospectors surged on close behind them. The first herds of cattle and mobs of horses pushed up from the south even while the telegraph line was lengthening. Manned repeater stations were erected along the line at intervals of two or three hundred kilometres, to service faults and to boost the feeble morse code signals which put Australian cities within less than two days reach of London. For migrants whose passage out had taken months, and whose letters to Britain took ten weeks, this modern communications system was a true symbol of progress.

Success boosted the conviction that colonists were destined to inherit the land, and the line enabled the instant occupation of remote Australia by a few determined and armed Europeans. Each repeater station, based on a natural water supply, provided a base for supplies, communications and law enforcement. The wire strand between stations acted like a safety net in the wilderness, making epic droving feats possible along its length, and also at right angles to it. The first cattlemen to open up the Barkly Tableland, drove their stock west in the direction of Tennant Creek or Powell Creek Telegraph Stations. John Forrest headed east across the hostile Gibson desert during 1874, until he reached the security of the line. Hitherto unknown Aboriginal societies suddenly were in contact with expanding frontiers of occupation. Their scale compared with that of the simultaneous, but more celebrated, American westward expansion. Within a decade, huge inland tracts were taken up for pastoral exploitation, with waterholes the focus of attention.

Iron poles replaced white-anted original poles; copper wire and successive technological improvements increased the line's efficiency. Eventually, other forms of telecommunication rendered the system redundant, and the central base at Alice Springs closed in 1932. Some repeater stations have survived the abandonment of the service and the demolition of the line. A few places linked with the Overland Telegraph are listed, appropriately, in the Register of the National Estate. No stretch of the line was preserved. Near Deep Well, south of Alice Springs, a forlorn line of wire-less iron poles marches parallel with the now abandoned railway track, across the sandy plain towards the southern horizon.

A few kilometres to the east of the track, in the Ooraminna Range, is a surviving relic of the original vehicle track from Oodnadatta to Alice Springs. As it is in the sandstone hills not far from Ooraminna rockhole, a traveller on the mail coach from Oodnadatta was already about twelve days out on the track when this tough stretch was reached. The surviving section includes the approach to a hill which is so steep and narrow that it was termed "the Pinch". A weary traveller described it: "in reality, it forms a kind of . . . smooth rock ladder, up which the horses stumble as best they can". Nothing better encapsulates the sense of the discomfort of travel along the Overland Telegraph track, or of the determination of Europeans to subdue the environment, than this rock-hewn Pinch. For these reasons it is listed in the Register.

The purpose of the telegraph stations may have puzzled Aborigines along the track. Their own systems of information transmission, using messengers, ceremonial gift exchange networks and smoke indicators, were efficient and more social in nature. Aboriginal people, uncluttered with the hot and bulky clothing of Europeans, were better adapted to this beautiful but tough environment. Sympathetic contemporaries believed that the contacts established with Aborigines following the opening of the Overland Telegraph Line would prove fatal to their culture and that all Aborigines would die. That the story was not simply one of decay and social destruction, is evident today. The depth of spiritual and ceremonial life in the modern Centre, and the continued bonds between people and their clan estates, are proof that cultural strength may persist through adversity.

The Alice Springs, Barrow Creek and Tennant Creek Telegraph Stations survive substantially as originally built. They are listed in the Register. The influx of fringe-dwelling Aborigines around such stations has been explained as the result of the attractions of novelty and "handouts". The availability of new forms of labour-saving food, especially flour, tea and sugar, together with tobacco and grog, acted as magnets. They drew in people from the bush and created attendant shanty annexes.

Such simplistic explanations omit the crucial factor that pastoralists disrupted the systematic seasonal cycle of land settlement and resource use across the entire region. Much of this drift to the telegraph stations was a necessary response to economic conditions, particularly where pastoralists barred

"The Pinch" was cut into the sandstone Ooraminna Range, on the original Oodnadatta-Alice Springs track. Baldwin Spencer photographed it in 1901. (Baldwin Spencer, *Across Australia*, 1912, fig. 87)

The Pinch today, a fossilised communications system symbolic of outback travel hardships. (D.J. Mulvaney)

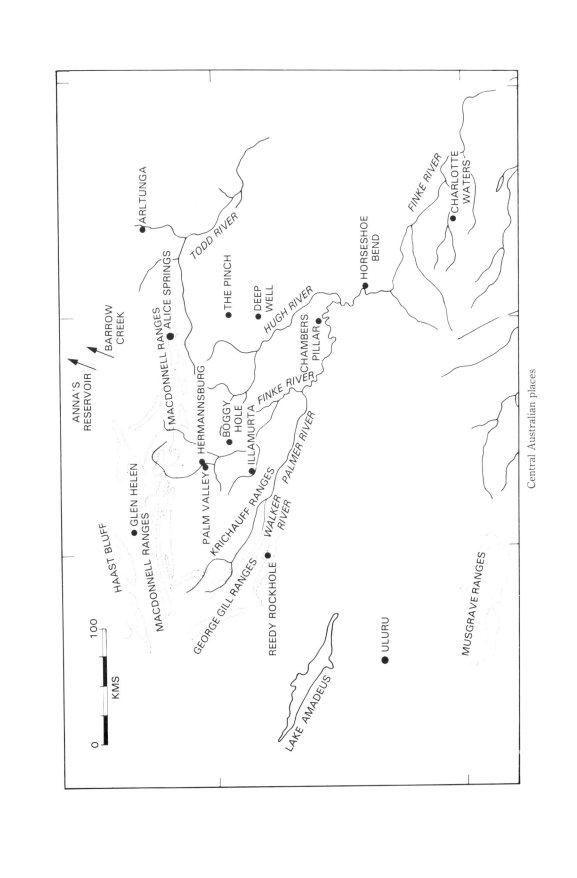

Central Australian places

Aboriginal use of waterholes, or even occupancy anywhere on their leases. In this sense, the telegraph stations served a rudimentary social welfare role, while the officer in charge was the local administrative officer. The Aboriginal connection with these stations must be included in any true history of their role. In the case of F.J. Gillen, the Alice Springs post and telegraph stationmaster through the nineties, he was the only justice of the peace in the Centre and he also served as the district Sub-Protector of Aborigines. For the same period, telegraph stations became ration depots. There is a popular belief that the line also lured "stone age" craftsmen to the telegraph poles for the insulators. Insulators provide excellent raw material for flaking tools, but their appeal may have been transitory. Alternative materials including glass, wire, hoop iron and metal tools proved welcome substitutes for stone tools. It is unfortunate that there was little interest in collecting specimens which documented acculturation and the adaptation of European goods to traditional uses. The early ethnographers sought "pure" pre-European institutions and technologies. Mounted trooper E.C. Cowle, who collected items for the Melbourne museum, obtained five adzes in 1900. He wrote to inform the director that these adzes had iron tips, "which I am getting replaced with flints". Here, then, was the preoccupation with the savage as a primitive, in which change was denied him, as "untypical".

Another stereotype was the savage as blithely ignorant and therefore suitable for the butt of wit. Surveyor-General Goyder retailed such a joke, which reflected Eurocentric superiority, rather than native innocence. According to Goyder, upon first seeing the Overland Telegraph wire, an Aborigine observed, "What plurri fool white feller put up this one feller fence? It no stop 'em horse."

From the time that construction began on the Overland Telegraph, travellers along the sandy track to Alice Springs were drawn to the soaring pinnacle of Chambers Pillar, visible across the undulating red sand dunes. This remnant of a Cretaceous ocean floor consists of friable and variegated pale cream and red-brown sandstone, rising vertically from a broad, sloping base to a fiery height of about fifty metres. Thrusting strongly against the blue sky and surrounding dull green vegetation, it is a striking monument, meriting its listing in the Register. John McDouall Stuart, the first European to visit it, prosaically named it for an Adelaide backer, James Chambers; he then called the next substantial range to the north, James. Some form of self-promotion must explain the reaction of other early visitors, including engineers, explorers and police, who climbed to the column's base and carved their names on its attractive surface. In this manner, it has become a monumental autograph album of European pioneers.

Aboriginal society places much greater value on this place, and to Aborigines these engravings represent both vandalism and desecration. They know it is Itirkawara, the transformed fossil of a knob-tailed gecko, a sandhill lizard. It was a place of deep significance and wide renown when Stuart arrived there, for it testifies to an important series of Dreaming events. This ancestral gecko was an aggressive warrior who travelled far across the desert, even into Queensland. He killed many men with his stone knife and captured their women. He was so evil that he even lived with women who belonged to the wrong kin-group, so he was incestuous under Aboriginal law. Eventually, he brought a young female captive of the inappropriate group to the camp of his own family. They were outraged and exiled him. As he led the girl across the dunes they became weary and rested.

They remained there for ever, for Itirkawara turned into the luminous pillar of sand, this latter being his male organ. This is not some "just so story", therefore, because like the Biblical Lot's wife, Itirkawara is a perpetual testimony for all who see it, to the primacy of observing moral laws. So is nearby Castle Hill, for Itirkawara's companion crouched down in her shame and averted her face. She huddles there still, separated from the pillar by a few hundred metres. This smaller hill's turrets impressed Stuart as "a number of old castles in ruins", and so they were drawn, in the fanciful picture in his published journal.

Chambers Pillar, a remnant of an ancient ocean floor. Aboriginal people knew it as Itirkawara, a Dreaming place where an ancestral gecko transgressed kinship rules and became a pillar of sandstone. (D.J. Mulvaney)

It is impossible to ascertain the extent of the impact upon Aboriginal morale and spiritual well being resulting from unthinking European visitation to places such as Chambers Pillar. It is certain that the marks of their presence, which bit deeply into this Dreaming rock of ages, gave offence and created resentment. Such encounters by colonists with Dreaming places occurred across Australia. Naturally, many sacred places were waterholes. They must have caused many of the retaliatory attacks on European persons and property, which the victims claimed as treacherous and unprovoked.

Nothing surpassed the actions of an 1884 visitor to Chambers Pillar for symbolising the arrogance and contempt of the new order for the old. "W.H. Willshire", police trooper, scourge of Aborigines and boastful violator of their moral laws, carved his name firmly. For good measure, he added his initials elsewhere.

Modern Australians should respect the awe in which this column is held by original Australians. It is ironic, however, that a century after these European pioneers carved their initials, they have become part of the region's historical process. Their engraved record of visits also requires protection, as part of the

Historical graffiti on Chambers Pillar rock face. Many of these names are celebrated in the European history of the Centre. Top right, "Basedow" was Herbert Basedow, geologist, doctor and ethnologist; F. Wallis opened one of Alice Springs' first stores; B.C. Besley was inspector of police and W. Bennett was a mounted constable; H.G. Swan (top) and C. Eaton Taplin (extreme right) visited Hermannsburg in 1890, to investigate police treatment of Aborigines; their chief concern was "W.H. Willshire 1883", "WHW 1884" (both top left). (D.J. Mulvaney)

A third attempt at immortality by Mounted Constable Willshire. Note how carefully earlier visitors inscribed their names, never superimposing on previous inscriptions, whereas modern visitors often deface the rock by careless, large and overlapping graffiti. (D.J. Mulvaney)

story of this place. The reality is, of course, that a continuation of this process must be opposed as vandalism in the secular sense, irrespective of the spiritual significance of this Dreaming place. This may seem contradictory, but it is essential.

The volume of visitation is magnified today; names are carelessly superimposed and crudely carved over the early engravings, and large scratches deface surfaces mindlessly. There is reason to suspect that vandals obliterated the initials of Ernest Giles, last of the "great" explorers. This beautiful environmental sculpture should be left untouched by modern visitors, as a monument which perpetuates both Dreaming concepts and prominent Europeans at the historical interface of two cultures. It is worth reflecting that both cultures have humanised this colourful but harsh environment, through their different responses to its immensity. Itirkawara or Chambers Pillar is more meaningful than simply a geological formation in an uninhabited landscape.

The Horn scientific expedition visited Chambers Pillar in 1894. When the expedition biologist, Baldwin Spencer, subsequently met Frank Gillen at Alice Springs, Gillen told Spencer a version of the Itirkawara myth. As editor of the expedition reports, Spencer included this first recorded account. He explained that it referred to Alcheringa times, "(or as Mr Gillen appropriately renders it 'dream times')".

This was the first published general application of the concept of the "Dreamtime", although precedence in its use belongs to a German missionary at Hermannsburg. Because Spencer and Gillen published a number of influential books, it is appropriate to link them with the popular adoption of "Dreamtime" or "Dreaming", terms used also by modern Aboriginal people.

It may be claimed that one of the most significant consequences of the Overland Telegraph Line for Aboriginal culture was the anthropological collaboration of Spencer and Gillen, which recorded the ethnography of Aboriginal societies along the line. Once the Horn expedition reports were completed, the two men produced their most important work. *The Native Tribes of Central Australia* (Macmillan, 1899) was the result of fieldwork completed during the 1896–97 summer, conducted in secluded bush immediately behind the Alice Springs Telegraph Station. Gillen enjoyed high prestige amongst Aranda elders because of his sympathetic concern for their society and his firm stand against police brutality. As the most senior official in the Centre, he was well placed to promote ritual activities with the elders, using funds provided by Spencer.

An exhausting year of fieldwork followed during 1901–2, when Spencer and Gillen drove along the line, with a diversion to Borroloola, on the Gulf of Carpentaria. They recorded a wide range of ethnography in a more systematic and detailed manner than had been attempted previously in Australia. The telegraph stations served as bases — Charlotte Waters on the South Australian border, Alice Springs, and Powell, Barrow and Tennant Creeks. In every case, their success depended upon the use of station facilities and the co-operation of Aboriginal elders who visited them there. Alice Springs, Barrow and Tennant Creeks would merit their listing on the Register solely because of this anthropological connection.

Except for a general ability in Aranda, neither Gillen nor Spencer spoke any Aboriginal language. Consequently they relied upon English-speaking elders or

Spencer and Gillen conducted their most celebrated anthropological research with Aranda elders on the other side of the hill from which Spencer took this photograph in 1896. It looks south over the rear of the post and telegraph station towards the MacDonnell Ranges. (Baldwin Spencer; pers. coll.)

Gillen (left) and Spencer with their Aranda informants, Alice Springs, 1896. The two visitors slept in this shelter during several weeks of intensive work with the elders. (Baldwin Spencer; pers. coll.)

interpreters. This imposed weaknesses in the reliability of their data, especially as they concentrated on esoteric spiritual matters. It is remarkable, therefore, that their material proves to be as dependable as it is. They published five major books concerned with societies along the Overland Telegraph Line, source books of inestimable value to Aborigines today.

Fortunately, two Southern Aranda men from near Charlotte Waters accompanied them. Erlikiliaka and Purunda eventually returned home from Boorooloola, arriving back in Charlotte Waters with their horses and equipment in good condition. Erlikiliaka proved invaluable at Barrow Creek, because he conversed with Kaytej men and interpreted.

It was during this expedition that Spencer made movie films and recorded sound on cumbersome and fragile wax cylinders. They were the second fieldworkers in anthropological history to attempt such recording. Some of these precious images and sounds survive, and all Australians are indebted to these pioneers for this priceless record.

Spencer became honorary director of the National Museum of Victoria in 1899, and his enthusiasm for building up the museum's ethnographic collections stimulated some officials along the Overland Telegraph Line to redouble their ethnographic collecting efforts. Such men merit praise, although there are contemporary critics who treat them as though they were criminals. Certainly, they collected sacred ceremonial objects, but many of them were given to them freely. Most of the objects were everyday items, with a concentration on male artefacts, such as shields, spears, knives and boomerangs. These objects were not stolen, nor were they very valuable at the time. Primarily through Spencer's example, many of these collections were donated or sold to the Adelaide and Melbourne museums, so that they exist today as national treasures.

Apart from collections made by Spencer throughout his career, and all donated to the nation, Gillen supplied numerous items from the Alice Springs district. The Tennant Creek stationmaster in 1901 was J.F. Field. Spencer purchased Field's collection of 600 items, primarily Wurumungu material, for his museum in 1907. This period was the climax, also, of collection building by the Lutheran pastors at Hermannsburg, who sent rich material back to German institutions.

Stirling, director of the South Australian museum, and Spencer, used duplicate ethnographic items as a medium of exchange during a period when museum budgets were minimal. Consequently, objects representative of cultures along the Overland Telegraph Line joined the Hermannsburg material in European museums, and in America. It is not surprising, therefore, that the world came to know Aboriginal decorative arts and material culture chiefly through the example of Central Australian culture. This served both to emphasise the secret-sacred elements of Aboriginal life and its "desert" aspect. Other regions were comparatively unrepresented in the early decades of this century.

The Native Tribes of Central Australia (1899) became one of the most influential books in anthropological history, widely quarried by overseas social and political theorists, historians of the origin of art, religion and ritual, and of the evolution of technology. Malinowski, a formative figure in the next generation of anthropology, claimed that by 1913, "half the total production in anthropological theory has been based on their work, and nine-tenths affected or modified by it". The celebrated author of *The Golden Bough*, Sir James Frazer, pronounced that they had "immortalised" Aranda society.

There is little doubt that Aranda rules and customs came to typify those of all Aboriginal societies. Consequently, Aborigines became known by a minority of the population, inhabiting a more arid environment than most. This set the intellectual context for "desert nomads" becoming synonymous with Aboriginal

Australians, and the failure of administrations to grasp the enormous cultural diversity and environmental complexity of Australian societies.

The energy and dedication of Spencer and Gillen are undeniable. They set new standards in comprehensive recording and established the importance of depositing material — ethnographic objects, pictorial images, sound records, field notes — in public collections. Modern Aboriginal people seeking closer cultural identity with their past should acknowledge their efforts, rather than condemn them as robbers of their heritage. The role of the Overland Telegraph Line in this research effort was paramount. For that reason, it is disappointing to visit the Alice Springs Telegraph Station National Park today. In all its historical exhibition there is no reference to the fact that the Spencer-Gillen partnership commenced in the stationmaster's house during 1894, and that it culminated in 1896–97 with the intensive fieldwork in the bush behind the station. Australia's heritage of traditional Aboriginal culture would have been greatly impoverished if this partnership along the line had never occurred.

Spencer, however, was a man of his period — a convinced Darwinian evolutionary biologist, who transferred what are now recognised to be simplistic and Eurocentric notions to the explanation of Aboriginal society. While he should be assessed within the context of his times, it is evident that his prestige had unfortunate repercussions. His opinions added academic respectability to those racial dogmatists who assumed that all Aborigines would soon die out (as Spencer believed), and that their social institutions were simply primitive fossil survivals from remote times, while their brains were not developed as fully as those of other races. So fixed were these preconceptions that, as late as 1927, Spencer prefaced their most detailed study, *The Arunta*, with this condemnatory assertion:

> Australia is the present home and refuge of creatures, often crude and quaint, that have elsewhere passed away and given place to higher forms. This applies equally to the aboriginal as to the platypus and kangaroo. Just as the platypus laying its eggs and feebly suckling its young, reveals a mammal in the making, so does the Aboriginal show us . . . what early man must have been like . . . .

Such forthright opinions reinforced racial prejudices. An improved understanding of the context in which racial encounters occurred may engender greater tolerance and respect for places which possess cultural values.

Barrow Creek Repeater Station possesses such value. Its chief claim to notoriety concerns the attack made upon its staff by Aborigines one summer evening in 1874. The complex of buildings survives virtually intact, placed immediately below a steep, rocky hill. The graves of the two men killed in the attack are situated in a walled enclosure in front of the station.

This was the only occasion in the history of the Overland Telegraph Line that staff and property were attacked violently by numerous Aborigines in a planned assault. The cautious administration-designed telegraph stations were like fortresses — stone buildings, erected around a courtyard, with an entrance at one end capable of closure. Windows were barred and loop-holes penetrated the thick walls. Such solid structures proved safe from attack. In this case, however, the surprise attack came while the staff relaxed outside the front of the station. The attackers approached along a wooded gully in the hill directly behind the complex. Twenty or more warriors suddenly crowded round, as the men retreated, desperately attempting to reach the rear gateway. One man fell dead and the

Barrow Creek Repeater Station. On the evening of the Aboriginal attack in 1874, the staff was sitting outside the front (right). The attackers came from the hill (left), and the staff had to run around the house to the rear. (D.J. Mulvaney)

stationmaster was mortally wounded. He was dragged to the safety of the courtyard and the gate was bolted behind them.

Warning messages sped both directions along the line and rescue parties set out from Alice Springs and Tennant Creek. Down in the Adelaide head office, young Frank Gillen was on duty that day. He received a message sent on behalf of the dying stationmaster and then transmitted a reply from the man's wife. When Gillen and Spencer worked at Barrow Creek for some weeks in 1901, their chief informant was a Kaytej elder, Tungulla, who had participated in that fatal raid.

Tungulla was fortunate to have survived, for terrible reprisals resulted once the relief parties arrived. The Aboriginal attack obviously was unexpected, and its cause remains unknown and the officers may have been entirely innocent. It is perhaps significant that the Europeans were alerted by one of their servants. This Aboriginal "boy" fired his revolver, which granted them the few seconds respite which enabled them to reach security. For this "friendly black boy", as Spencer called him, to have acted against his people, suggests that he was not a local Kaytej man. As he was armed and had status as a station attendant, it seems possible that he had taken advantage of Kaytej women. If so, he may have been the cause of the attack. An Aboriginal tradition accuses the white staff of this same offence, but as this is a common general tradition, there is no positive evidence. The attack is counted as uprovoked. As Strehlow remarked wryly, however, if an administrative centre in occupied territory in another country was to be attacked, it would be termed guerilla warfare, and the partisans would be patriotic resistance fighters.

Under normal rules of British law, the offenders would have been traced, tried and executed. The Kaytej would have understood such a reprisal. What happened, however, was a massive destruction of life, directed by police trooper Samuel Gason. Spencer was there a quarter of a century later. He reported that, after the relief parties arrived from the two other telegraph stations, "they rode out over the surrounding country, and the natives had such a lesson that they never again attempted an attack". Tungulla told him how he lay concealed and trembling in a crevice within a few metres of his pursuers. "For our own sakes we were glad that the old rascal had not been shot, though he richly deserved it", Spencer cheerfully observed.

T.G.H. Strehlow was in the area in 1932 and he questioned people about the incident. He concluded that "native and white evidence alike indicates that whole camps of natives were shot down at sight, often miles from the scene". Skull Creek, eight kilometres south of Barrow Creek, was such a place and the indiscriminate violence is perpetuated in the name. It was in Unmatjera territory, people unconnected with the attack. So also was the important ceremonial centre at Lukara, about eighty kilometres southeast of Barrow Creek. It was destroyed and sacred objects were broken so effectively that it was never again used for rituals. Such wanton reprisals on life and cultural property increase the importance of the research recorded by Spencer and Gillen during their attachment to the Barrow Creek Telegraph Station. The positive co-operation of Kaytej people with them needs to be recalled in addition to journalistic accounts of the Barrow Creek massacre.

The Alice Springs Telegraph Station impinged directly on Aboriginal affairs again in 1932. In that year, technological changes in communications rendered the Overland Telegraph system redundant, and the base was closed. The area was proclaimed an Aboriginal Reserve on 8 December 1932, and four years later its area of 273 hectares was enlarged to 437 hectares. The Department of Native Affairs administered it as a home and a school for part-Aboriginal children brought there from all parts of the Northern Territory below Pine Creek, regardless of the wishes of the Aboriginal parents. It was here that the future secretary of the Department of Aboriginal Affairs was born. Charles Perkins was delivered on a table in the former telegraph office, in 1936.

Ten years after it became home to these administratively orphaned children, the Japanese bombing of Darwin led to their abrupt evacuation. The place was required for other purposes. The children ended up in distant country, Mulgoa, New South Wales and South Australia, where the premier queried the wisdom of disrupting their lives by such a drastic move from familiar places.

For the war's duration, the Aboriginal Reserve was taken over by the army as the Native Labour Corps headquarters. The role of Aborigines as an alternative labour force is an important episode. (In August 1944, there were 209 Aborigines employed by the army in Central Australia and 510 around Darwin.) Vic Hall, who was sergeant in charge for a period, evidently improved their conditions. He praised their "keenness and good work", but found at the time he assumed control in 1942, that "they did all the dirty work for sevenpence per day. Native Affairs fed, or rather . . . half-fed, the dusky workers on a diet unfit for anybody. They were accommodated in the Native Affairs' settlement at night and delivered to the Army each morning by Army truck." Hall considered that "the conditions in which their families were forced to live on the Reserve were scandalous. Several visits to the . . . Reserve proved that . . . the menfolk were mostly in the Native Labour Camps . . . while their women and children starved." Clearly, this is a subject meriting research.

The Department of Native Affairs resumed control of the Aboriginal Reserve in 1945, until it was vacated in 1963. In that year the Aboriginal residents were moved to Amoonguna, twenty-one kilometres out of town.

The Alice Springs Telegraph Station therefore was home to various Aboriginal groups for over thirty years, one-third of its history prior to its National Park status. It is surprising that no reference to this important phase occurs in the existing public exhibitions. Its role as the "bungalow", when children lived there, or its importance during the war years, merit emphasis. Unfortunately, also, when the complex was "restored", the decision was taken to reproduce a photographic copy of its nineteenth century appearance. Consequently, numerous corrugated iron structures and other unsightly additions were demolished. The grounds are sanitised and watered in a manner which no resident there during its dusty heyday of camels and horses would recognise.

Such historical restorations should take account of the totality of the history of a place. Australia is signatory to an international Unesco agreement, the ICOMOS charter. This charter on the protection of monuments and sites lays down that conservation proposals and management practices should relate sympathetically to the entire historical development of a place. In this case, at least some of those corrugated iron additions and shanties should have been left, while the internal furnishings and interpretive displays also should reflect its Aboriginal occupancy.

Human affairs are never static, so it is unreal to fossilise a building in an idealised era, or to isolate it from the environmental and social changes which occurred within and around it. Even after an absence of about three years, Gillen was struck by the changes upon his return there in 1901. Drought had seared the area and killed the vegetation which screened the 1896 ceremonies. Overcome with nostalgia on his first day back at the station where all the staff was new, Gillen pondered on the reality, "that I am here a stranger in the place over which I ruled so long". Aranda people had even greater reason to reach the same conclusion about their lands.

Alice Springs

CHAPTER
EIGHTEEN

Central Australia: "Land of the Dawning"

At what he judged to be the appropriate geographic heart of Australia, John McDouall Stuart erected a cairn of stones on Central Mount Stuart. The date was 23 April 1860, only twelve years before a line of telegraph poles marched across the continent, bearing the single wire which tied Australia to Britain. "We then gave three hearty cheers for the flag", Stuart recorded proudly, "the emblem of civil and religious liberty, and may it be a sign to the natives that the dawn of liberty, civilization, and Christianity is about to break upon them." Unfortunately for peoples such as the Aranda, Loritja, Matuntara, Kaytej and Unmatjera, protection of their civil liberties was not scheduled as a priority on the duty statements of those South Australian mounted police who arrived in the Centre. Once the construction of the Overland Telegraph Line opened the region to pastoral occupation, priorities ensured white supremacy. As for religious freedom, even few sympathetic European contemporaries believed that Aboriginal people possessed any religious beliefs or values. Stuart's optimism was unfounded.

Second Class Mounted Constable William Henry Willshire (1852–1925) was amongst the earliest of the small band of police to be stationed in the Alice Springs pastoral district. He arrived there in 1882. His career symbolises racial encounter in Central Australia. Willshire was soon provided with a lesson in the need of bushcraft for survival. He set out to trace a missing police party from Barrow Creek, under Mounted Constable Shirley. He found their bodies, the killer being the environment — heat and lack of water.

Willshire proved an energetic and competent officer and his promotion to first class followed within a year. He was entrusted with special projects, such as forming and training native police groups. He also supervised the establishment of police stations. An obituary praised his Northern Territory service, "where he achieved universal popularity, and esteem for his daring and efficient devotion to duty". No Aborigine would have described his career in that manner, however, because he ranks in Australian history as a callous butcher of humanity. Willshire was an unusual character. Even his approving Adelaide superiors eventually found him to be insubordinate and reckless on occasion. After his acquittal on a murder charge, they thought it prudent to transfer him to another district. His early resignation from the police force, aged forty-five, may have resulted from his rustication to settled districts, his last post being on the Yorke Peninsula.

Unusual amongst his peers, Willshire published four accounts of his experiences in the Centre, although there was considerable repetition. He included material on Aboriginal ethnology and language. In keeping with his personality, these publications are dramatic, tinged with romance, uninhibited, and therefore very quotable. The title of his last book, chiefly concerned with his version of the Victoria River district in the nineties, is typical of his free interpretation of evidence. *The Land of the Dawning; Being Facts Gleaned from Cannibals in the Australian Stone Age*, was published in 1896. Evidently he saw himself as an heroic frontiersman, in the American Western mould, with savage, although inferior, black warriors substituting for Indian braves. Possibly he yearned to be an explorer of new lands. At least his *A Thrilling Tale of Real Life in the Wilds of Australia* (1895), appears to be based on a visit to the hills north of Lake Amadeus, rather beyond the range of settlement or normal patrol duty in 1890. Whatever his personal drives, Willshire was popular with pastoralists. At his trial for murder in 1891, they subscribed up to two thousand pounds for his bail and his court case, enough to retain the services of an eminent Queen's Counsel.

The remains of three of the police stations established by Willshire are in the Register. Another two listed places (Illamurta and Gordon Creek, on Victoria Downs) were directly associated with his activities. These police stations symbolise the official means by which outback areas were made safe for European pastoralism, through "pacifying" and "dispersing" the original inhabitants. The Alice Springs Police Station and the Post and Telegraph Station (both in the Register) provided the basic administrative structure for Central Australia.

The first two of Willshire's buildings are sited on the same block. In 1886 he supervised the relocation of the police station which previously was associated with the Post and Telegraph Station at Alice Springs. Its new strategic site was six kilometres south, nestled at the southern approach to Heavitree Gap. Only a few dislodged foundation stones survive, lying next to the railway line and directly outside the gateway to the second structure. This later solid sandstone building was erected during 1888–89, and it served as the police station until 1909, when the township had developed at its present location two or three kilometres north. This house survives in its restored condition, attractively screened by pepper trees. Surprisingly, the impressive centennial plinth and plaque erected in the grounds make no reference to the adjacent original temporary building whose centenary was their occasion.

The other police station ruins associated with Willshire's career are more remote. A room and fireplace stand to shoulder height on the flood plain above the Finke River, thirty-five kilometres downstream from Hermannsburg. White people called the place Boggy Hole, Boggy Waterhole, or Boggy Waters. Boggy it may prove upon seasonal conditions, but the prosaic name is unfortunate, for it often forms a long, shady and majestic pool. As mighty floods gushing down the gorge occasionally uproot the trees, the trunks of the present ghost gums are not as stout as those in Willshire's time, while the reeds are again reclaiming the pool's margins. Immense numbers of stone artefacts and broken grindstones, littered across the sandy spread on which the sandstone police building stands, testify to the ancient importance of this place as an Aboriginal base camp.

During 1887 Willshire and Wurmbrand and four native police escorted Aboriginal prisoners to Port Augusta. This posed studio photograph was taken there, in January 1888. Willshire is standing and Wurmbrand is crouched. Martini carbines are prominent. (The Mortlock Library of South Australiana)

Willshire established this police station at strategic Alitera, Boggy Waterhole, at the point where the Finke River emerges from a gorge downstream from Hermannsburg. The river is concealed by the trees. (D.J. Mulvaney)

Aranda people knew Boggy Hole by a more poetic title, Alitera, named for two ghost-gum serpents and an ancestral wallaby who came here. As they had travelled west from the Hale River, during the Dreaming, they linked different Aranda groups through associated ceremonies. As befits such a beautiful place of tumbled red rocks (one of which is the ancestral wallaby), massive cliffs, water and related life-forms, it features in the Register as part of the Finke Gorge National Park. Willshire also moved from the east to found the police station in 1889. It effectively marks the end of the Dreaming, because by siting the building on such an economically and ceremonially important waterhole, Willshire denied the Aranda free access both to its resources and to the route along the Finke gorge.

Another police station established as a consequence of Willshire's activities, is situated by the perennial water of Illamurta Springs, across the jagged ridges of the James Range, over forty kilometres southwest of Hermannsburg as the crow flies, but many more on horseback. It dates from 1892–93, when the Boggy Hole station was abandoned by official direction, because the Lutheran missionaries complained about the proximity downstream of Willshire's warlike base. The chief purpose of Illamurta was to safeguard the economic interests of Tempe Downs cattle station, then centred upon the Walker River. Illamurta and Old Tempe Downs are deserted ruins today. The former is included in the Register as the Illamurta Springs Conservation Reserve, but the original Tempe Downs homestead is a pile of rubble on the broad, sandy bed of the Walker River. Massive erosion at a river bend undermined the entire landscape. While Willshire was stationed at Boggy Hole to prevent the spearing of stock, his men exacted a terrible price from the poachers. His successors at Illamurta proved less bloodthirsty.

The newly discovered grassed plains located within the valleys of the Finke, Palmer and Hale in the central mountainous belt attracted optimistic but inexperienced pastoralists. Even by 1880, the few immense pastoral leases centred upon Alice Springs supported over 13,000 cattle, 1,200 horses and 6,500 sheep. Misplaced optimism and a run of good seasons resulted in expanded pastoral leases and greatly increased stock numbers. By 1889, cattle numbered about 50,000, horses 4,400, and sheep 10,000. Even though Tempe Downs was over 200 difficult kilometres from Alice Springs, it was occupied by 1881. Within eight years it was stocked with 6,000 cattle. With competition between stock and Aborigines for access to water, trouble was certain even without droughts and drastic ecological changes induced by grazing stock and muddying of pools.

Demographic statistics also are ominously revealing. The 1881 census (although understating males) indicated that between the modern South Australian border and Barrow Creek, there were only seventy-nine males and three females of non-Aboriginal descent. Although numbers rose during the eighties, the massive disparity between men and women continued. Even in 1901, there were only nine women in Alice Springs. Aboriginal women therefore satisfied the sexual needs of many settlers. The outspoken Willshire offered relevant comment. "Men would not remain so many years in a country like this if there were no women", he reflected later, "and perhaps the Almighty meant them for use as He has placed them wherever the pioneers go." "What I am speaking about is only natural", he continued, "especially for men who are isolated . . . where women of all ages and

Aboriginal Perceptions of Contact: A Pictorial Essay

Plate 1 Hermannsburg Mission painted by Albert Namatjira early in his career. This delicate image recalls the home of his youth. The whiteness of the buildings obviously impressed him. Watercolour over pencil 27.5cm x 37.5 cm. (Courtesy Alan D. Hickinbotham and the Ntaria Council Inc.; photographer Julie Byron)

Plate 2 A figure in European dress holding a rifle as though it was a spear-thrower, western Arnhem Land. Is this one of the earliest images of European contact in northern Australia? (Robert Edwards)

Plate 3 For comparison, a man preparing to throw a spear using a spear-thrower, from the same region. (Darrell Lewis)

Plate 4 Figure with rifles, western Arnhem Land. (D.J. Mulvaney)

Plate 5 On Innesvale Station, guns and revolvers were prominent in the perceptions of these artists. (Robert Edwards)

Plate 6 Images of contact in Wardaman territory include a horseback rider; two revolvers are to the left of the standing man. (Robert Edwards)

Plate 7 On the East Alligator River, a buffalo hunter, pipe in mouth, hunts a buffalo (out of picture). His Martini-Henry rifle has a deadly bullet in its barrel, while he has extra bullets in the belt (upper right). Aborigines were hunted with this armament across the Outback. (Darrell Lewis)

Plate 8 A drover and packhorses cross Willeroo Station, southwest of Katherine. (Robert Edwards)

Plate 9 Horse and rider in western Arnhem Land. (Paul Tacon)

Plate 10 Horse with rider, South Australia. Note the plan view of the hooves, drawn in twisted perspective. (Robert Edwards)

Plate 11–12 Introduced species: (*above*) a pig drawn in a sandstone shelter, Laura area, north Queensland; (*below*) the image of a giant horse from the same area. (Grahame L. Walsh)

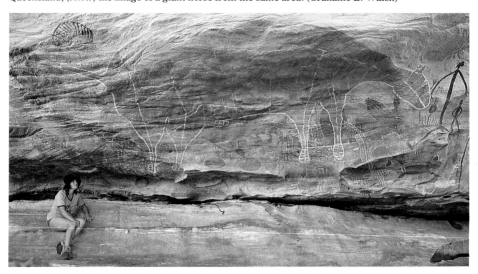

Plate 13 Buffalo and hunter outlined in beeswax, Kakadu Park, Arnhem Land. (Paul Tacon)

Plate 14 A camel and cameleer image pecked into rock at The Granites, Central Australia. (R.G. Kimber)

Plate 15 Darwin harbour busy with shipping in the 1890s, evidently a memory recorded by a visitor from the distant Alligator Rivers area. (George Chaloupka)

Plate 16 This lugger sails across the rock on an island in Princess Charlotte Bay. (Joan Goodrum)

Plate 17 This steam launch, painted in the Wellington Range, Arnhem Land, south of Goulburn Island, possibly transported the Darwin official who collected taxes from Macassan trepangers during the 1880s. (George Chaloupka)

Plate 18 Twentieth century technology depicted on this Arnhem Land rock: a biplane and ships. (George Chaloupka)

Plate 19 A RAAF bomber of World War II vintage in western Arnhem Land. (Paul Tacon)

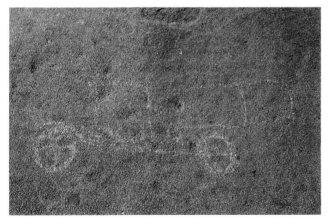

Plate 20 A truck at The Granites, where the first motorised vehicles arrived during 1927. (R.G. Kimber)

Plates 21–23   Technological borrowing. In plate 21 (*top left*), the tomahawk stencil from the Alligator Rivers region looks totally European, while in plate 22 (*bottom left*), the red stencil on sandstone north of Injune, Queensland, is improvised. Its blade may be a piece of hoop iron. In plate 23 (*above*), the artist at Little Nourlangie used Reckitt's "Bag Blue" to provide this attractive composition in a colour not used in pre-European Aboriginal art. (Paul Tacon, plate 21; D.J. Mulvaney, plate 22; Robert Edwards, plate 23)

Plate 24 Chinese migrants in this remarkable cross-cultural image (*above*) construct the Darwin to Pine Creek railway line during the 1880s. European technology, Chinese labourers and Aboriginal artistic perception combine in this western Arnhem Land rock shelter. (Robert Edwards)

Plate 25 Chinese prospectors (*below*) flooded into the Palmer River goldfields from the 1870s. These pigtailed men were painted near Laura, Cape York. (Grahame L. Walsh)

Plate 26 A Macassan prau, Groote Eylandt, with dugout canoe (right). Praus from Macassar ceased their visits soon after 1900. (Campbell Macknight)

Plate 27 Macassan visits were commemorated in stone arrangements on the northeastern tip of Arnhem Land. A prau is shown here; its mast is the triangular section, with the hold to the left. (Campbell Macknight)

Plate 28 The Sir Edward Pellew Islands from a satellite. The McArthur River enters the sea south of the islands. This Landsat imagery shows dense mangroves in red-brown. Vanderlin Island is the largest island (right) and Karruwa (Little Vanderlin) Island is the tiny islet near its southeastern extremity. This image shows the shallow water and the numerous sandy beaches which made these islands so favoured for trepanging. Flinders reported extensive remains at various places throughout the group. Major sites still exist on North Island (projecting farthest north) and on Centre Island (large, central). (Landsat imagery provided by the Australian Centre for Remote Sensing, Division of National Mapping)

Plate 29 The cairn on Possession Point, King George Sound, which claims to approximate the spot where Vancouver took possession of the southwest in 1791. (D.J. Mulvaney)

Plate 30 Itirkawara, Chambers Pillar, a sandstone column which proved a landmark in early European settlement times, but which featured in Aboriginal mythology. (D.J. Mulvaney)

Plate 31 Itirkawara's female companion, crouching in shame near her lover. The explorer Stuart named it Castle Hill. (D.J. Mulvaney)

Plate 32 Battle Mountain, northwest of Cloncurry, scene of Aboriginal resistance in 1884. (D.J. Mulvaney)

sizes are running at large." Not surprisingly, Willshire asserted that Aboriginal women were "good, but the men are bad".

In a grotesque semi-fictionalised, but autobiographical story, partly set in a cave north of Lake Amadeus, Willshire, playing the role of Oleara, entered a black harem. He "walked about like a sultan in his seraglio", and stamped round naked contemplating the "black beauties". In more serious vein, he recorded the personal names of only eleven men, but *seventy* "lubras", and a word list which included many sexual themes. Such was the mind of the most powerful man in the Centre during the eighties.

Another factor in this racial encounter was the enormous task assigned to the police. During the first decade of European expansion, the only police were stationed at Charlotte Waters and Barrow Creek. Before 1894 there were never more than six police within this immense tract. As patrols sometimes covered over 600 kilometres, even a conscientious policeman had little incentive to investigate carefully complaints against Aborigines or to take prisoners. In fact, no arrests were made before 1887, and very few before Willshire's own arrest in 1891. As court attendance cost settlers time and money, they eagerly supported police direct action. As Willshire advised later, "a good Winchester or Martini carbine, in conjunction with a Colt's revolver . . . are your best friends, and you must use them too".

Willshire became involved in a major "dispersion" in 1884, while he was based at the Post and Telegraph Station. In probable reprisal for the wounding of Aborigines by police from Barrow Creek, Unmatjera warriors attacked and burned Anna's Reservoir homestead, to the northwest, severely injuring two Europeans. The place was abandoned and its ruins are included in the Register. It proved a Pyrrhic victory. Willshire set out at once, captured four women from whom he extracted "useful information", and soon located over sixty warriors. He shot two and wounded three men, which more than repaid the blood debt. However, he continued raids for ten months, after which he boasted, "and now I say, 'All's well that ends well'". His meaning became apparent in 1901, when Baldwin Spencer visited the area for anthropological research. He found that the Unmatjera were "nearly wiped out", having been "what is called 'dispersed' ", for attacking Anna's Reservoir. Aborigines called a place Blackfellow's Bones, where men, women and children had been shot.

Willshire's general efficiency attracted the attention of his Adelaide superiors. During 1884, some Europeans in the Daly River area of the "Top End" were speared. Willshire was transferred to Darwin to pacify the area and to train a troop of native police. His model was the Queensland native police, troops who in that year were ruthlessly solving the so-called Kalkadoon problem, north of Cloncurry (see chapter 24). His troop of six men was drawn mostly from the Peake district, near Lake Eyre, so it worked in a totally alien region. Because Willshire's men had no kinship, ceremonial or linguistic ties in the region, they were trespassers. Fear must have added to their zealous pursuit of people of their own race, but different culture. Historians also correctly emphasise the rewards received by native police — firearms, horses and colourful uniforms — which brought some sense of status to fringe-dwelling men whose traditional existence had been disrupted.

In Willshire's case, there was also the sadistic manner in which he dominated his men, by destroying their traditions and allegiances. Willshire once referred to his later actions at Alice Springs, when he formed another detachment of native police, this time employing men from the Top End. When one recruit refused to eat brush turkey because of ceremonial taboos, "I insisted, and stood over him". On another occasion, when skeletons were found in a cave, "I screwed two of the skulls off, but my boys shuddered at the action. They were afraid to touch them".

His brutal contempt, made known to Aborigines, is evident from two other actions. At the important male ceremonial site at Emily Gap, he forced a group of women to pass through an area absolutely forbidden to them at pain of death. When Willshire was posted to the Victoria Downs district, he reported, that some months after two Aborigines had been shot and buried in 1895, "I went out and brought both their sculls [sic] in and buried them in my garden at Garden Creek, as the late John Watson Manager for Goldsborough Mort . . . stated that he wanted Pompeys scull for a spitoon." Elsewhere, he wrote with enjoyment about shooting at an old man to frighten him, and the humour of whipping another man.

Meantime, while Willshire spent part of 1884–85 with his new force, where he "worked" the Daly and Roper Rivers, two other police continued his repressive policy in the Centre. Thomas Daer came up temporarily from Charlotte Waters and Erwein Wurmbrand became the second staff member at Alice Springs. Wurmbrand, an aristocrat from the Austrian Tyrol, who returned there after 1888, emulated Willshire as a "hammer of the blacks". Daer and Wurmbrand ranged widely. Daer "dispersed" around Simpson Gap in September 1884 and next month at Glen Helen. During November, Wurmbrand arrested three men at Hermannsburg, neck-chained them, and shot them in the back when they allegedly attempted to escape in a gorge. This action was reported to Adelaide authorities by a missionary. Wurmbrand, indifferent to criticism, proceeded to shoot four more men at Mt Sonder. After Willshire returned from the north, he trained another native police troop. With Wurmbrand, they began the first of four patrols amongst the eastern Aranda. Oral tradition reports heavy casualties, but the police made no arrests and never submitted any report on their activities.

Whether the following manhunt occurred on one of these patrols, or whether it was a separate incident, is uncertain. Aboriginal tradition assigns it to Willshire and Wurmbrand. A version purporting to be told by a white participant was recorded in 1929. It claims that about twenty police and pastoralists were involved in reprisals for Aboriginal attacks at Owen Springs, southwest of Alice Springs, on the Hugh River. It may describe the most savage reprisal of that era. "After chasing 'em along the valley we rounded 'em up on that razorback hill over there. Then we let go. We ran a cordon round the hill 'an peppered 'em until there wasn't a 'nig' showing . . . . Poor devils . . . . There must have been 150 to 170 of 'em on that hill and I reckon that few . . . got away . . . . But what could we do? We have to live up here. That was the trouble of it."

It has been estimated that, during the period from 1881 to 1891, from 500 to 1,000 Aboriginal people were shot in the Alice Springs pastoral district. It must be remembered that relatively few Europeans were killed. Even Willshire claimed that only sixteen Europeans died from Aboriginal action in the entire Northern Territory between 1873 and 1892. Police "dispersion" related essentially to punishing cattle killers. It was human lives for bullocks.

With most areas subdued or depleted of its warriors, by 1887 the centre of action moved to Tempe Downs, in the vivid-hued and rugged Krichauff Range, through which the Palmer and Walker Rivers flow. This period coincided with drought, when the overstocked country accelerated the depletion of water supplies. Not surprisingly, cattle spearing increased. Whereas only twelve beasts were speared early in 1887, the total reached 1,000 animals by 1892. As the Tempe Downs Pastoral Company was based in Adelaide, with useful parliamentary connections, it is not surprising that Boggy Waterhole Police Station was established. Willshire was instructed to form his third corps of native police, this time four Aranda men, and move to this Finke gorge base. This time, the unit was independent of the South Australian police, thereby paralleling the Queensland force. Willshire was transferred to the Northern Territory police, as "officer in charge of police patrol party for the interior".

Willshire obviously enjoyed life in the bush, with sole command over his men and the willing co-operation of pastoralists. While undertaking similar duties in the Victoria River area during 1894–95, while based at Gordon Creek, he described his feelings as a killer in lyrical terms. The setting in the Krichauff Range and his sentiments were similar.

> At 3 o'clock we came upon a large mob of natives camped among the rocks. They scattered in all directions. It's no use mincing matters — the Martini-Henry carbines at the critical moment were talking English in the silent majesty of those eternal rocks. The mountain was swathed in a regal robe of fiery grandeur, and its ominous roar was close upon us. The weird, awful beauty of the scene held us spellbound for a few seconds.

Willshire discovered that his Boggy Waterhole base imposed irritating limitations. Complaints concerning police brutality were lodged by the Hermannsburg missionaries. In particular, the earlier actions of Wurmbrand in shooting chained captives was condemned. Yet such was the influence of Willshire and the Tempe Downs Pastoral Company, that the South Australian minister actually reprimanded the Hermannsburg mission in April 1890, for harbouring Aboriginal criminals and impeding police action. Even so, public pressure resulted in the appointment of two government commissioners to investigate the charges on the spot. Their report, presented in September 1890, "whitewashed" the police. They found that there was "no foundation for any charge" that Willshire or Wurmbrand were guilty of "shooting down the blacks". This meant that the commissioners accepted the conventional fiction that Aborigines were shot only in self-defence or when attempting to escape from custody. As Willshire prudently wrote in his current publication, "it is the rule with police patrols never to commence hostilities".

Willshire therefore believed that it was safe to renew hostilities. He mistakenly confused his campaign of terrorism, however, with traditional Aranda-Matuntara enmity. The father of one of his Aranda troopers had been speared by Mantuntara warriors while camped at Boggy Waterhole. The man had been guilty of an offence years before, so his death was traditionally determined. Willshire chose to call it an attack on his police station, so it provided him with an excuse for an offensive. At dawn in February 1891, his men opened fire on the sleeping Matuntara camp near Tempe Downs Station, killing two men. It is evident that the station people supported this outright massacre, because once firing ceased, Willshire and his troop breakfasted at the homestead. After their meal, one of the station hands helped remove the bodies to a sufficient distance from the house to allow their cremation. Presumably, the evidence was to be destroyed.

This was Willshire's last violent action in the Alice Springs area. Emboldened by the recent public disquiet and the fact that an official inquiry had occurred, Frank Gillen acted. Gillen was the only justice of the peace in the Centre, and had been appointed recently as Sub-Protector of Aborigines. Wurmbrand had been replaced in Alice Springs by a less trigger-happy policeman, W.G. South, whose rank equalled Willshire's. Gillen and South went out to the scene of the crime and Gillen eventually charged Willshire with murder. South escorted him to Port Augusta, where he spent some days in prison before pastoralists raised his bail. Sir John Downer, QC, a former premier, defended him. Although Willshire was declared innocent, he never returned to the Centre. After two years policing southern towns, however, he was sent to Victoria River to renew his murderous onslaught. The ruins of this police station at Gordon Creek are also in the Register. It lies twenty-seven kilometres south of Victoria River Downs homestead, having been established in 1888, six years before Willshire's arrival.

In Willshire's subsequent writing, and in country newspapers which supported the cattlemen's cause, Gillen and South were ridiculed. "The country J.P. . . . with the double chin", was one of his malicious jibes. Misguided "pompous dignity", railed the *Kadina and Wallaroo Times*, had persecuted Willshire. "As an author and a *savant* Willshire has shown that his mind is far above the commonplace level of his detractors. Much of what is known regarding the enthology . . . of Central Australia" was the result of his work.

Yet the future rewards went to just men. Gillen's reputation was so enhanced amongst Aranda elders because of his firm actions, that they treated him with the respect and status of an initiated elder. This was Willshire's greatest contribution to Australian ethnology. Gillen's acceptance was the initial step in a sequence of events which launched Gillen and Spencer on the path to anthropological fame. Because Aranda men accepted Gillen and his energetic biologist partner, they were admitted to secret rituals. *The Native Tribes of Central Australia* (1899) soon made the Aranda (Arunta as they called them) internationally the most celebrated of all Aboriginal societies. They retain this status in anthropology overseas today.

In 1908, Willshire had the effrontery to apply for the post of South Australian Protector of Aborigines. His old rival W.G. South was appointed. At this point, Willshire resigned from the police force. He later spent twelve years as nightwatchman at the Adelaide abattoir, a post for which his career made him admirably qualified.

CHAPTER NINETEEN

Sacred Storehouses: Illamurta's Role

In deference to complaints lodged by Hermannsburg missionaries, the 1890 investigation into police activities in the James and Krichauff Ranges recommended the abandonment of Boggy Waterhole Police Station, in the Finke gorge. Soon after W.H. Willshire's posting south, the outpost was transferred to the more remote site of Illamurta Springs, 220 kilometres southwest of Alice Springs. This secluded place, with perennial water in the shady, rocky creek which divided the living area from the horse paddock, was closer to the cattle spearing action on Tempe Downs Station. It was manned by two mounted police and six Aboriginal troopers from early 1893. Tom Daer took command and C.E. Cowle supported him. The story of Illamurta Springs is included as an analogue of those insignificant seeming places, which assisted the rape of Aboriginal culture.

The spring is overgrown today, but there is water amongst the matted reeds and tangled brush. During rains, this tributary creek of the Finke runs down from the foothills of the James Range through a broad rocky valley until it reaches the spring. Below here it changes into a braided sandy stream winding across the plain. This is an attractive, sheltered place, recessed into the red and orange rocky hills which rise directly behind the site. It supports welcome tree cover and faces southwest across the grassy plain to the Palmer River. A visitor there in 1894 remarked upon the carefully tended vegetable garden by the creek. Although the station was abandoned around 1912, many traces survive. Fortunately, the area is included within the 129 hectare Illamurta Springs Conservation Reserve, so it is in the Register. A detailed archaeological record of this frontier outpost is warranted. Most prominent is a sandstone building, preserved to roof height, but there are footings of other structures. Aboriginal stone artefacts, including fragments of grindstones lie around the site. Whether they predate the police phase, or whether they belonged to Aboriginal women associated with the native police, is an issue which excavations might establish. It is important that the place should be respected and conserved, for the hints it offers of past lifeways.

Across the creek bed are the remnants of post and rail fences. Some tall posts suggest the location of a horse paddock. A hollowed log may be a remnant water trough. As Cowle arrived back from Adelaide leave in 1897 with a camera, two photographs now in the Mortlock Library, Adelaide, may have been taken by him between that time and his departure in 1903. A wooden trough is prominent in one, with goats or sheep behind it. The top background of that view overlays with the left of the other photograph which is too faint to reproduce. It shows insubstantial brush structures, possibly the native police quarters and storage facilities. Stone alignments visible today in that area probably belonged to these structures. The stone buildings, presumably the police residence, are out of sight to the left in the image reproduced, screened by the brush around the spring. It is possible that none of the surviving foundations was a gaol. This was an area where potential prisoners were black, and normally they would be neck-chained and shackled to a tree, so a gaol was superfluous.

A sandstone building at the Illamurta Springs police post. The creek bed and the springs are concealed by the vegetation. (D.J. Mulvaney)

Despite the appearance of solidity in the stone masonry, sleeping quarters may have been less substantial. In correspondence, Cowle referred to "lying on my blankets in front of the wurley". (That is, he was lying on the ground.) He mentioned this, because a snake crawled leisurely across his chest. This was his fourth snake scare within the late summer. His previous encounter also is

Mounted Constable E.C. Cowle probably took this photograph around 1897, looking towards the Illamurta Springs police settlement. Water has accumulated in the creek, downstream from the springs (in the brush); portion of the hollowed log trough survives at this spot today. Beyond the nearest fence, through the butchering gallows, is the fence of the presumed horse paddock. That identical corner survives today. (The Mortlock Library of South Australiana)

The corner of the presumed horse paddock, 1986, with luxuriant growth in the springs behind. (D.J. Mulvaney)

revealing of station architecture. He was at tea; "when I looked up, a snake was hanging out of the bough roof just above my head".

One further feature on the site merits comment. About fifty metres on the far side of the spring, on higher land immediately at the foot of a hill, stands a small stone pile. It may be a grave. As Daer probably died at Illamurta in 1895, he may be buried there. As he was aged only forty-two, his death so far from any available medical services, is a reminder that, apart from snakes and bullets, conditions in the outback were hazardous.

Charles Ernest Cowle (1863–1922) assumed command of the outpost upon Daer's death. He was an educated man with an inquisitive mind, a cynical turn of phrase and an unquenchable thirst. Willshire wrote suggesting that he replace him at Gordon Creek in 1895, but Cowle preferred the solitude at Illamurta. Despite annual invitations to spend Christmas with the Gillen family in Alice Springs, he stayed at base, ate the puddings which Mrs Gillen sent him and read Ruskin. He was promoted to second class while at Illamurta, but his career was terminated, because by 1903 he was crippled by arthritis and he was invalided out of the force. Cowle's name would be little known today if he had not been deputed to lead a party of scientists to Uluru (Ayers Rock) in 1894. It was from Illamurta that he left to collect members of the Horn scientific exploring expedition. On their fourteen-day safari, his talents impressed Baldwin Spencer, then a biologist, particularly when they arrived back at Glen Helen base camp within minutes of the agreed time, after travelling over 500 kilometres.

Cowle and Spencer formed a firm friendship and it was Cowle who became Spencer's first important ethnological informant. In retrospect, the mounted police do not seem the most appropriate authoritative sources of data about Aboriginal society. Yet Cowle was a critical correspondent who assisted Spencer in interpreting Aranda life. In addition, his letters provide invaluable insight into the life and times of a frontier policeman in the aftermath of the Willshire trial.

"I am not advocating shooting for a moment in the so called good old style", he assured Spencer in 1899, "but they should be made to respect the law of the land that has been taken from them and it would be better for them." Obviously, Cowle was a stern realist, for whom white supremacy was a fact of life. His sympathies lay with the pastoralists, yet he attempted to understand Aborigines. He arrested them, rather than use bullets, and he brought many into Alice Springs for sentencing. During one year he arrested sixteen offenders, six of them being taken there at once. It is evident that, to achieve this alone, it required feats of horsemanship and endurance, as he combed the rocky hills. (During the search for a missing European youth, whose remains Cowle found, he covered 1,000 kilometres.)

When a prisoner was taken, neck-chains ensured his captivity. These instruments are never referred to in Cowle's correspondence, probably because they were taken for granted. Their use for Aboriginal prisoners was universal in outback Australia (see chapter 26). Over thirty years later, a traveller in this same region witnessed a mounted trooper escorting four prisoners to Alice Springs. They bore neck-chains, in addition to leg-chains. If challenged, possibly Cowle would have offered the same defence as was voiced on this 1929 occasion. The trooper "would rather have brought them in unshackled, only . . . no man on earth could bring prisoners out of that lone wilderness, through weeks of bush and desert riding, other than in this iron-handed way; he would certainly lose his prisoners; he might very well happen to lose his life".

Cowle was prepared, also, to be heavy-handed. He admitted to beating prisoners. He frightened them also. Gillen was amused to see him in 1901, complete with massive beard, "looking more like a Greek bandit . . . his belt laden with cartridges, revolver and handcuffs and altogether he presents a formidable appearance". His letters also record gruff kindnesses, such as a Christmas party when he deluged Illamurta Aborigines with five gallons of ginger beer and three bottles of raspberry vinegar. He claimed to be strict with his native police, while looking after them "in sickness and feed them on a scale and style different to anywhere else".

In those post-Willshire days, three other evils of European contact proved potent killers and destroyers of culture, rather than rifles. Cowle made incidental references to the first scourge, introduced diseases, in his letters to Spencer. During early 1899, he knew of about thirty deaths within his district from measles; a year later, six children at Hermannsburg died from whooping cough.

Cowle was a perceptive ecologist, although that concept was unknown to him. His letters contain observations on the consequences of the introduction of animal species into the fragile habitat. He reported the appearance of rabbits at Haast Bluff in 1896. In that same year, he observed that, because the drought concentrated cattle round perennial rock pools in the Gill Range, "all the fern and reeds [were] eaten or trampled to pieces by the cattle". As 2,500 cattle moved about the region, he posed the crucial question — "how should this affect the country biologically . . . ?" He grasped the fact that cattle destroyed Aboriginal food sources. He deplored "handouts" of food to Aborigines who drifted in to stations, because "if they remained in their own country in little groups they would be fat". Cowle worried over these social and economic problems, yet he was an administrative agent appointed to facilitate these destructive impacts, and to ensure that the rights of pastoralists were paramount over Aboriginal or environmental interests.

Cowle became deeply involved at Illamurta, also, in a more subtle but socially more destructive form of racial encounter, the traffic in sacred ceremonial objects. This was the period when Aboriginal secret regalia and sacred engraved boards and stones became fashionable museum pieces and art curios. Of all Aboriginal sacred items, the tjurunga of Central Australia attracted most attention. Caves and crevices on rocky hills were searched by Europeans, as though hunting veritable Aladdin's caves. This pillage and desecration of these most valued and esoteric components of Aboriginal culture, under the guise of scientific interest, may have done more to arouse racial animosity or to destroy morale, than the mayhem committed with rifles in the name of the law. Generations later, the whirlwind is being reaped.

The Horn expedition accelerated this plunder. Previously, curious settlers, such as Frank Gillen, had assembled assorted Aboriginal artefacts. Their collections were varied and relatively small, though they were intrigued by the difficulty that they had in obtaining tjurungas. Probably because they were difficult to obtain, this stimulated them to greater effort. As it happened, the director of the South Australian Museum, E.C. Stirling, was a member of the Horn party, while Spencer became National Museum of Victoria director within five years. Stirling claimed that the interests of science warranted wholesale collection. This was the period when impecunious museums bartered, arranging extensive international exchanges in order to optimise collections. Portable, attractive and enigmatic items such as painted or engraved tjurungas proved admirable for postal exchange. Within twenty years, most major European and American museums displayed collections of such items. Many of them were obtained from these two museums, or from the Hermannsburg missionaries. From Russia to Melbourne with care, was sent a Samoyed sledge, stuffed reindeer team and human apparel, for such a consignment.

Although such sacrilegious robbery cannot be justified, a sense of historical perspective is needed. In the nineties, few Europeans believed that Aboriginal people held deep spiritual values, or comprehended that a person's life could depend upon maintaining total secrecy about these objects and their hiding places. Even sympathetic residents, Gillen being a prime example, failed to appreciate the intense depth of attachment between clan members, their emblems, and their spiritual sense of place. They regarded them as being in "the curious habits of the natives" category. The challenge was to coax or bribe somebody into producing a curio. Even though Gillen knew that they were valued deeply and that they passed from generation to generation, he still failed to grasp their full significance. Within the context of his times, this must be regretted, but he cannot be denigrated because otherwise, he was far ahead of his peers in his tolerance.

It is also a matter of historical reality that many sacred objects were stolen by Aboriginal people, not only by Europeans. At a time when they underwent intense social pressures, sometimes young men reacted against the elders; some were urged on by a desire for alcohol; others curried European favour.

At a different intellectual plane, this was the heyday of evolutionary theory overseas. It was assumed that all social institutions, religious beliefs included, evolved from the simple to the complex; that some societies were fossilised survivals from the dawn of time; amongst these fossils, Aboriginal society was considered the most archaic of them all. Writers of books on the origins of religion, such as James Frazer's *The Golden Bough*, claimed that primitive beliefs began with simple magic; therefore Aborigines lacked religion, but they practised magic rituals. Baldwin Spencer was a convinced evolutionist, so he subscribed to this theory. The word "religion" never appeared in the index to any Spencer and Gillen book. Aboriginal beliefs and rituals were interpreted as simple magical increase ceremonies, intended to maintain the supply of food plants, animals or water. Significantly, *The Arunta* is dedicated to "Our Master Sir James Frazer". These naturalistic concepts lacked spiritual depth or real humanity. As the years passed, both Gillen and Spencer deepened their perception of the significance of ceremonial life, but it was too late to save the cultural heritage of clanspeople across the Centre.

Tempe Downs and Illamurta played their part in this tragic drama. While Cowle was leading Spencer and party to Uluru, the balance of the expedition members spent some time at Tempe Downs. The station manager tempted Stirling with stories about a major cache of "corroboree stones" in a cavity on a hill east of Haast Bluff. Stirling was determined to find it. The expedition surveyor, Charles Winnecke, assisted him, "as these rare and interesting stones are of special interest and value to the ethnological department". This was Kukatja territory and their terrified Kukatja guide, whom they called Racehorse, attempted to prevent them approaching the area. The unfortunate man was browbeaten and tricked in the camp that night and became so confused that he revealed sufficient clues concerning its location, even though he then vanished. Stirling simply remarked obtusely "with some difficulty we persuaded our local guide to take us to the locality". The sanctuary was a well-concealed fissure on a hill, no more than a metre wide and two metres deep. The carefully stacked tjurungas were covered with gum and mulga branches. "The concealment was perfect", Stirling observed. Quite obviously the place was actively used, but this counted for nothing. In fact, it was highly significant to both Kukatja and Aranda elders and it is not inappropriate to compare the rape of this place with a Greek's view of Lord Elgin's removal of the Parthenon frieze.

About seventy-five sacred incised boards and stones were handled. Stirling took away two-thirds of them, including all the stone specimens. In a statement which revealed gross misunderstanding of the true worth of these links between men, land and Dreaming, Winnecke reduced robbery to shopkeeping. "I left a number of tomahawks, large knives, and other things in their place, sufficient commercially to make the transaction an equitable exchange." A few trinkets for the natives could not suffice, however, for these objects were beyond price to the culture which revered them. As for Stirling's "scientific" haul, after taking them to Adelaide, he confessed, that "I am not in a position to throw very much further light on their meaning."

Poor Racehorse, who tried to keep the secret safe, was later executed for his part in the affair. Entry to the cache occurred during Spencer's absence at Uluru. Over thirty years later, Spencer recorded his regret at the consequences. "We learned, later on, that the loss of these Churinga was very severely felt and mourned over by the natives, who remained in camp for two weeks, smearing their bodies over with pipeclay, the emblem of mourning."

Tragic futility: rubble from Tempe Downs homestead lies on the bed of the Walker River, after erosion destroyed it. It was here that Willshire breakfasted after shooting Aborigines, and the Horn expedition stayed in 1894. (D.J. Mulvaney)

Stockyard fences at Tempe Downs, set further from the river than the homestead, which was abandoned in 1902. (D.J. Mulvaney)

Although sacred objects were sought previously, Stirling's example unleashed a phase of plundering. Some of it was undertaken with the high-minded intention of increasing knowledge through museum studies, but much of it consisted of rapacious collecting by private individuals. Gillen's interest in sacred objects was rekindled. He heard of a cache northwest of Alice Springs, and soon added twenty-five tjurungas to his collection. This brought it to over one hundred specimens, all destined for museums. Out at Illamurta, Cowle was enlisted as an ethnographic collector and he acted with enthusiasm. It became his hobby, as he sent consignments of tjurungas and other artefacts off to Melbourne's museum. He was shocked, however, as he told Spencer in 1897, "that they had killed some old blackfellow for giving me some information". Gillen's reaction to this news was to express deep regret. He ordered Cowle to return some tjurungas to individual men known to him. "There must be no more . . . robberies", Gillen abruptly informed Spencer, "I bitterly regret ever having countenanced such a thing and can only say that I did so when in ignorance of what they meant to the natives."

Although Cowle grumbled about these restrictions, he continued to collect, whenever Aborigines offered items. He had his eye on a superb specimen which he intended presenting as a farewell present on Gillen's departure from Alice Springs. He was forestalled by a passing adventurer-explorer, who obtained it from an Aborigine and who would sell it for profit, something which Cowle never did. As the sacred items continued to flow in Spencer's direction, he must have accepted Cowle's assurances that all items were freely given, never stolen. "The whole secret lies in not appearing grasping and stifling covetous thoughts when viewing objects", Cowle wrote, "*later* they will be offered to you." Cowle omitted to explain, however, whether each offer came from the appropriate custodian, or whether it was assisted by fear or favour. It is relevant that he even interrogated his prisoners about ethnological matters; several prisoners set out from Mount Connor, each burdened with a pitchi for Spencer's museum. Despite Gillen's protest, therefore, crates of ethnographic material made long journeys south. One consignment, in 1900, contained fifty tjurunga and two years later nineteen more followed.

It is ironic, therefore, that those in positions of authority who attempted to administer Aboriginal affairs with a rough sense of justice, undermined the authority of clan elders and the fabric of Aboriginal society. Their hobbies or scientific interests were unrelated to their routine tasks. Presumably Gillen, Cowle and a few other local identities would have justified their collecting because it assisted science and it added to European knowledge of the indigenous population. Unfortunately, few Territorians ever read the results of such research in the latest Spencer and Gillen. Their main readers were overseas scholars, none of whom was involved in native administration or welfare. Even Cowle, a substantial contributor to the first *Native Tribes*, dismissed that notable book in terms reminiscent of recent Territorian reaction to academic scholarship. "'Grimm's Fairy Tales' up to date by S & G", he wrote upon first reading *The Native Tribes of Central Australia*. He continued: "Do you honestly think you and Gillen saw any natives as ordinary beings . . . wherever either of you met them, were they not always on their good behaviour . . . they would be rewarded with tobacco or flour?"

The inhabitants of the central ranges were subjected to various encounters during the last decades of the nineteenth century. The incoming herds and flocks ruined their traditional economy; pastoralists and police challenged their pattern of land use and settlement; new diseases added to the toll of bullets. Perhaps most importantly, their sacred storehouses were robbed and therefore clans lost their spiritual title deeds to a place in their land. In all these dramatic changes, the tiny Illamurta Springs outpost played a part, often unintentionally and in ignorance of the consequences.

Illamurta's chief official role was to safeguard the fortunes of a handful of cattle stations, especially Tempe Downs on the Walker plains. Those fortunes were never viable in its early decades. Drought, distance from markets, and the massive southern economic depression, all doomed this lonely enterprise. The cattle spearing which dominated parliamentary and newspaper propaganda and which determined police activities was a secondary issue. Aboriginal predation on the herds served as a useful scapegoat for this foolhardy enterprise of land taking in an unfamiliar environment. It is interesting to reflect that, only a decade later, the depredations of white cattle and horse duffers were as severe as this phase of cattle spearing. Yet nobody was shot, and efficient thieves gained grudging admiration around the outback.

The writing was on the wall, even in the year when Illamurta was established. The Tempe Downs Pastoral Company sold out in 1893 to its manager, for a reported net loss of £27,000. The price paid was £2,500. Spencer called at Tempe Downs a few months later, on his Uluru journey, and described the station as merely "one or two little huts". The place was later offered to Cowle for £800, but he had gambled his savings on the reluctant Arltunga gold field. Kidman gobbled up the offer, taking the stock and the plant. The homestead was abandoned by 1902 and later a less remote, new Tempe Downs Station was established further east, on the Palmer River, where it stands today.

Within twenty years, therefore, this optimistic cattle venture on the Walker River had become worthless. Over time, swirling flood waters eroded the sandy plain. The building where Willshire breakfasted after his native troops shot defenceless people, became a small pile of rubble on the river floor. A few surviving stockyard posts lean crazily amongst the brush above the river. The cost of maintaining the police posts at Boggy Waterhole and Illamurta Springs during all these years imposed an imprudent burden upon South Australian taxpayers. For the Aranda and all inhabitants of the ranges to the west, it was a senseless tragedy.

CHAPTER
TWENTY

● Hermannsburg

Hermannsburg

The Ntaria twins emerged during the Dreaming from Ntaria waterhole on the Finke River. About two kilometres downstream, Lutheran missionaries established Hermannsburg (today renamed Ntaria) in 1877. This is the colourful heartland of the Western Aranda, 120 kilometres southwest of Alice Springs. Just to the south, white-trunked gums line the gorge which the Finke carved through the orange-hued Krichauff Range. In the purple northern distance across the red sands of Missionary Plain stands Mount Sonder, inspiration for Albert Namatjira, the great Hermannsburg artist.

Hermannsburg was the first Aboriginal mission in the Northern Territory, and for many years its solid stone church with massive desert oak beams was the only church in the Centre. The Lutheran Church maintained the pastoral lease until 1982, when freehold title to 3,807 square kilometres was returned to its traditional owners. Five separate Land Trusts are administered by the Ntaria Council, responsible for servicing more than 1,000 people.

Hermannsburg's celebrated era followed Pastor Carl Strehlow's arrival in 1894. Under his firmly paternalistic direction, pastoral care and religious conversion were emphasised. During his twenty-eight-year mission, 172 Aborigines were baptised. Strehlow possessed linguistic and anthropological skills. As he translated the New Testament, hymns, and the Lutheran catechism into Aranda, his message became more meaningful to his congregation. His anthropological studies were published in Germany.

Strehlow ran a strict society. Non-Christian Aranda were barred from living at the mission, so they camped on the fringe, excluded from material benefits such as food at the communal kitchen. He constructed separate dormitories for boys and girls, enforcing segregation at night by locking the doors, while teaching them at school by day. Despite his firmness, his determination and unstinting support gained respect. Life at Hermannsburg proved ordered and families kept together, unlike the rough conditions on stations in the Centre.

Strehlow's commanding zeal ushered in a building programme, utilising Aboriginal labour. The attractive surviving central core of his settlement is, like New Norcia, evocative of a non-British cultural tradition. It adds a dimension to the cultural heritage of Central Australia. In this instance, architecture was adapted to local resources and perceived climatic requirements to produce a unique precinct. Between 1896 and 1910 buildings rose on land above the Finke flood plain, associated with productive gardens on the river flats, and attractively shaded by planted trees. Simple whitewashed structures cluster around the church, centre in a "village" square. Lime for bonding the thick sandstone random rubble walls and for whitening them, was produced in a local kiln. Desert oak and mulga timbers supported thatch roofs (later replaced by imported corrugated iron). The thick walls, small windows and large fireplaces insulated against temperature extremes, but were more airless than conventional outback architecture.

Strehlow built, educated and baptised within a paternalistic milieu. His successor, Pastor W.F. Albrecht, was forced to integrate Hermannsburg society into the harsh world of the Depression. The year of his arrival, 1927, saw Hermannsburg linked to that world by the pedal wireless and morse keyboard. A severe drought set in. Scurvy killed many children within a year, so serious dietary deficiencies had to be countered. He attempted to bolster the economy and employ people, to make the station more self-supporting. He developed cattle production and established a tannery. Related leather and pokerwork crafts fostered latent artistic talent in this new medium. Albrecht's lasting engineering feat was the pipeline which pumped water downslope for seven kilometres from the shady Kaporilja Springs. It was a major contribution towards improving the settlement's quality of life and it supplied the tannery.

During these lean times, Albrecht's mark on Hermannsburg was considerable. The massive cement water tank received Kaporilja water; improvised cheap structures sprang up. Some survive today, with flattened 44-gallon drums used for roofing and as wall cladding, together with limewashed flourbags. Less

Hermannsburg in 1923, from different viewpoints. A fire shortly afterwards destroyed six of the circular Aboriginal huts. (Baldwin Spencer, Museum of Victoria)

The church erected by Pastor Carl Strehlow and now a museum. (D.J. Mulvaney)

The Hermannsburg water tank into which flowed the water from Kaporilja Springs. (D.J. Mulvaney)

aesthetic than earlier buildings, these adaptations reflect wartime shortages and the meagre funds available for Aboriginal welfare from the twenties to the fifties.

Hermannsburg's most famous son, Albert Namatjira, was born in 1902. He was educated under Strehlow, while occupying the boys' dormitory. He was confirmed into the Lutheran faith, but also he was an initiated Aranda elder. Albrecht's encouragement of craftwork first revealed Namatjira's artistic talents, chiefly in pokerwork. His subsequent apprenticeship with Rex Battarbee and his emergence as an artist of greatness is now part of Australian art history. It also

Improvised building materials adapted during the lean years by Pastor Albrecht — flattened petrol drums. (D.J. Mulvaney)

The cottage built by Albert Namatjira during the early years of his success. (D.J. Mulvaney)

provides a melancholy episode in social history. Feted in capital cities, he mingled with white celebrities, yet it was only two years before his death in 1959 that he was granted full citizenship. Even then, it did not entitle him to the right to purchase property in the Northern Territory, while it denied him the dignity of sharing a drink with his people. When he did so, as a man finally succumbing to pressures, he was sentenced to six months hard labour (later modified to detention at Papunya).

Namatjira lived in a house over four kilometres from Hermannsburg during the early years of his success. He built a neat two-roomed cottage made of stone and lime mortar, after the Hermannsburg model. That lonely place survives today as a ruin. Namatjira's tragedy was personal. Yet, had he not abandoned his home for life in the white man's world of Alice Springs, with all its indignities, other Australians would not have been made so sharply aware of the racial discrimination under which his people suffered. His fate may have stimulated some Aborigines towards direct political action.

Missionaries substained Hermannsburg for over a century. As a consequence, Aranda people were sheltered to some extent during those harsh years. They maintained their sense of place and participated in a community which recognised the importance of spiritual life. The contrast is with Namatjira, who was broken by the tensions between homeland obligations and the demands and incentives of fame in another society. Hermannsburg, transformed back into Ntaria, is in the Register because it provides material evidence evocative of that century of cultural encounter.

CHAPTER TWENTY-ONE

Coranderrk

Self-determination at Coranderrk

Conventional estimates of Victoria's population at the time of European settlement in 1835 number it around 10,000 to 12,000 people. Recent archaeological and historical reappraisals suggest a greater density, possibly double that number. It is a sad demographic reality that, by 1863, fewer than 2,000 Aborigines of full descent were counted in Victoria. When the next reasonably accurate census was attempted in 1877, the number had fallen to a meagre 774. Ominously, there were only 138 children.

Public attention has focused upon the misfortunes of the original Tasmanians, whose number declined from possibly 5,000 in 1800, to a handful during forty years of European contact. These Victorian statistics over a comparable time span are almost as drastic, for this much larger population declined by ninety per cent, or more. While settler's bullets and poisoned flour accounted for a proportion of this mortality rate, the vast majority of deaths must be attributed to introduced contagious diseases associated with sub-standard European-style housing and diet and unsuitable dress, or to socio-psychological factors.

The 2,000 hectare Aboriginal government station at Coranderrk, near Healesville, offers insight into the problems facing Aboriginal communities after the initial trauma of colonial occupation. Set in attractive bushland on Badger Creek and the Yarra River, this area extended from river flats to the mountains five kilometres away. Coranderrk was named by its inhabitants for the Victorian species of Christmas bush, *Prostanthera lasianthos*. During about sixty years from 1863, it was an important focus for Woiwurung, Bunurong, Wurundjeri, Taungurong and other central Victorian groups. About 300 Aborigines are buried in the cemetery, where the Christmas bush still flowers.

Coranderrk was a sizeable and successful settlement over a century ago, close enough to Melbourne for interested overseas tourists to visit and to recall in their

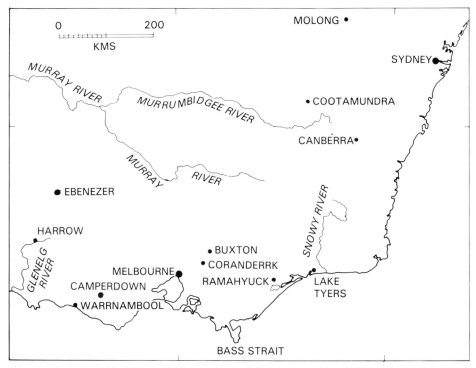

Southeastern Australia

reminiscences. Many took their cameras or bought craftwork there. As two government inquiries investigated Coranderrk affairs and the Aboriginal community developed an exceptional flair for media publicity, the documentation concerning conditions there is admirably full. Achieving its peak of success by 1870, the place was abandoned in the early twenties and most buildings were demolished around 1942. The area is indicated today by a number of planted trees and the remnants of an avenue of pines. The attractive two-storey multi-coloured brick manager's house, built in 1883, and the cemetery, dominated by an ornate memorial to William Barak, are the only major surviving features. Both places are listed in the Register of the National Estate.

Because Coranderrk's status in the history of Australian race relations is considerable, a brief excursion into its background is necessary. It was perhaps the earliest example of a large Aboriginal community which accepted the realities of a lifeway and rules of conduct adapted to the European mode. In volunteering to modify, the community still imposed its individuality and asserted its right to follow its own traditional decision making processes. It is a social tragedy that the spirit and initiative of the people conflicted both with the heavy-handed paternalism and evolutionary ideology of the times and with the economic interests of local settlers. If administrators had heeded the advice and requests of the resilient Aboriginal leaders, the subsequent role of Victorian Aborigines could have proved a happier and more positive one.

A parliamentary Select Committee on Aborigines investigated the Victorian situation during 1858–59, but failed to consult Aboriginal people concerning their needs. The inquiry was supported by philanthropic and humanitarian interests. Such was the state of anthropological ignorance in 1859, that celebrated year in which Charles Darwin published *Origin of Species*, that Aboriginal society remained grossly misunderstood. For example, the committee was widely informed that Aboriginal people had no religious or spiritual beliefs. As a result of the inquiry, a Board for the Protection of the Aborigines was established. It received statutory authority by the Aborigines Protection Act 1869. Its broad definition of an Aborigine included part-Aborigines, if "habitually associating and living with aboriginals". Regulations under this Act gave the Board far-reaching powers over such matters as domicile, contracts, money, and child custody. These original Australians had few freedoms in their own land.

It should be acknowledged, however, that at a time when social justice and social welfare were concepts seldom applied to the urban poor, over £11,000 per annum was expanded by the Board. Had it been spent on the Aborigines, this would have represented reasonable charity for those times. Unfortunately a high proportion was swallowed by the administrative structure, such as salaries for white managers. On the principle, presumably, that cleanliness was the most important virtue next to godliness, about 5,000 kilograms of soap was supplied to Aborigines in 1877; little was spent, however, on providing a protein diet.

In its first report for 1861, the Board accepted "the bounden duty of the people who have taken possession of their country to protect them", chiefly through the creation of reserves, where "they should be confined as closely as possible". This was humanitarianism implemented through compulsion, compassion based upon assumed racial and intellectual superiority, rather than compensation for lands lost. As the Board's second annual report emphasised, "they are, indeed, but helpless children, whose state was deplorable enough when this country was their own; but is now worse, for they have adopted all the vices of the superior race, and gained nothing from the exhibition of its virtues".

These assumptions already had been refuted by the actions of perceptive and adaptive Aboriginal elders in the Melbourne district. Even before the Board was established, they took advantage of the sympathetic public mood early in 1859, when seven Yarra and Goulburn River clan leaders approached William Thomas, their long term official Guardian. They requested a block of land, chosen freely by themselves, on the Acheron River, near Buxton. Their initiative succeeded, when the Board of Land and Works granted them almost 2,000 hectares at that site. About eighty enthusiastic people moved there at once and invested considerable labour. At a time of intense European land selection, when white settlers were confirmed in their blocks through the evidence of improvements and effort, the Aborigines obviously believed that their group selection now belonged to them. Thomas was assured that "they would cultivate and set down on the land like white men".

Regrettably, the government failed to follow up its grant immediately with any provision for implements, stock or housing, until months passed. It is significant that, although the government tacitly accepted the Select Committee's opinion that land should be granted as compensation for the loss of tribal territories, it neither conferred legal title nor left them free to control their estate. Trustees of the Acheron station were appointed from amongst local self-interested European settlers. Although these men never visited the station, they soon devised means of shifting the Aboriginal settlers to the less desirable Mohican run in the nearby hills. Greedy whites profited by the transaction, but Aboriginal optimism was replaced by frustration and resentment at this unjust interference. Most of them refused to undertake the task of resettlement, and a few months later rejected a further offer. Settler opposition late in 1862 blocked another grant which would have proved acceptable.

Thomas advised originally that the leaders should be permitted to select their own place. Within a year, he informed the Board that the Aborigines objected to the Mohican expedient, because "that is not the country they selected, it is too cold and blackfellows soon die there". Unfortunately, Thomas lost his credibility over the Acheron transaction, a block which "I had promised them ever should be theirs". The disillusioned Aborigines had learned that "ever" in white man's language meant a few months.

John Green now took over the mantle of Aboriginal champion from the aged William Thomas. He was appointed Inspector of Aborigines in the colony by the Board, and he made the welfare of the Yarra and Goulburn people his own special concern. Early in 1863 Green accompanied forty Aborigines from the Acheron to Badger Creek. The men selected a place which had been a traditional site for ceremonial activities. On 30 June about 1,000 hectares was gazetted as a reserve (the area was doubled in 1866).

The place had been chosen by the elders. The Yarra people knew it as Coranderrk, but this white flowered tea-tree (Christmas bush) was called Geringdah by the Taungurong Goulburn residents. It retains both names today. Neighbouring Europeans named their settlement Healesville, in honour of a politician. The Board expected Green to superintend activities, and he resided there. However, he wisely left matters to Aboriginal discretion, including communal discipline and movement and work beyond the reserve. From 1865 the adult males decided to terminate traditional marriage rules involving bestowal. They substituted Presbyterian ceremonies, and required two years residence before a man could marry. Green informed R. Brough Smyth, the opinionated Board secretary, that "my method of managing the blacks is to allow them to rule themselves as much as possible". His trust in communal wisdom and respect for the good intentions of the leaders made Green virtually unique in his time. It was to ensure his own downfall and the failure of Coranderrk, because the authoritarian and paternalistic Board shared none of these beliefs.

Evidence often is capable of conflicting interpretation. Coranderrk's history is no exception. Contemporary critics found the Aborigines to be lazy and unreliable, while the place was a drain on the public purse. There also was an optimistic, positive aspect to the station's early development, and it is appropriate to begin by examining that situation. During its first decade under its popular first manager, John Green, Coranderrk exhibited economic promise and evident Aboriginal input and communal well-being. This existed despite inadequate funding by the Board to provide equipment and stock, and the high mortality rate. Under Green's benign oversight, work duties were divided by community leaders into four "companies", presumably based upon tribal or clan affiliations. The station was home to people from several tribal areas, although it is relevant that most of them possessed traditional linguistic, ceremonial and marriage affiliations.

The first arrivals settled down to serious labour, clearing and fencing within the strict limits imposed by available utensils and equipment. Within the first four months, also, nine split log slab and bark roofed huts were built after the European model. They had large fireplaces, with log chimneys, plastered internally with mud. Skin rugs covered earth floors of huts comparable to those occupied by European pioneers. As the Board was reluctant to invest a higher proportion of its relatively meagre funds, the community practised self-help. Through the sale of possum skin cloaks, baskets, boomerangs and other artefacts, capital was raised to purchase necessities, such as tools, boots and clothing. Indeed, Coranderrk became an important supplier of material culture items to museums and tourists through the century.

Green sensed a feeling of achievement amongst the community, which was set firmly upon the path of adaptation to European economic and social goals. By 1867, they ground some flour from their own grain. Within a decade the settlement comprised thirty-two cottages and five other buildings, while 300 hectares of grazing land was fenced and about sixty hectares was under cultivation. (Some years later, 1,200 hectares was classed as "improved pasture".) Sawn timber and planks were produced at their sawmill, powered by water from Badger Creek, so the cottages were more secure. There was a school, bakery, butcher's shop, slaughter house, barns, milking sheds and a dairy. In this pioneering landscape, here was a township of about 125 people with an air of permanence. Its inhabitants had adapted to European-style architecture years before most Aboriginal people elsewhere, for they actually inhabited the houses, rather than camping outside. Traditionally, houses were burned after a family death and the family moved elsewhere, but that was not so here, where occupancy was continuous.

Coranderrk during its early years. Cottages have bark roofs, while distant ones have bark walls. All have wooden chimneys, plastered internally with mud. Even the children wear European dress. The quality of this housing was comparable with that of European pioneers. This image is attributed to Kruger c. 1876, but it must belong to an earlier camera, possibly Charles Walter, 1867. (Museum of Victoria, Coranderrk 13; BPA photo 145)

Housing had improved by 1877, with some buildings roofed with metal and brick chimneys on official buildings at least. The hop kiln (left) dominates the sizeable township. (National Gallery of Victoria and Mrs B.M. Curl; photographer, Fred Kruger)

Viewed in 1986 from a comparable vantage point, the 1884 manager's house chimneys appear above the trees (right, above the shed in the foreground). The mature pine trees, across the middle distance, line the former station road. Presumably the hop kiln stood near the left of this image, near that track. (D.J. Mulvaney)

Financial shortage hampered sound economic growth, for large herds were needed to feed the community if self-sufficiency and an adequate diet were to be sustained. Problems were aggravated by the obligation to feed numbers of needy Aboriginal visitors and numerous orphans. Traditional forms of charity persisted at Coranderrk, based upon obligations which were less marked in European settlements. Because the Board did not pay wages, men undertook part-time work outside the station, which depleted the available work force for extending the productive area of the station. These wages during harvesting or shearing seasons provided an important supplement.

There is a sense, therefore, in which Coranderrk resembled any pioneer rural bush community. It was no less agricultural, pastoral or horticultural ("neolithic") than its white neighbours. It offered striking testimony to an economic and technological transition of which contemporary theorists believed Aborigines to be intellectually and physically incapable. Importantly for its social cohesion, this society retained familiar and consoling links with its past culture in various ways. Its leaders were its traditional elders. Because the domestic livestock available was insufficient, two days weekly were set aside for hunting and fishing activities, so providing a customary food supplement. The emphasis upon arts and crafts production ensured the persistence of material culture skills within that generation. One of the most significant figures was William Barak, a Woiwurung elder, who adapted his artistic creativity to produce lively pictures on paper of ceremonial activities. They maintained an inner cultural authenticity, while providing meaningful drawings for a European market. Arnhem Land bark painters who have adapted to European perceptions command great respect today; earlier artists such as Barak merit closer attention for their response under more difficult circumstances.

The community moved, also, towards the deliberate acceptance of the social lifestyle of Europeans. Its firm leadership included Barak and Simon Wonga, another Woiwurrung man, and Birdarak (Thomas Banfield), a Taungurong. Most inhabitants were photographed individually by Charles Walter in 1867. Proudly posed in their fashionable Victorian clothing, smart coiffure or trim beards, they reflect a striking elegance and formality. Another series of 1876 photographs confirms the continuance of European normality. So did the contents of some cottages, furnished with sofas, chiffoniers, harmoniums, clocks, curtains and wallpaper. Flowers and vegetables grew in many gardens.

These people were set on their integrating course of acculturation even before Coranderrk was gazetted. It was Wonga who planned an Aboriginal presence at Governor Barkly's Queen's Birthday levee on 24 May 1863. In suited formality, but wearing traditional skin cloaks, a male group presented the Queen with traditional male weapons and female basketwork; a crochet lace collar symbolised the new culture. As the Queen's letter of thanks assuring them of her continuing interest and protection, coincided with the gazettal of the reserve, it is small wonder that the community believed that the land was conveyed to them in perpetuity.

This community was no seething hotbed of racial "resistance", but a loyal peasant society seeking to improve its condition by lawful means within a British

Men from Coranderrk at Governor Barkly's Queen's Birthday levee in 1863, shown in a picture titled *Deputation of Victorian Aborigines at the Governor's levee*. The deputation was arranged by Simon Wonga. On the floor are craft gifts for Queen Victoria, including traditional artefacts and a crochet lace. This was dignified, self-reliant acculturation. (*Illustrated Melbourne Post*, 18 June 1863; National Library of Australia)

colonial context. It was their chosen course of action. It is fashionable today for some white historians and Aboriginal activists to emphasise the thread of resistance which united all underprivileged Aboriginal groups. They also should acknowledge that there were communities such as Coranderrk which chose a very different response. Simply because they conformed to European ways does not constitute the despised "Uncle Tom" syndrome. These people retained their individual self-respect and group dignity. Later actions showed that, when they did resist the imposed system, they opposed it through accepted European channels, especially political lobbying and the press.

Another choice concerned religion. Although this was not a Christian mission establishment, the community practised Christianity, officially at least. They even held a thanksgiving service upon their arrival at Coranderrk. Presumably John Greene's role was influential, for he was a zealous lay preacher, although without any formal church support. Even so, at least an external conformity continued in Green's absence. Diane Barwick, that devoted historian of Coranderrk, observed that the Sabbath was observed generally "with Presbyterian rigour".

If the community did not adhere to the Established Church, it followed the establishment sport. Cricket was played there with enthusiasm, as photographs of games around 1880 and 1890 testify. The best account of their English cricketing mores was supplied by H.N. Moseley, who saw them play in 1874. Moseley was a naturalist on the HMS *Challenger* scientific expedition. He arrived there in search of a live platypus, but cricketers and spectators were too involved to hunt one for him. ". . . we found the cricket party in high spirits, shouting with laughter, rows of spectators being seated on logs and chaffing the players with old English sallies: 'well hit'; 'run it out'; 'butter fingers' ". Moseley also noted that they "all dressed as Europeans; they knew all about Mr W.G. Grace and the All-England Eleven".

A passing visitor would have been justified in assuming that this village green merrymaking and the productive lands indicated a state of well-being. Yet, even during this first decade of promise and initiative, problems existed. The population of the settlement passed one hundred by 1865 and fluctuated between 120 and 150 until 1878. The estate's resources could not sustain such numbers. The Board provided insufficient funds for adequate stocking and maintenance, arguing that the estate should become self-sufficient and also sell its surplus in Melbourne to make some financial return to the Board. Yet they opposed Green's attempts to extend its area. No other farm with a few hundred hectares of grazing land attempted to sustain so many residents. Unfortunately, the climate proved unsuitable for wheat and local farmers soon abandoned dairy farming because of the adverse conditions. Aboriginal farmers cannot be blamed for poor yields of flour and milk which, together with meat, were the basic requirements for self-sufficiency. Although hunting, fishing and gathering traditional food resources offered enjoyable interludes, this large standing population imposed undue pressure on those resources on the estate. Within a few years the effective return was meagre.

It is evident that the supplies of fresh meat, milk and vegetables were insufficient to feed a labouring population adequately. Public health was affected, and it already was subject to the onslaught of introduced diseases from which there was no immunity. In a measles epidemic during 1875, thirty-one people died of measles or from subsequent pleuro-pneumonia. This constituted one-fifth of the community. A list of causes of death of another 120 people during the post-1875 period, attributed sixty-two of them to respiratory ailments. It is ironic that all these diseases were contagious, so that the decision by residents to become "civilised" and not to burn personal possessions and cottages of deceased kin, facilitated their spread. The advice of an enlightened doctor in 1876 was ignored by the Board. He claimed that poor sanitation and drainage contributed to the problem. In their contemporary ignorance of contagion, however, medical authorities blamed Coranderrk's damp climate. This fuelled demands by covetous local settlers that the station should be abandoned. It proved convenient to urge humanitarian causes, rather than reveal naked greed for fertile land.

Desperate to resist settler demands and to placate the Board by producing a viable estate, Green encouraged hop cultivation from 1872. The case was attractive, for the environment was suitable. Hops provided constant employment, and the varied tasks involved, such as weeding, poling, pruning, tying and picking, could be shared by all the community. This work proved appropriate to those many who were weakened by respiratory ailments or malnutrition, for the labour was not intense. Production expanded and the 1874 crop yielded a Board profit of £983. Coranderrk hops won a gold medal at the 1883 Melbourne Show.

This proved little consolation for the community. The cost of diverting labour to hop processing resulted in a dramatic decline in grain, butter, bacon and vegetable yield. A potentially viable peasant society now was producing a mono-cultural cash crop. Equally serious was the Board's initial refusal to pay any wages to the labourers, and its subsequent agreement to a rate which was one-third of that paid to non-Aboriginal workers.

In effect, once hop processing began, Green lost management of the estate to the Board, which treated it as an economic investment rather than as a fragile human welfare situation. More importantly, the community lost its former freedom of action, while the quality of its already meagre diet worsened and its income virtually ceased.

Involved in a series of petty disputes during 1874, Green became increasingly frustrated until, to the dismay of the community, the Board dismissed him. Over the next decade there was a succession of inept and unpopular managers, for whom self-management by the community was anathema. The community's independent spirit survived, however, and leaders showed remarkable toughness and knowledge of European modes of protest. The Melbourne press printed many letters from Aborigines or their well-wishers, Aboriginal petitions flowed, politicians were lobbied; strikes were declared; deputations marched from Coranderrk to Melbourne's parliament; there were rumbles about rebellion.

The direct consequence was a Royal Commission, in 1877, and a Parliamentary Board of Inquiry during 1881. The Board for the Protection of the Aborigines alleged that the Coranderrk malcontents were being manipulated by outside interests. This was demonstrably untrue, but outside farming interests certainly attempted the reverse, to get the Aborigines evicted. The Aboriginal protest movement won, it seemed, when Coranderrk was gazetted as a "permanent reservation" in 1884. Parliamentary approval, rather than Board orders, was required in future before the station could be resumed. The Aborigines assumed, therefore, that their tenure was secure. However, their other demand, for the re-instatement of John Green, was ignored.

The peace secured through verbal battle was short-lived. The part-Aboriginal population was growing, while those of full Aboriginal descent were in evident decline. There was a general community acceptance that these latter must be sustained until their total extinction, but that part-Aborigines ("half-castes") should not become a burden on the public purse. Some critics claimed that they were the ringleaders of protest at various stations. The Aborigines Protection Act 1886 redefined the nature of Aboriginality. It excluded from the definition all those of mixed descent under the age of thirty-four. Without a special Board permit, such people were excluded from residence on any reserve. This legal device virtually halved both the population and the annual budget. Figures provide some idea of the trauma involved for communities arbitrarily divided. By 1893, 227 persons of mixed descent out of a total of 233 resident on Victorian stations had left for more hostile environments.

At Coranderrk, over sixty people were exiled over the next few years, while the dependent children of those who were eligible to remain, were sent away once they reached the age of fourteen. This terrible family disruption coincided with the era of depression from 1890, and so added to the hardship. Fewer people needed fewer stations, so Board policy moved towards consolidation. As reserves were resumed, they were made available to European settlers. Coranderrk had half its area excised during 1893, so farmers encroached on the rich river flats. However, it maintained a population of sixty to ninety over the next twenty years, because people were transferred there from distant centres. These newcomers lacked the consoling ties of close kinship and ceremonial obligation of the original Coranderrk pioneers. As a result, further tensions must have been introduced into life there.

The end came in 1917, when the Board resolved to close the station and transfer residents to Lake Tyers. Police escorted the people there during 1922 and 1923, although six old people were permitted to remain in their cottages on fifty acres, after another public clamour. The last resident died there in 1944. The "permanent" reservation which the community had achieved in 1884, was revoked by parliament in 1948. Despite fine words and promises, therefore, the only permanence which Aboriginal people gained at Coranderrk, are the graves of some 300 people on the hillside overlooking the station.

As a result of the 1881 inquiry, the government made funds available to repair some cottages. The most substantial material change resulting in the settlement, however, was the construction of the solid brick structure, to house a white manager whom nobody wanted. While all trace of the cottages was swept away years ago, that attractive house is a landmark today.

The model European-style village of the 1870s housed a community with which all Australians nurtured on the concept of "a fair go" should identify. The co-ordinated, law-abiding public protest by that community was a landmark in post-1788 Aboriginal political history. It is appropriate to conclude by letting two of its wise leaders express their dissent.

At the 1881 government inquiry, optimistic William Barak pleaded forthrightly for freedom from Board control. "Why do not the people do it themselves? We don't want any Board nor inspecting . . . over us . . . only Mr Green . . . and the station to be under the Chief Secretary; and then we will show to the country that we can work it and make it pay, and I know it will.''

Birdarak (Banfield), the Taungurong elder, complained that neighbouring settlers grazed 300 stock on Coranderrk land, because fencing and other management processes had lapsed since John Green's departure. With some wistful exaggeration, he told the inquiry, that ''we used to kill our own cattle, and grow our own potatoes, cabbages, onions, carrots and pumpkins . . . . We had plenty of milk, butter and cheese. We get nothing like that now . . . I think they have done enough in this country to ruin the natives without taking it from us any more.''

CHAPTER
TWENTY-TWO

The Peppers of Ebenezer

Overlanders bound for Adelaide drove cattle through Wutjubaluk territory during 1838. Led by E.J. Eyre, the party followed the Wimmera River to Lake Hindmarsh. It proved a blind alley, because despite its abundant water, cattle could not cross the waterless horizon, so they retraced their long drive. Along the river between future Dimboola and the lake, Eyre reported that "kangaroos and emus abounded", while the lake supported "innumerable" waterfowl. Beyond the chain of ponds along the river's course, however, the hinterland was "a dreary, sandy, barren, scrubby flat looking country". They met Aborigines at intervals, so the impression which Eyre derived was unfavourable for pastoral or agricultural purposes; yet it was an environment well suited for a sparsely populated hunting, fishing and gathering economy.

Four years later, men gambled with drought and depastured their flocks in the region. H.C. Ellerman, a Belgian migrant, established Antwerp Station in 1846, about fifteen kilometres south of Lake Hindmarsh. Ellerman prospered. He repressed Aborigines initially, but later came to feel sympathy for their welfare. Late in 1858, he welcomed missionaries and made available about 260 hectares of his run, situated above the Wimmera flood plain.

During the intervening years, pastoral expansion had completed Victoria's occupation, just as the surging tide of gold prospectors multiplied the human population. The ecological and social havoc wrought by domesticated animals and colonists, combined with the deadly onslaught of introduced diseases, decimated Victoria's Aboriginal population. Because of humanitarian concern about their plight, the Victorian Legislative Council appointed a Select Committee, in 1858, "to enquire into the present condition of the Aborigines . . . and the best means of alleviating their absolute wants". The committee was appalled to find that only "a few hundred" Aborigines survived a population in 1835 which they (under-)

estimated at 7,000. In most areas, they found that people were "in a state of abject want".

The Select Committee found "that great injustice has been perpetrated". It advised the establishment of mission reserves, to succour "the remnants . . . in comparative plenty. This is a duty incumbent upon the community . . . so long neglected". Their report led directly to the creation of the Board for the Protection of the Aborigines. It also stimulated some denominations to found missions. Even while the committee deliberated, two missionaries took up the challenge. The Moravian Board of Missions in Europe had sent two missionaries from Germany in 1858, F.W. Spieseke and F.A. Hagenauer. During the following years, the Moravian authorities collaborated with the Presbyterian Church in Victoria.

Both missionaries toured the Wimmera district to select a suitably segregated site, deciding upon the out-station on Ellerman's run. It was near the river, but conveniently remote from townships and grog shanties. They initially used the shepherd's hut as a school. Wutjubaluk people knew this place as Punyo Bunnutt, but the mission was named Ebenezer; often it was called Lake Hindmarsh.

The number of people attracted to Ebenezer fluctuated. Sixty attended a religious service in March 1859. Perhaps they assembled for other reasons because much to missionary displeasure, they dispersed after holding their own traditional ceremony. After a subsequent return and further ceremonies, pagan rites were banned by the missionaries. These men placed solemnity and righteousness before their stern God ahead of other considerations. Not surprisingly Ebenezer's first year was characterised by lack of harmony and direction. Spieseke already had demonstrated his inability to comprehend or adapt to Aboriginal ways, when he abandoned a mission at Lake Boga and returned to Germany in 1856.

Ebenezer possibly was saved through the intervention of a teen-aged Aboriginal youth. He was called Pepper, after John Pepper, who took up land during the forties in that region, when "Pepper" and his brother Charley were young. Both lads spoke English. The brothers remained at the mission after the older people left, and built a bark hut. Later, they visited their kin in the bush, telling them stories from the Bible. About fifty people returned to live at Ebenezer early in 1860, under their encouragement.

Pepper was baptised in August 1860, taking the name of Nathaniel. He is claimed as the first Victorian convert to Christianity. Charley was baptised later, becoming known as Phillip Pepper. The brothers remained active within the community. They are credited with later enticing wayward people back from Dimboola, after a shanty bar opened there. Hagenauer left Ebenezer in 1862, to found a new mission in Gippsland, called Ramahyuck. Both these mission sites are in the Register, although little remains at Ramahyuck. Seven years after Hagenauer's departure, Nathaniel joined him, where he played an influential role amongst Kurnai people, in developing Ramahyuck, until his death there in 1877. Both in its educational and agricultural policies, it was one of Victoria's few successful Aboriginal stations. Apart from its surviving monuments, Ebenezer is significant because of its positive Aboriginal involvement.

Nathaniel Pepper's life span of about thirty-five years symbolises the vast social changes accompanying European settlement. Almost certainly initiated into the

first stages as a Wutjubaluk clansmen, he became a convinced Christian, adopting
European ways. He married Rachel, a Nyungar girl from Albany. She was one of
a group of mission educated girls sent to Victoria on the initiative of Poonindie's
founder, Bishop Hale of Perth. She died at Ebenezer six years later, from
tuberculosis, the same introduced disease which killed Nathaniel at Ramahyuck.
By that time he was married to a Kurnai girl. This mingling of Nyungar, Kurnai
and Wutjubaluk was sudden, and it constituted such a break with the territorial
bonds of traditional society, that comparable dramatic culture shocks must
account for many problems of Aboriginal adjustment across the continent.

Yet some Aborigines were so adaptable and resilient that, like Nathaniel, they
survived the social stress, only to succumb to alien diseases. Nathaniel died a
dignified, Christian death, respected by the Kurnai people.

Although Ebenezer's lands were increased to about 700 hectares by 1871 and
1,500 hectares in the nineties, it never was a viable economic prospect. As its
sandy soil supported only mallee scrub, and limited rainfall restricted agriculture
or horticulture, gainful employment opportunities were few. It served, however,
as a useful staging post for people moving around their ancient cycle of contacts.
In later years, it became a focal point for the displaced and the feeble. About 150
Aboriginal people died there before it was abandoned in 1904.

All that remains at Ebenezer today are what the ravages of bushfires and
neglect have left. An archaeological survey could locate much of the settlement,
but the chief visible structures are the ruined church, the restored kitchen, a
storehouse and a latrine. All buildings consist of limestone rubble walls, thick,
solid, but attractive examples of vernacular architecture. Nearby is a cart shed
with wooden posts and brush roof, another fine regional design.

Aboriginal people and missionaries at Ebenezer, c. 1892. The church was opened in 1875. (Museum of
Victoria)

The roofless limestone Ebenezer church today, framed by a house or store and a privy block, restored in recent years. (D.J. Mulvaney)

Phillip Pepper was a Wutjubaluk leader. He and his brother Nathaniel, who moved on to help found Ramahyuck mission, played a vital role in establishing Ebenezer. Phillip died in 1873 and is buried close to the church. (D.J. Mulvaney)

The existing church was opened in 1875, after H.C. Ellerman (by now, the reverend) laid its foundation stone. Its square bell-tower and primitive Norman style form an exotic import in this mallee landscape. It deserved a better fate than its present neglect. Once, with its plastered interior walls and varnished wooden floor and ceiling, it seated 120 people. Considerable Aboriginal labour was involved in quarrying the rock and erecting the walls.

The graveyard behind the church is the most precious feature for Aborigines. Very few of the graves are marked, but the headstone over Phillip Pepper is prominent. He died in 1873, after serving the mission faithfully as an evangelist.

The names are known of 89 people who died between 1875 and 1905, together with the cause of death of 84 of them. They are a sad reflection upon the state of medical health and the unbalanced diet. Twenty-five infants died aged three years or under. Many diagnoses are vague, but it is evident that at least fifty per cent of deaths (mostly adults) were attributable to chest and lung conditions; others simply "wasted away". Alongside these Aboriginal graves lie the remains of two female and three male Moravian missionaries, testimony to the sacrifices incurred by both races in this encounter of mercy.

The fact that these were indeed dedicated missionaries, and that Aboriginal people felt love and gratitude for their efforts, is overlooked today by many critics. It is facile to criticise missionaries for their lack of anthropological understanding, for their solemnity, their heavy, voluminous clothes, their prudery, and their failure to win many to their faith. Their cheerful flock had different moral values and expectations. This is to judge them out of the context of their moralising and formalistic Victorian period. Nathaniel Pepper's grandson, another Phillip Pepper, emphasised the positive achievements of mission life. He recorded his gratitude in 1980, and many Aborigines elsewhere would echo his sentiments:

> Only for the missionaries there wouldn't be so many Aborigines walking around today . . . . Our people were finished before the mission men came . . . . Old Hagenauer took them sick ones in and gave them medicine and food too.

The annual reports of the Board for the Protection of the Aborigines provide insight into dietary and legal aspects of life in protective custody. As for Ebenezer, the 1863 report indicated that about 100 people frequented it (an average of 33 received rations), "and look upon it as their home". With so many people congregated around Ebenezer, the return from traditional hunting and collecting activities must have declined sharply. Although the station killed its own sheep, meat was never abundant. Consequently, like other settlements, diet was predominantly European and unbalanced. Consider the government rations supplied to Ebenezer during 1863, in pounds weight: flour — 10,000; oatmeal — 100; rice — 400; sugar — 2,500; tea — 160; peas — 224; tobacco — 75 (and 864 pipes); Epsom salts — 6; soap — 350.

A census of Victorian Aborigines was attempted in 1877. It is significant that of the 60 residents at Ebenezer, 28 were described as mixed race. Of those of full Aboriginal descent, there were 17 men, 4 women and only 11 children. Within a few years the government determined to economise by redefining those eligible. The Aborigines Protection Act 1886 excluded "half-castes" from mission residence or from sharing in charity. This excluded up to 261 of the 585 people resident on Victorian stations in 1884. Not surprisingly, this cruel decision to redefine Aboriginality saved money. By 1890, Ebenezer's population had fallen to 35, following the exclusion of 25 "half-castes".

Ebenezer's fate was sealed. Its maintenance during forty years cost the Moravian mission authorities £11,377. The legal expedient of exclusion ensured that numbers were too small to maintain the institution. The Board report for 1902 announced its impending closure. The Lake Hindmarsh Land Act 1904 revoked the Reserve, except for the central cemetery area, and the land was thrown open for selection. Indeed, between 1887 and 1902, about 6,000 hectares of Victorian reserve lands were relinquished. The 1902 report predicted that, "in another twenty years [Aborigines] will probably be extinct". A systematic policy of closure and amalgamation culminated in 1923, when residents from all other reserves had been transferred to Lake Tyers. Hardships incurred by those transplanted from familiar places may be imagined. The Board's actions failed to match its fine sentiments when it announced Ebenezer's closure. Survivors, it proclaimed, "should be dealt with kindly, wisely, and generously".

CHAPTER
TWENTY-THREE

Esperance

Camperdown

Bicheno

Epitaphs of Friendship:
Camperdown, Esperance, Bicheno

James Dawson of Camperdown published his *Australian Aborigines* in 1881. He wrote it in the hope that greater understanding and charity would be extended to "an ill-used and interesting people". Two years later, Dawson appealed for funds to honour the memory of the local Aborigines, whose last member, Wombeetch Puuyuum, had died. Few local landholders contributed, despite the fact that they were proud sheepmasters of some of the colony's best land. Dawson erected the monument largely at his own expense. The grey granite obelisk stands about eight metres tall in the Camperdown cemetery, with Wombeetch Puuyuum's remains buried beneath it. The dates inscribed, "1840–1883", are less than a normal life span. In that district during the period, however, every person of full Aboriginal descent died. Dawson's conservative estimate for that population at contact was a minimal 120 persons. The monument is in the Register as a solemn reminder of the massive impact of white settlement and a reflection that while most settlers were uncaring, genuine humanitarian concern existed amongst a minority.

John Forrest, the Western Australian, also expressed sympathy for Aboriginal people and he felt obliged to those who accompanied him on his explorations. A Beverley district Nyungar man, Billy Noongale (William Kickett) travelled with Forrest in 1870. Forrest was shocked when Noongale died suddenly in 1904 and ordered an inquiry into the circumstances. The local doctor had refused to visit the sick man, although he was within five minutes of the hospital. He sent a bottle of medicine instead, and this possibly accelerated his death. This was not the only case of serious malpractice cited, but no action was taken against this doctor. Forrest paid for a finely inscribed marble headstone in the Beverley cemetery, for "one of his faithful companions".

Forrest already had acted to perpetuate the memory of his chief Aboriginal guide, Windiitj. Tommy Windich, as he was known, was born near Mount Stirling around 1840. As a native policeman, he accompanied landseekers during the 1860s into new country. John Forrest learned of his bushcraft and horsemanship, so he joined all three of Forrest's expeditions in 1869, 1870 and 1874, as well as Alexander Forrest's party in 1871. He was a good rifle shot and proved invaluable in obtaining food and at locating water.

On the famous 1874 crossing from Geraldton to the overland telegraph line, Forrest named Windich Springs after "my old and well tried companion". In this manner, capable Windiitj, a Nyungar man, assisted the European penetration of an Aboriginal desert heartland. His Europeanised name was fixed to a rare waterhole, 150 kilometres northeast of the future Wiluna. In retrospect, one wonders what he thought of such a close identification with an almost certain sacred place in another people's country, with names and associations as old as the Dreaming. Such unauthorised trespassing must have caused Aboriginal "trusty guides" deep psychological unease. It may help to explain why so many apparently acculturated men of full Aboriginal descent died young, or later took to drink.

During the 1870 expedition they passed along the southern coast through Esperance. Five years later, energetic colonists erected the first telegraph pole at Albany, for a line to link the isolated west with easterners. Because of his familiarity with the route, Windich was employed as a guide on the project. He was with a construction party at Esperance in February 1876, when he contracted pneumonia and died. He was buried on Dempster Head.

When John Forrest heard the sad news, he dubbed him "the most experienced and best bushman in the colony . . . an old and well-tried companion and friend". He and Alexander paid for an elaborate black slate headstone, whose inscription reads: "Erected by John and Alexander Forrest, in memory of Tommy Windich. Born near Mt Stirling, 1840. Died at Esperance Bay, 1876. He was an aboriginal native of Western Australia, of great intelligence and fidelity, who accompanied them on exploring expeditions into the interior of Australia, two of which were from Perth to Adelaide. Be Ye Also Ready."

The name Windich has become part of the state's nomenclature. There are a Windich Place and Street in Perth, Bunbury has a Windich Way and Windich Street is a main Esperance route. He gained a sesqui-centenary footpath tablet in Perth's St George's Terrace. His grave in Hughes Road is listed in tourist brochures of Esperance as a place to see. It is in the Register, but more as a symbol than a reality.

The grave today sits neatly by the road, while bulk wheat trucks thunder past to the nearby terminal. Early accounts refer to the grave situated amongst sand dunes overlooking the sea. Today, it is on solid earth, with no view. Presumably it was moved to allow road and port development. Unfortunately, the headstone is not in place either. Fear of vandalism resulted in its removal to an obscure and dim corner in the Esperance Municipal Museum. A granite rock and a neat bronze plaque, which reproduces the original inscription, substitute for the Forrest memorial. "Gone but not forgotten", would seem a more appropriate epitaph for this example of municipal tidying up.

The memory is all that lingers on at Waubadebar's grave, a monument which is in the Register. Waubadebar was buried at Bicheno, Tasmania, on the grassy

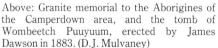

Above: Granite memorial to the Aborigines of the Camperdown area, and the tomb of Wombeetch Puuyuum, erected by James Dawson in 1883. (D.J. Mulvaney)

Above right: When Windiitj died at Esperance in 1876, John Forrest had this headstone engraved for his former guide. It has been removed to the Esperance museum. (Courtesy Battye Library, 2904B)

Right: The memorial today, in Hughes Road, Esperance: a new site and a different, potentially more vandal-proof headstone. (D.J. Mulvaney)

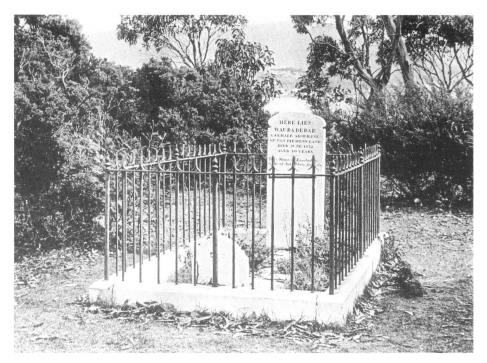

In 1832, Waubadebar's white friends buried her in a pleasant place above Bicheno harbour. Friends were rare at that time. This is an old image. Today the inscription is less evenly lettered. (Courtesy John Hamilton, Bligh Museum, Bruny Island, from the late Dr Bruce Hamilton; photographer D.J. Mulvaney)

slope above Waub's boat harbour. The inscription on the simple gravestone informs the visitor, that "Here lies Waubadebar a female Aborigine of Van Diemens land. Died June 1832. Aged 40 years. This Stone is Erected by a few of her White friends." The grave is surrounded by a neat wrought iron fence of later date; snowdrops are said to bloom there.

Local tradition maintains that Waubadebar was taken from Oyster Bay by sealers when a girl. She passed her life with the sealers and assisted them by swimming amongst seals and clubbing them. Once when their boat was wrecked in a storm, and the man with whom she lived broke his arm, she swam with him to the shore, then returned to rescue his companion. This is a reminder that, although conditions for captive Tasmanian women were tough, bonds developed between the sealers and their women. The hardy offspring of such unions were the ancestors of most of today's Tasmanian Aboriginal population.

Unfortunately, although the grave survives in good condition, despite rather amateurish retouching of its inscription, it may be empty. Possibly Waubadebar's remains were removed, allegedly for scientific purposes. It is claimed that they formed part of the collection of Tasmanian remains returned to the Aboriginal community and cremated at Oyster Cove in 1985.

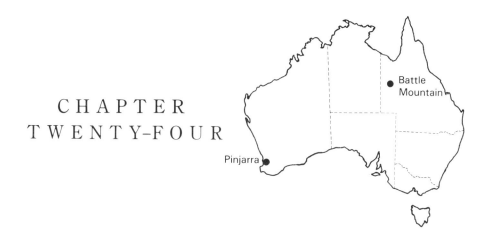

Battle
Mountain

Pinjarra

Battles in the Bush: Pinjarra and Battle Mountain

An Australian contributor proudly informed readers of a recent prestigious American publication, that Australia "is the only country in the world, outside the great neutralist tradition of Europe, where in its whole modern history less than one thousand men have lost their lives under enemy fire on native soil". He referred chiefly to the 1942 Darwin air raids, having overlooked the violent deaths of over 20,000 Aboriginal men, women and children on their own soil. Skirmishes, reprisal raids, massacres and euphemistic "dispersions" were commonplace in every state, while folklore elevated at least two killing grounds to battle status. Participants and their heirs on both sides have different perceptions of these military actions, the Battles of Pinjarra, 1834, and of Battle Mountain, northwest of Cloncurry, in 1884. Both places are in the Register because, no matter how those encounters are interpreted, they had great significance for Aboriginal people.

Pinjarra

Once Britain colonised the Swan River in 1829, settlers quickly expanded along fertile valleys. Aboriginal resistance to dispossession resulted in British casualties. The reprisals which followed prompted pay-back killings, traditional under Aboriginal law. One of the most celebrated series of encounters centred round the activities of Yagan, a Nyungar elder.

The reluctance of modern society to recall the conditions under which land was occupied, is reflected at All Saints Church, Henley Brook, Upper Swan. This charming place merits its Register listing. A notice there records that this was the farthest point inland reached during Stirling's 1827 exploration of the Swan; that the attractive church opened in 1841; that pioneers rest in its graveyard. The river flats immediately below, at the junction of the Swan and the Brook, were important and productive Aboriginal lands, and it was in the vicinity in 1833, that Yagan was treacherously shot and buried. References to these matters merit inclusion in notices.

The need for public information is even more necessary concerning the so-called Battle of Pinjarra. Although much of the site is on public land, there is no reference at that place to the events which occurred there. Settlers by 1834 felt it imperative to occupy the rich soils in the Mandurah-Murray River area. As the Nyungar reacted to encroachment under Calyute as the local leader, deaths and property damage occurred on both sides. Thomas Peel's aim was to develop Pinjarra, but hostilities restricted him.

Peel lobbied Governor Stirling for increased military protection, involving "a complete and satisfactory lesson to these desperate offenders". European tradition maintains that Stirling's Pinjarra intervention was accidental, during an inspection tour with Surveyor-General J.S. Roe. Neville Green's analysis demonstrates, however, that the prior arrangements "indicated that Sir James Stirling was preparing to launch an attack on Calyute". In justifying his actions to the English colonial secretary, Stirling revealingly stated that it "became an urgent Necessity, that a Check should be put upon the Career, of that particular Tribe". It is relevant, also, that when Stirling's party left Peel's Mandurah property on 27 October, it numbered twenty-five, including eleven soldiers and five mounted police; only Roe was unarmed; Peel took his dog pack.

The river ford at Pinjarra was a nodal point for Aboriginal trackways and it was

The Murray River at Pinjarra. The Nyungar people were camped in the vicinity on the near bank. When they attempted to escape across the river, they came under fire from Governor Stirling's men lining the higher opposite bank. (D.J. Mulvaney)

a place of ceremonial significance. Indications pointed to an Aboriginal presence there, so the fact that Stirling's force moved at a leisurely pace and camped overnight within striking distance, suggests a planned early morning assault. The force set out before dawn on a foggy Spring morning. By the time they approached the river opposite the encampment it was raining, which drowned out their shouts to people in the awakening encampment. So five men crossed the ford to ascertain whether the camp consisted of Calyute's people. "A preconcerted Signal to me", Stirling reported, set actions in train for what must have been a planned ambush. As the five riders advanced over the river flat towards the surprised camp of seventy or eighty people, spears wounded one and the force of another unseated the police captain, who died later from concussion. As the Nyungar retreated to gain presumed safety across the river, they came under the raking fire of the main party, lining that higher opposite bank. No wounded men were spared. Others attempted escape downstream, but were picked off by men stationed at the second ford. It was over within an hour, though escapees were hunted through the bush for some time.

So ended the Battle of Pinjarra, which Stirling simply termed a "skirmish". There were only two casualties in his party, but he needed to explain this incident of deadly crossfire to Stanley, the humanitarian colonial secretary. Minimising Aboriginal losses, Stirling reported that these "amounted probably to 15 Men". The number is disputed, but the names of known dead or seriously wounded included three wives and a girl; Roe reported "several children" dead. Roe and another witness estimated about thirty killed, while thirty-five was the figure reported in Perth. It is likely to be somewhat more, to judge from Roe's diary entries. Although an Aboriginal oral tradition, recorded in 1973, claimed an impossible 750 deaths, the loss of half the population of this community (and those largely adult males), virtually terminated the Pinjarra clans as social units. In terms of political, economic and cultural effects, it was as traumatic as this tradition implies.

Stirling's terror tactics were extended to captured women and children, who were released with the threat that, should any settler be killed henceforth, "not one would be allowed, to remain alive on this side of the Mountains". Despite these dire warnings, and armed patrols in case of Nyungar reprisals, the survivors returned to bury their dead under three mass grave mounds and thirteen other graves. For modern Nyungar, therefore, this place is doubly meaningful. It was a ceremonial centre before colonists made of it a massacre and burial site.

It is also understandable that settlers stressed the necessity for savage action by assigning battle status to this bloody frontier raid. Charles Bussell, a contemporary, did not mince matters. "It is absurd to hope to dwell in peace in any country", he stated, "until the aboriginal inhabitants have been subdued." Even the more sympathetic George Fletcher Moore consoled himself that the episode "was a painful but urgent necessity, and likely to be the most humane policy in the end".

Convenient for colonists, certainly, but the humanity implicit for the original inhabitants is difficult to perceive. These events occurred over 150 years ago. While time cannot diminish their barbarity, the work of a mature society should be to accept their reality, and to work to establish more harmonious racial relations. An extensive tract of land alongside the Murray River is public land. It offers the opportunity to educate the public in a bipartisan manner about the terrible events which occurred there.

Battle Mountain

Opposite the Kajabbi bush pub, northwest of Cloncurry, Aborigines erected a stone cairn in 1984. This centennial tribute to the Kalkatunga (Kalkadoon) people was unveiled jointly by a Kalkatungu elder, George Thorpe, and Charles Perkins, secretary, Department of Aboriginal Affairs. Its plaque commemorates "one of Australia's historical battles of resistance", at Battle Mountain, some twenty kilometres southwest of Kajabbi. A settler tradition stationed 600 to 1,000 warriors there, whose "downhill charge may be equated with the charge of the Light Brigade — brave, but a tactical misjudgement".

Such a field of military actions merits Register inclusion, although it is difficult to visit. It is situated within the rugged and ancient rocks of the spinifex covered Argylla Range mineral belt, between Mt Remarkable and Prospector Creek, a Leichhardt River tributary.

Given claims about the Aboriginal spear-power (exceeding "the number of riflemen in an Australian Infantry Battalion"), the evidence for the encounter is suprisingly meagre. Without doubting Kalkatungu courage and sacrifice, it is probable that Battle Mountain justifies its Register listing because it symbolises the end of a major campaign of resistance and because of what both black and white people *believe* happened there, rather than the incident itself. Oral traditions and European folk lore combine to project a frontier epic of filmic proportions, but dubious authenticity.

No eyewitness accounts are known, except that one survivor, "Tubbie Terrier", was sheltered at Glenroy Station. Aboriginal informants consulted by modern historians and linguists were born after that event. The closest approximations to first-hand settler versions are two reminiscences by contemporaries, both written half a century later. S.E. Pearson worked in the Cloncurry region, while Hudson Fysh, the Qantas pioneer, obtained his information from pastoralist Alexander Kennedy. Kennedy participated in earlier reprisals but evidently he was not present on the mountain. The sympathies of Fysh's interpretation are revealed by his title, *Taming the North*.

The encounter involved the Queensland Native Mounted Police, under young F.C. Urquhart. Sources agree that, at this period, officers rarely reported officially on the details of frontier incidents or the number of Aboriginal casualties. European or Chinese murders, however, were highlighted by police and public. For a man with such a distinguished career, Urquhart (1858–1935) proved remarkably reticent. Although he became Queensland's police commissioner in 1917 and he served as Northern Territory administrator 1921–26, apparently he left no account of his various activities. His role during 1884 proved so formative according to Fysh, that "he was the man who made the Cloncurry district safe for white men". A cynic may conclude that these were the characteristics which ensured his later high office. Regrettably, the author was informed that Urquhart's file was missing, when he visited the Queensland State Archives.

Pastoralists settled along the Cloncurry River in 1864, and conditions remained peaceful until the late 1870s. By that time the heartland of Kalkatungu country was occupied and the competition between cattle and Aborigines for access to natural resources became acute. The Kalkatungu survived longer than most plains people, because of their ready access to mountainous terrain. Ironically, even these rocky fastnesses were penetrated peacefully. Despite the settler tradition that Kalkatungu were aggressive, nowhere in Australia were Aboriginal guides of more assistance to eager prospectors. Cloncurry mining pioneer, Ernest Henry, was led to promising stained outcrops of bright green and red ores through these ranges. His original labour force at the Argylla copper mine was Kalkatungu; in 1880, even after he was speared in a dispute, Aboriginal women cared for him.

Beginning in 1878, Kalkatungu attacked cattle, bush camps and settlers in numerous incidents, provoking harsh reprisals in which Kennedy was prominent. One of the region's first settlers, Edward Palmer, who was untroubled by Aboriginal attacks, was sufficiently interested in Aboriginal society to publish ethnographic studies. He reflected later, that "the white pioneers were harder on the blacks in the way of reprisals . . . for spearing their men . . . cattle or horses even than the Native Police". Even so, he could not imagine any alternative to "some summary system of retribution". He was unusual in that these moral issues bothered him.

In any assessment of the battle, the preceding events are relevant. The first massive attack on Kalkatungu followed the murder of settlers who had occupied Woonamo waterhole, south of Cloncurry. One claim was that 300 Aborigines were shot. Fysh contemptuously observed, that they "did not reckon on the deadly carbines . . . who speedily shot the warlike bucks down".

The hazards faced by settlers in these years of guerilla warfare must be admitted. Numerous cattle were speared, some camps were raided and at least eight men were murdered in five incidents. Even so, these deaths were used to justify mayhem. Indeed, Fysh generalised from the murder of three people on the distant Normanby River, to assert that, "before condemning any measures that were taken against blacks, the reader should study . . . this terrible outrage". Possibly irate pastoralists fostered a general sense of panic in order to ensure police support and to excuse violence. Rumour spread that Cloncurry was to be wiped out. In this instance, and in another tale that the Kalkatungu had challenged the native police to pursue them, settlers willingly relied upon the allegations of single Aboriginal informers. This is interesting, for it suggests that it suited the settlers to do so, because nobody would accept Aboriginal testimony in a court of law anywhere in Australia.

Kennedy visited the chief of police in Brisbane during this period of tension and departed with official assurances of increased police protection, and the private advice that, "if you have trouble you know what to do".

Cloncurry duly received its native police troop, which was active in pursuit and retribution until their officer, Beresford, and most of the troop were killed in the bush by escaping Aboriginal prisoners. Sub-Inspector Urquhart arrived in March 1884 to restore law and order. In July, Kennedy's partner, J.W. Powell, was murdered north of Kajabbi. According to Pearson, "the murder of Powell marked the point at which it was officially decided to break the strength of the

Kalkadoons. They were hunted by armed whites, and by Native Mounted Police." Kennedy joined Urquhart in a savage manhunt, shooting a large but undisclosed number. Urquhart now initiated a campaign of systematic punitive raids, which must have been in progress in September, when a Chinese servant was murdered on Granada Station. Another combined force set out in the pursuit which ended at Battle Mountain.

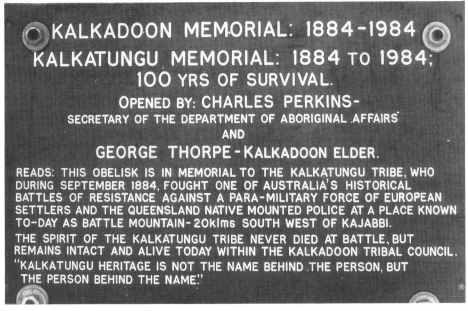

An Aboriginal memorial to a resistance movement, Kajabbi, Queensland. Whether it was a major battle is less certain than the fact that these were spirited people. (D.J. Mulvaney)

Consider the unfortunate Kalkatungu about to face the virtual end of their armed resistance. With so many brutal "dispersions" during the previous six years, their dead probably numbered more adult males than the living. Their waterholes, food resources and ceremonial life were disrupted, so their diet must have shrunk and their morale sunk; add to this the debilitating diseases always associated with European contact, especially measles and chest ailments. Given these factors and the population density in normal hunter-gathering societies, it is inconceivable that 600 warriors or more congregated on the mountain. On those hot, rocky slopes they also were high above water supplies.

From below, in their boulder-strewn spinifex cover, Urquhart demonstrated his suitability as a future imperial administrator, by shouting the Queen's regulations command to the beseiged, "Stand in the name of the Queen". He was answered with a shower of spears and stones, and later, by a lump of hurled ant-bed which felled him temporarily. Stiff resistance continued from the Kalkatungu vantage point, so Urquhart devised a flanking movement, thereby dividing the attention of the defenders.

Whether there was a terminal heroic charge downhill in face of withering fire is a decision best left to personal preference. The two oldest European versions are

Somewhere in this ancient rocky area of the Argylla Range, Aboriginal warriors looked down upon F.C. Urquhart and his native mounted police. Their defence gave these ramparts the name, Battle Mountain. Numerous termite nests are visible (left centre). Urquhart was felled by a lump of this material. (D.J. Mulvaney)

less dramatic. Fysh, following Kennedy, termed the events a "skirmish" in which "a number" fell, hardly implying hundreds of warriors. He paid an uncharacteristic tribute, however, to "the natives [who] stood up to an attack . . . by fire-arms, and fought it out". Pearson seems to echo Fysh in his later publication: Kalkatungu went "down to history as one of the few native tribes . . . that have stood up to the whites in open battle". His comment that "a number of their best warriors were slain" is hardly testimony to the largeness of their force. It seems probable that this was indeed the desperate last stand of the Kalkatungu, but that their number was few. The downhill charge may have been an attempt to elude the flanking attack, and some men certainly escaped from the field.

While Urquhart set off immediately in ruthless pursuit of the survivors, the guerilla resistance had ended. Battle Mountain witnessed the final symbolic action of brave people. Several days later the police passed by the battlefield and saw women and children there. Uncharitable and uncomprehending to the end, they believed that the corpses were being eaten by cannibals. More probably, the survivors were arranging mortuary ceremonies for the vanquished, because the victors treated them with such contempt that they ignored even the normal human values respecting the dignity and disposal of the dead.

Carl Lumholtz visited Queensland in the early 1880s. If this incident, entitled *Native police dispersing the blacks*, does not depict Battle Mountain, it typifies the situation in the Cloncurry region at that time. (C. Lumholtz, *Among Cannibals*, London 1890, p. 348)

CHAPTER TWENTY-FIVE

Afghans and Aborigines at Marree

Camels facilitated the occupation of arid Australia. During the period 1866 to 1907, between ten and twenty thousand camels were imported, more than half of them landing at Port Augusta. As the railhead pushed north from Beltana in 1881, to Farina in 1882 and Marree in 1884, camel pads radiated towards distant stations. Demand during 1883-87 resulted in the importation of 1,142 camels. Railway construction continued to Oodnadatta and eventually to Alice Springs, stimulating camel supply transport; along the Birdsville track during 1901, 1,000 camels entered Queensland. Outback freight transport depended upon camels until the 1930s.

Each camel shipment was accompanied by handlers, possibly totalling 3,000 men, many of whom later returned home. These hardy cameleers, who boarded ship at Karachi, mostly originated in Rajasthan or Baluchistan. Australians were crassly ignorant of Asian geography, so cameleers entered folklore as "Afghans". While some were from Afghanistan, the term was equivalent to labelling migrants from Wales as Cornishmen.

Afghans normally proved quiet, industrious and religious men. Their race, Islamic creed and humble origins ensured discriminatory actions during this era of "white Australia". Their willingness to work for low wages under rough conditions added "unfair competition" to their sins, because they out-freighted European hauliers. Except for a few financially successful individuals, they enjoyed little social contact with white settlers.

Marree's layout reflected this lowly Afghan status with geometric precision, because that multi-cultural community was divided socially by the railway track. European Australian homes and official buildings occupied the western side, where the massive two-storey pub still dominates the thirsty landscape. East of the tracks was a clutter of irregular corrugated iron Afghan huts and sheds. A post and brush mosque with earth floor offset the pub; the town was "dry" on this side of the line. In this zone, also, were the humpies of Aboriginal fringe dwellers.

The Afghans were a minority group everywhere, despite their economic importance. During half a century of racial encounter, they interacted strongly with Aboriginal people. Their camel strings ventured into remote territory, first as most explorers after Ernest Giles relied upon camels and their attendants, and later, as pastoralists depended upon their freight. Many accounts recall the fear evident amongst Aboriginal groups who, for the first time, saw camels and turbaned Afghans. They soon overcame their initial fright and friendly relations developed. The passage of camel-strings, or temporary halts en route, became woven into the social life and oral traditions of communities. Aboriginal encampments were associated with camel depots.

Cameleers were tough men and they were not in the business of racial interaction for sentimental reasons. They are said to have carried arms. However, despite some mutual distrust, they were drawn into association with Aborigines. Few Afghan women ever accompanied their menfolk to Australia; racial prejudice meant that white women were scarce. As Afghan culture promoted the ideal of the ample female figure, Aboriginal women satisfied their requirements. Arabana traditions recall Afghan sexual escapades and the warnings with which mothers protected their daughters from surprise encounters (including the notion that Afghans were cannibals). Many unions proved more permanent and Afghan genes are represented in many outback populations.

An important facet of economic life was the employment of young Aboriginal males to handle camels. Although they were rarely entrusted with the main driving duties, they walked alongside the string, keeping camels moving at a steady pace, watering and saddling them, or fixing snapped noselines. Many journalists have written about the romance of the camel days and praised the Afghans, while overlooking the major labour contribution from Aboriginal communities. Until traffic declined, Afghans retained their ownership monopoly. Aboriginal cameleers then entered the trade. Walter Smith, a part-Aranda man, worked as an offsider for Alice Springs cameleer, Charlie Saadadeen, before running his own string. He employed Aboriginal assistants. During recent times feral camels have been tamed and used by Aboriginal communities.

Two places in Marree are in the Register because they signify Afghan-Aboriginal associations, and also they are representative of the Afghan contribution to Australian history. On the scorched, treeless plain stands the fenced Marree cemetery, divided internally by invisible barriers neatly separating this multi-cultural community even in death. The ornate monuments covering European graves stand at the eastern end. The largest obelisk commemorates a railway construction accident on the Oodnadatta line north of Marree, which killed four men, a reminder that white settlers also faced dangers.

In the northwestern corner of the cemetery are about sixty Afghan graves. Two of them encapsulate the Afghan story. The oldest dated grave is that of Wahub, who died in 1895. The finely contrived bilingual inscription reflects the importance of the Arabic script and of the Koran to his mourners. The two decaying posts marking Syed Goolamdeen's grave provide mute testimony to change. Syed Goolamdeen (1870–1963) arrived in Australia in 1901. He prospered, and at a time when about sixty Afghans worshipped in Marree's

There are some 60 Afghan graves in the Marree cemetery. That of Wahub who died in 1895 is one of the finest. (D.J. Mulvaney)

The grave of Syed Goolamdeen is the most forlorn at Marree. He died in 1963, the last of the important migrant Afghan cameleers. (D.J. Mulvaney)

mosque, he owned ninety camels. By 1956, when he was the last surviving migrant cameleer there, he supervised the demolition of the mosque, "rather than become a playhouse for children, who would not treat it with the respect due".

Isolated in another zone are the graves of Aboriginal people. Their burial here commenced under police order during the mid-1950s. Previously, the deceased were wrapped in blankets and carried northeast of Marree to be interred in the sands of the Frome River.

Bejah Dervish and his son, Jack Bejah (Abdul Jubbar), were celebrated names in Marree and made distinguished contributions to the last phase of European explorations. They also established enduring relationships with Aboriginal people. Their home is in the Register. It consists of unpainted corrugated iron and weatherboard, with a clump of date palms to one side. The palms were planted and tended lovingly by Bejah Dervish, but his cottage was more rudimentary (including an earth floor) until his son improved it.

The Marree residence of famed cameleers and explorers, Bejah Dervish and Jack Bejah. (D.J. Mulvaney)

Bejah Dervish (1862?–1957) attained the rank of sergeant in the British Indian army, before migrating to Australia in 1890. He established a reputation for endurance, reliability and good camel management on the 1896–97 Calvert scientific exploring expedition in northwestern deserts. Two of the small party perished and the return of the other members was due largely to him. The leader, L.A. Wells, recorded an occasion upon which Bejah stoically refused breakfast when his camels were hungry: "camel no eat, me no eat". He proved less impassive when a group of excitable Aborigines approached. According to Wells, he "kept calling to me not to let them get too close, as I should not be able to shoot them".

Despite his martial prudence, he enjoyed good relations with Aborigines and employed them on his extended camel routes. Indeed, a Diyari speaker with an Arabana mother claims Bejah as his father. Upon his return from the Calvert expedition, Bejah was feted. He dined at Adelaide's Government House, while every visitor to Marree was shown proudly the brass-boxed compass which Wells inscribed and gave him. He had retired before 1939, when C.T. Madigan sought his guidance. Consequently Jack Bejah supplied and led the camels for Madigan's Simpson Desert expedition. This was the first European party to cross that desert. As was the case with the Calvert expedition, Afghan cameleers deserve much credit for the successful outcome. That expedition in the first year of World War II, marked the end of a transport era. Camels already were so little used that Oodnadatta residents flocked to see the party pass through.

The inclusion of Bejah Dervish's place in the Register is an appropriate symbol of the Afghan role in outback history. That the grounds include date palms is a bonus, because Afghan initiative at Marree and Lake Harry produced Australia's first attempt to cultivate dates commercially. These few survivors are forlorn testimony to a failed enterprise. While popular imagery associates date palms with camels and deserts, unfortunately artesian bores do not constitute oases.

Along the Birdsville track about thirty kilometres from Marree, the first bore was sunk at Lake Harry in 1890. Like the Marree bore sunk six years earlier, daily flow exceeded 450,000 litres. Date palms were planted using the excess run-off from both bores. There were a few hundred palms at Marree, irrigated over

This Alice Springs memorial to district cameleers includes Walter Smith, an Aranda man. (D.J. Mulvaney)

more than three hectares, but Lake Harry plantation numbered at least 2,200 palms by 1907.

This is an astonishing fact for any visitor today. Lake Harry is a flat salt pan in a gravel and sand wasteland. The bore and Lake Harry homestead ruins stand near the Birdsville road. The area is in the Register because it epitomises the changing environmental and social fortunes along "the track".

Pastoral occupation of this region commenced in 1870. The unsuitability of this country is reflected in the lease transfers. At least four occurred (including a bank) before it was acquired in 1900 by the government Water Conservation Commission. It became a camel depot, where camels were depastured for use in the important tasks of pulling bore drilling rigs or constructing dams along the stock route. It served also as a main halt for camel caravans. It was a busy place, because hundreds of camels passed back and forth early this century.

Lake Harry was closed as a government depot in 1918, although it had been used decreasingly since 1906. It returned to leasehold pastoral purposes under several different lessees, belonging for a time to the Sidney Kidman cattle empire. Perhaps Kidman's exploitative and environmentally destructive control contributed to its barren, eaten-out aspect.

The timber-framed stone and galvanised iron homestead, using local stone and gypsum plaster, dates from around 1905. After several owners and alterations, it was abandoned in 1953. Its walls still stand, but it has been savagely vandalised.

Lake Harry homestead, once a camel depot and date plantation on the Birdsville track. (D.J. Mulvaney)

A solitary dead date palm in the saltbush at Lake Harry, 1986. (D.J. Mulvaney)

Some of the 2,200 date palms at Lake Harry around 1907. (D.J. Gordon, *Handbook of South Australian Progress and Resources*, Adelaide 1908, p. 215)

Its surrounds merit systematic archaeological survey and preservation. The soil must conceal traces of its varied occupation. The sheds and yards of its camel depot phase require definition; traces of Afghan activities need locating; as it is probable that an Aboriginal fringe camp existed, its location should be sought. Foundations of extensive structures surround the homestead. Rusted traces of a large rectangular iron structure, either a tank or a shed, invite investigation.

The most fleeting of all evidence concerns the date plantation. One dead palm stands desolately a few hundred metres from the homestead, challenging the imagination to restore greenery to a dead landscape, where eighty years ago a boat could have negotiated the irrigation channels. Circumstances predestined failure for the date industry. Because the appropriate bee is absent in Australia, natural pollination is impossible. Afghans were engaged to pollinate the plants manually, a tedious task which younger men declined. Besides, it added to the costs of an industry which had marketed only 250 kilograms of dates in 1906.

More importantly, the artesian water proved unsuitable. It emerged at 46°C, which may explain the use of a bulky iron container at the borehead. Possibly it cooled the water slightly before it passed through pipes to the channels. The palms developed and fruited, but as salinity increased, they ceased bearing. The scheme had failed by about 1914, although some palms survived to suggest to visitors during the thirties that they were in foreign lands.

Although this chapter has featured Afghans in the inter-racial encounter at Marree, it must be remembered that the written sources have been influenced by the exotic cameleers. An old Arabana woman, who saw a television feature, remarked with some annoyance: "They only showed [pictures of] Afghans: the Afghans used to travel here and there, the Afghans went on the Birdsville track, the Afghans went with their camels! They didn't show . . . Aborigines. But I've seen Aborigines working [with camels] . . . and get lots of money . . . . When I was a big girl a lot of Aborigines from Marree were working [with camels], they are dead now. . . ."

CHAPTER TWENTY-SIX

Dorre and
Bernier Islands

Bernier and Dorre: "Isles of the Dead"

At the northwestern extremity of Shark Bay, some forty-five kilometres from the coast at Carnarvon, the Indian Ocean beats upon the tumbled rocky shore of the two uninhabited islands, Bernier and Dorre. They are listed in the Register for their scientific flora and fauna values. Although their brief and forlorn episode in Aboriginal history merits greater recognition, it is forgotten today except by Aboriginal communities of the region. For little more than a decade early this century, the islands were designated as Lock hospitals, virtual prisons, where segregated Aboriginal victims of venereal diseases were detained and given compulsory medical treatment. Males occupied Bernier Island, while Dorre Island became a female reserve.

Venereal diseases were one of the ravages of Aboriginal society from the time of European contact. Although the contagion was spread by European colonists, and greatly aggravated in the Aboriginal community by the shortage of European women on the frontiers of white settlement, it proved convenient to blame the morals of other races. Western Australians denounced the lack of moral constraints in "savage" society, the promiscuity of Aboriginal women, and the immorality of Asians along the pearling coast. Little attention was given to treating the afflicted Aborigines. A sympathetic colonist who was familiar with the area from Perth to Geraldton during the later nineteenth century concluded that "not a moment of medical attention was being given to them".

With the new century, worried citizens believed that the incidence of venereal diseases was increasing rapidly. Perhaps their indignation and social concern were activated by the growing number and increasing respectability of white women in the outback. Two regions aroused particular anxiety, Broome and the Ashburton area inland from Onslow. A proposed solution was outlined by the Chief Protector of Aborigines, in his 1903 report to parliament. Patients should be

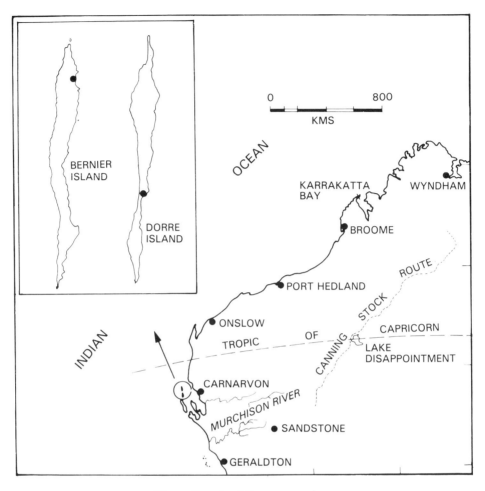

The northwest and Carnarvon regions

held under permanent medical supervision in special Aboriginal hospitals at Broome and Onslow, while the entry of Aborigines into Broome needed strict control. Using the phraseology of current racialist ideology, the Chief Protector noted that restrictions on the movement of Aboriginal women were the only means of preventing them "pandering to [the] lusts", of "Asiatics, who are so numerous and ubiquitous". While it seemed appropriate to use the law to regulate the personal lives of alien races, such as wily orientals and savages, nothing was proposed to limit the propensity for spreading disease by randy European bushmen, armed with rifles and grog to ensure their domination. Such was the current attitude to sexuality, that Aboriginal women were blamed as the purveyors of the disease.

A Royal Commission on the Condition of Natives reported widely and critically upon the social and economic plight of Western Australian Aborigines in 1905. The commissioner was W.E. Roth, a Queensland medical officer and ethnologist, whose solutions involved a harsh and compulsive paternalism. "The wrongs and injustices . . . and the cruelties and abuses met with in the unsettled districts", Roth proclaimed, "cannot be longer hidden or tolerated." A year later, a German scientist who visited Wyndham supported Roth's allegations. He found "every white person being regarded with the dread that natives attached to police officers, who . . . were likened to dangerous animals".

Roth's report assisted humanitarian calls (mostly from outside the state) for action on various fronts, although little positive change actually resulted. One major innovation, which affected the lives of several hundred Aboriginal people, resulted from a conference of medical officers held during 1907. The Chief Protector's recommendation, that isolated Lock hospitals should be established to restrict the spread of venereal diseases, was adopted. This proposal was motivated more by concern for the welfare of Europeans, than by humanitarian feelings for Aboriginal patients. "The menace to the white population", the Chief Protector observed, "although probably the seeds of evil have been sown by them in the first instance, is becoming so great that . . . some drastic steps should be taken to check the spread of the disease."

In selecting Bernier and Dorre Islands, the government reacted with surprising resolution, compensating a Carnarvon pastoralist with £1,000 for resuming his grazing lease on Bernier Island and spending considerable funds on the hospitals. The first bewildered patients arrived on 6 October 1908. The men were housed at the northern end of Bernier, and the women at White Beach, two-thirds of the way down the east cost of Dorre.

Bernier and Dorre are elongated, narrow limestone and dune sand fingers, running north-south. They are remnants of ice age dunes, formed on a landscape which was drowned as seas rose following the melting of ice sheets. Bernier, the northern island, is twenty-six kilometres long, but little more than two kilometres wide at its broadest. Dorre is a few kilometres longer, but equally narrow. Over sixty kilometres of western coast are exposed to the Indian Ocean, whose great rollers smash on the fringing reef of submerged coral rock. A welcome cooling breeze normally blows across the islands, restricting the flies, although a visitor deplored "the horror of flies in summer-time". Cyclones of great intensity fling themselves at these flat-topped islands. They terrified early maritime explorers and occasionally proved a destructive and hazardous force for patients. Stunted vegetation covers the extensive sandy plains, running to the abrupt cliff edge which surrounds most of the islands. No springs or natural reservoirs of fresh water supply either island, and rain is infrequent. The calm sea and scattered beaches along the eastern shores, however, teem with marine life. As the islands abound with reptiles and small marsupials, traditional food collecting activities were possible for those well enough to undertake them.

Isolated at Australia's furthest western extension, and separated from each other by rapid tidal races, these islands may have seemed to offer tropical rest cures for patients. In reality, they were natural prisons for their reluctant inmates, of whom almost one person in three would die there. For Aboriginal people firmly oriented within their clan territories and kinship structure, this uprooting to unknown islands was a traumatic psychological experience, even without the burden of a diseased body. Amongst the first batch of fifty-eight women to arrive on Bernier were people who had been "collected from Wyndham downwards". This means that some unfortunate women, already seriously ill, were deposited over 2,000 kilometres from their homelands and mixed with people whose languages and customs were unknown to them.

When Daisy Bates was working about 700 kilometres inland from Carnarvon, she witnessed the commencement of a journey to Bernier and Dorre by some of her former informants. "I shall never forget the anguish and despair on those aged faces", she recalled, "The poor decrepit creatures were leaving their own country for a destination unknown, a fate they could not understand, and their woe was pitiful." Part-Aboriginal children were taken from their mothers during this same traumatic period.

It is small wonder that official reports on the condition of the enterprise referred to "a natural longing to go back to their native homes". Unfortunately for the peace of mind of both patients and their kin at home, it was only during the closing months of the system that officials accepted the need to inform kin of a patient's progress. There even was a utilitarian purpose behind this humane service. As the Chief Protector reported in 1917:

> At the request of the natives in several places, I was able to . . . supply periodical progress reports as to the condition of . . . relatives in hospitals, to . . . the districts from whence the patients came, an arrangement which gave much satisfaction, and the absence of which was causing much trouble when attempting to examine the healthy, and inducing the sick ones found inland to journey to the coast.

Even when patients were declared cured and shipped back to Carnarvon or some other port, it seems problematical whether many actually returned to their homelands, a thousand or more kilometres east or north. The police "facilities" of forced marches did not apply in reverse. The chief source of information, Daisy Bates, implies that many people would not have attempted to cross regions with which they had no traditional affiliation. It must be concluded that a majority of those who were suddenly torn from place and kin never returned. There is no evidence to suggest that the Aborigines Department questioned its right to treat and isolate Aborigines compulsorily. For individuals who were neither slaves nor convicts, this is a grave indictment of a democratic system.

Nothing reveals the terrifying authoritarianism better than a telegraphic exchange between Roebourne police and the Chief Prosecutor in 1912. Roebourne asked, "What about syphilitic. reply. constable leaving tomorrow". The Perth response was "Bring in syphilitic patient with other and place under doctors treatment until can be sent island". So a prisoner probably was neck-chained to an infected non-offender!

Some unusual circumstances resulted in a visit to the islands during 1910 by a team of anthropologists. Their experiences provided invaluable insights into the conditions under which patients were located on the mainland, brought to Carnarvon, and transported to the islands. It all began at a remote inland Aboriginal camp at Sandstone, southeast of Meekatharra. The English anthropologist A.R. Brown (later Radcliffe-Brown) was collecting genealogical data, assisted by a young Cambridge biological science graduate, Grant Watson. Collaborating with Brown in this research was Daisy Bates. The camp was raided suddenly by a posse of uncouth police, in search of alleged murderers. They departed with prisoners, probably not guilty parties, and so frightened the community that the camp was deserted. Possibly the raid was intended to dislodge the Europeans, because such Aboriginal studies were unlikely to find favour with local settlers.

Determined to continue research into that particular social group, Brown set off for Dorre Island, where he knew kindred people were lodged. Watson accompanied him, while Daisy Bates joined them there later. Years afterwards, Bates commented critically on the conditions of Aboriginal patients. Within four years, Grant Watson based the first of his Australia-centred novels, *Where Bonds are Loosed*, entirely upon his experiences, "with but little deviation from the actual events".

The power to determine the fate of Aboriginal people judged to be suffering from venereal diseases, rested primarily with police troopers. One police expedition collected 99 people in 1911. They "inspected" populations in outback camps and settlements, both males and females. "I regret to say", the Chief Protector blandly reported in 1911, "that at times force has to be used." As Watson testified around that time, "the method of collecting patients was neither humane nor scientific". The police, who had no medical training, selected those women and men who appeared to be diseased, or whom they suspected of infection. It is obvious that they were unqualified to make medical diagnoses. Superficial visual inspection could also confuse other diseases, particularly yaws, which was passed by social contact rather than by sexual contact.

Despite the tragic probability of error, suspects were immediately and unceremoniously removed from their communities. Such arbitrary treatment in no way differed from the handling of criminals. It had its parallel three decades earlier in the British Contagious Diseases Acts, under which prostitutes were held

Although the date and location of this Western Australian image are unknown, it exemplifies the physical discomfort of neck chains. Nine men are chained together and handcuffed. Note that the unfortunate man at left has to support the weight of the spare chains and a heavy padlock. (Courtesy Battye Library, 7816B, and Mrs H. Stretch, Kojonup)

Even in police custody at Wyndham c. 1905, prisoners were handcuffed and neck-chained in groups of three. *Black prisoners, chained in threes* illustrated an article in the first volume of *Inlander* (1913–14), edited by Reverend John Flynn. Its author favoured neck-chains as being "more comfortable than to be chained by the arms or legs." (*Inlander*, vol.1 (1913–14), p. 154; courtesy National Library of Australia)

under laws which differed little from those governing contagious diseases in animals. Daisy Bates, who witnessed the police raid on the Aboriginal camp, the "inspection" and selection of potential patients, reported that they departed on the first leg of their long journey, to Sandstone gaol, by cart. It was more common to walk. In both cases, all patients were restrained by neck-chains, which bound them in close proximity to each other, thereby ensuring cross infection of other ills, in addition to the discomfort involved.

Roth condemned the use of neck-chains for prisoners in his Royal Commission report and provided glaring examples of inhumane practices. Police normally were equipped to collect up to fifteen prisoners and it was common to walk the gang from place to place until all neck-bands were occupied. Roth found examples of chained women being sexually abused; prisoners were forced to cross rivers in chains; chains might be fastened to saddles, a cause of horrible injuries should a horse bolt; even after three years, some prisoners still wore their chains while performing hard manual tropical labour.

The Western Australian government considered Roth's objections and responded, that "it has been conclusively proved by all medical and other evidence that this is most humane". So the system was retained. As late as 1958 the Western Australian Police Commissioner defended neck-chaining as the form preferred by Aborigines. There is no evidence, however, that either the police or European prisoners preferred such degrading communal chaining. Handcuffs were standard for non-Aboriginal people. In any case, Roth's criticisms referred to alleged criminals, not innocent patients, whose infected sores often must have added to the discomfort of chains. The authorities claimed that these chains were "light", such as weighing 28 ounces (791g). Roth found instances where the combined weight of neck-band and connecting links weighed 84 ounces (2,377g).

It has been possible to reconstruct the sheer discomforts and endurance imposed upon ailing people, from Grant Watson's incisive eyewitness accounts. The journey to Carnarvon "often took weeks, and many prisoners died by the way. Flies in clouds buzzed about suppurating sores [sometimes becoming fly-blown]. The chains were never removed, for if they had been the natives would have been quick to escape. Men and women mingled, and it was not surprising that all the survivors were thoroughly infected by a variety of ailments by the time they arrived at their destination."

Once they reached Carnarvon, patients awaited suitable weather for embarkation. In favourable conditions, the voyage took one day. Watson sailed on a stinking former pearling lugger, although the government later supplied a more substantial thirty-ton boat, with the incongruous name of *Venus*. Watson boarded shortly before the boat sailed, but the chained patients had been herded aboard the day before. "As most of them had never been to sea before", Watson observed, "they were very much frightened." "All the hatches were open, and in the shallow hold were standing some forty natives, pressed close together, their heads just coming above the level of the deck. They looked miserable and suffering pieces of humanity." Their discomfort increased during the crossing, because "most of them had been very sick and were cramped from being so closely packed". When Bates crossed, all the passengers were seasick on a terrifying voyage which took thirty-six hours. On an earlier occasion, when the boat became overloaded at Carnarvon, many of its frightened cargo had to get off, walk weary miles back to their camp (they were barred from town) and wait for another passage.

Exile on these islands may have come as a temporary relief after the horrors of reaching them. The government made a positive attempt to make the system work, and in most years spent between £4,000 and £6,000 on the project. This constituted a high proportion of its expenditure on Aboriginal welfare. The cynic, however, who reads the 1908 report by the Chief Protector with his approving quotation of the island's doctor, that efficient treatment was necessary, "not only for their sakes, but for the sake of the community at large", may conclude that European self-interest justified the expenditure. Besides, most of this expenditure was concerned with staff salaries and housing, and maintaining the boat.

The doctor was assisted by a matron, two nurses and a dispensary assistant, concentrated on Dorre, the female island. Hospitals were reasonably equipped for routine operations. A research bacteriologist worked there for some months. Periodic medical visits were made to Bernier, where those men who were well enough assisted the manager to maintain the sheep, goats, tracks, a cart and horse. In 1910, this cheap labour carted building timber, gathered 500 loads of coral, and mixed mortar.

It became necessary to erect a twenty-bed female hospital and a twelve-bed male building on concrete foundations. Their jarrah frames came from Perth, as did the corrugated iron roofs. Walls consisted chiefly of tarred canvas. They appear airy and orderly in photographs. As officials termed them "incurable wards", however, patient morale may have sunk as low as Watson portrayed it:

"Broken and helpless pieces of humanity who lay still all day and looked out across the bleak expanse of sand-dunes, under which they were destined to be buried, and thought regretfully of their beloved and far-away bush."

During the first months of the settlement, patients were encouraged to forage or hunt for much of their own food, although rations were supplied, including flour, tea, sugar and tobacco. However, many people were too feeble to undertake such activities, and Daisy Bates considered that people of inland origin were too unfamiliar with marine and coastal resources to adapt to the regime. Whatever the reasons, it appears that the plentiful natural food supplies, especially fish, crustacea, turtle eggs, wallaby and lizards, were not exploited to any extent after the first months of occupation. The communities were so dependent upon supplies by 1910, that Bates claimed "the position became pitiable", when climatic conditions delayed stores from Carnarvon.

Shelters, initially, were constructed largely of tarpaulins. They were avoided, and patients built their own brush shelters. With the advent of winter, however, it became necessary to provide more substantial protection. From Perth came more jarrah frames, two sheets of corrugated iron per shelter and canvas. The entire structure could be adjusted to wind direction, which provided better protection from the elements. Such siting rearrangements often meant the violation of traditional settlement patterns involving people from unrelated communities and mutually unintelligible languages. This imposed spiritually unsettling conditions at the very time when nature imposed greater environmental stress.

The greatest inhibitor of recovery was death. Emotional Daisy Bates termed the islands "tombs of the living dead". Death was always a factor, with burial grounds within sight of the ailing patients. In departmental annual reports there was never any computation of the number of sick people who died between the time of their capture, their enforced marches in chains and temporary lodgement in gaols, their wait for shipping outside Carnarvon and the voyage across. It must have amounted to a considerable total during the eleven years of its operation. By June 1910, however, 197 Aboriginal people reached the islands, of whom 37 were returned to the mainland as healed. The death toll exceeded the successes, for 41 died. Arriving on Bernier in November 1910, Daisy Bates found that only fifteen male patients survived, but she counted thirty-eight graves. At the end of June 1912, out of a total of 405 patients treated, the official death toll was 103.

The period of peak intake then passed. Although it has been claimed that over 800 persons were treated in Lock hospitals, admissions totalled 635, of whom 162 died during treatment. As those remaining after 1917 were described as incurable, a more realistic total would be about 180 deaths. Annual reports acknowledged that a death rate of one in four was high, but emphasised that many patients were critically ill at the time of their admission. It is likely that most people died from other infections, such as tuberculosis, and that they cross-infected each other.

Bates realistically appreciated the psychological stresses associated with an Aborigine dying in an alien place. "Some of them were alone of their group", and they could not undertake traditional mortuary rituals or present offerings to persons who were outside their ceremonial and kinship network, "for fear of evil magic. A woman could be called upon to bath and feed or bury another woman whose spirit she knew was certain to haunt her." The unfamiliar and

Female patients outside the Dorre Lock hospital, c. 1910, around the time of the visit by Daisy Bates. (Courtesy Battye Library 725 B/22)

Bernier Island ward for men, c. 1910. (Courtesy Battye Library 725 B/59)

incomprehensible medical system, however, may have provided the greatest terror. The fact that there were frequent changes of medical staff supports the impression conveyed in Grant Watson's novel that doctors were not highly motivated. Evidently, the male patients on Bernier were visited infrequently, even when weather conditions favoured the sea voyage from Dorre. Watson's version provides horrendous descriptions of feeble patients with fly-blown sores.

The pain of operations and injections, or the fear which unknown actions engendered, were further deterrents to an easy recovery. Current injected medications often had extremely painful consequences. Bates knew of one terrified man who hid in the bush and died there, rather than face an operation. Experiments were conducted during 1911 with Salvarsan, a new arsenic-based drug. The medical officer claimed improvement, but his successor refused to continue with it because it failed to achieve a cure. One unfortunate woman was injected with "various preparations of Mercury, with various of the Arlarsonates, and finally" Salvarsan, during the course of six months. Salvarsan injections took five minutes to flow into a vein, but patients had no option. The superintendent explained that "they are free to roam the islands at their own sweet will, provided, of course, that they obey regulations and attend at regular hours for their disease to be attended to". Punishment of defaulters was common and the unruly might be locked up — unusual powers for doctors whose normal concern is healing the sick.

One shocking accusation levelled by Biskup, however, must be refuted. When the superintendent ordered a bone crusher, to improve "the nutritive value of the

Inside the women's ward, c. 1910. The blankets were designed to honour Federation. Although only 4,000 were made, they obviously remained in supply nine years later, to conceal the dispirited patients. (Courtesy Battye Library 725 B/67)

soil", he was *not* using humans for fertiliser. His requisition form simply specified a "hand-bone crusher (small)", for fish and sheep bones.

In the face of all this human misery, A.R. Brown, that scientific anthropologist, methodically collected and checked geneaologies as his informants died around him. Evidently, he recorded nothing else about them or their present condition, even though he knew something of their vastly different traditional society. They existed for him simply as scientific specimens to be classified into kinship structures. Later, as Radcliffe-Brown, he delivered the 1930 presidential address to the anthropology section of the Australian and New Zealand Association for the Advancement of Science. His theme was "Applied Anthropology", but it was as lacking in human understanding or charity as was his research on Bernier Island.

Federation blankets kept out the draughts for those men who were well enough to fend for themselves in the lee of a dune. Boredom was a way of life. (Courtesy Battye Library 21075P)

It was evident that the costly system of treating venereal disease did not work. The outbreak of World War I also required "a considerable curtailment in expenditure" on Aboriginal affairs, even by the time the Chief Protector submitted his report for 1914/15. The medical reality, discovered just before the war, was that the ailment from which most Aborigines suffered was a variant of yaws, which produced the appearance of a venereal disease. It seems probable that many affected people had been incarcerated for the wrong disease. Reports stressed that the incidence of the disease had diminished, and claimed that this success was due to the Lock hospital programme. Mild cases now were treated on the spot, thereby decreasing those requiring hospitalisation. By 1917, it was argued of Bernier and Dorre that the "upkeep was out of all proportion to the benefit derived from the expenditure". During the next year, even though only twenty-four patients were left on the islands, it cost £3,112 to keep them there (one-fifth of the departmental budget).

The decreased incidence of the disease is heartening, and possibly the harsh policy resulted in the improvement. The logic of improving cost efficiency by 1918 seems undoubted. Yet an element of wishful thinking may have coloured the statistics. Numbers held on the islands decreased because fewer diseased people were being removed forcibly from their land. Over the last years "inspections" were made by one Protector on a circuit. Presumably he had better diagnostic knowledge than police showed in random actions. With the advent of war, probably there were fewer police, or they had other duties. There was less incentive to locate subjects, both on grounds of departmental economic policy and because Western Australian concerns rested more with men in France than with women in the Pilbara.

Despite the hysteria concerning venereal diseases earlier in the century, and the alleged role of Aborigines or Asians as their host carriers, it is ironic to consult the report presented by the combined state Medical and Health Departments in December 1917. A Contagious Diseases Act was passed in 1915, so venereal diseases were discussed at length. No reference was made to those races. It was noted that 2,653 persons in Western Australia were known to have contracted the disease. As this was coincident with the period when Aboriginal cases declined, presumably factors within European society were responsible. Even so, the firm measures recommended to safeguard white society made no reference to the arbitrary transport and confinement of patients in segregated prisons. Neither was the implicit immorality of that society castigated. The sad episode of Lock hospitals was a classic case of a righteous society with double standards, when race was involved.

The twenty-four surviving inmates on Bernier and Dorre at the end of 1918 knew that they were to return to the mainland. They waited ten months before a new "Depot for Diseased Natives" was opened at Port Hedland and they were transferred there. It was claimed that their health improved, due to new techniques involving injections of antimony. Some of the improvement, however, may have been a consequence of their return to familiar mainland surroundings from islands beyond the western shore. In any case, as antimony in excess is poisonous, it is a reminder that some earlier experimental injections may have killed more than they cured.

Bernier and Dorre Islands became uninhabited once more, and even the grazing licences which were granted subsequently were never taken up. In 1957, the Western Australian government gazetted both islands as Class A Reserves for the preservation of fauna, hence their listing in the Register.

A scientific expedition visited the island in 1959. On Dorre Island they noted the concrete floors, an underground tank and some other remains of the Lock hospital at White Beach. At the northern end of Bernier Island, near the boat-landing area, lay debris, including bottles, clay pipes and charred wallaby bone. On the higher ground was the concrete base of the hospital, while the remains of the cart lay in the scrub. When the nomination of the islands was lodged with the Australian Heritage Commission, their role in the fatal encounter between Aborigines and alien disease was so little recognised that no reference was made to it.

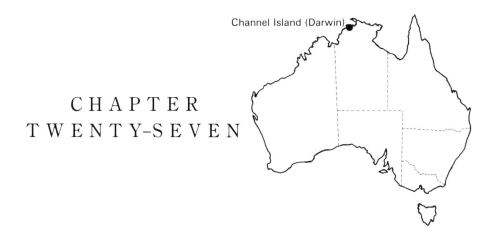
Channel Island (Darwin)

CHAPTER
TWENTY–SEVEN

"I am no loathsome leper" on Channel Island

The Channel Island leprosarium (1931–55) was within twelve kilometres of Darwin, yet it was and is a remote and desolate place. Mangroves on its rocky perimeter screen its low, waterless interior. The horizon across the waters of Middle Arm is a vista of sombre green mangroves rooted in salt flats. This unlovely place is in the Register as testimony to human suffering from an introduced disease. At least 443 lepers of different races were exiled here, although by the time of the leprosarium's transfer to East Arm in 1956, only 77 patients had been discharged; at least 142 died there. Over ninety-five per cent of all admissions were people of Aboriginal descent.

Leprosy and its supposed easy contagion fostered horrific folk lore long before Shakespeare's "loathsome" imagery. Presumably its persistence and very disfiguring nature, affecting the peripheral nerves, skin and other tissues, promoted some innate fear of pollution. Although the bacillus *Mycobacterium leprae*, which resembles the tuberculosis germ, can be transferred in droplets from sneezing or coughing, it is not very infectious, provided close personal contact is avoided. It is curable today with sulphones and associated drugs, and patients are no longer removed from their communities. The East Arm leprosarium closed in 1982, while the Derby leprosarium, established during an epidemic in 1936, was abandoned in 1986.

Medical science only recently mastered the cure. Traditional medical and societal responses enforced absolute segregation. Safety was rated more highly than compassion for the sufferers, so islands were selected as lazarets with a callous disregard for the comfort of sufferers of any race. Some Queensland communities bordered on hysteria, incarcerating lepers on virtually uninhabitable islands. South Australia's Darwin administration reacted similarly in 1884, when leprosy initially was diagnosed in a Chinese. The unfortunate man was marooned on Mud Island and left in a tent, literally, for dead.

Leprosy was endemic in China and Indonesia, but probably was unknown at first in Australia. Isolated cases were diagnosed in most states after 1855, involving Chinese. Whether its Northern Territory introduction resulted from Macassan contacts, or from the Chinese influx to the goldfields, remains uncertain. The first diagnosed cases, however, were Chinese. An American also died from leprosy near Darwin in 1889, and the first Aboriginal case was diagnosed in 1890; in Western Australia, a few Aborigines contracted leprosy in the Pilbara around 1910. Although a few white Territorians became infected (ten were admitted to Channel Island between 1931 and 1938), the Aboriginal population proved more susceptible. Their closer association with Chinese people and their squalid fringe-dwelling conditions were relevant to its spread.

During the early years, numbers diagnosed were few. Some Chinese lepers were repatriated, while Aborigines were returned to their own communities. This provided some solace, because sufferers died in their own country. It surely demonstrates European self-preservation, however, and an uncaring attitude for the consequences, because this was a period when leprosy was believed to be dangerously contagious.

Leprosy approached epidemic proportions amongst the Aboriginal community during the 1920s, when Mud Island was used as a leper station. Conditions there were appalling, while townspeople were concerned at its proximity to Darwin, because escape was possible at low tide. The former Channel Island Quarantine Station became a leprosarium in 1931. Unfortunately, just as authorities elaborated stronger policies to confine lepers, overseas research was demonstrating that strict segregation was unnecessary. Australia disregarded such encouraging signs. As the Chinese population diminished, from the thirties leprosy was envisaged as essentially an Aboriginal disease. Funds were expended, therefore, at the minimal rate which applied generally to Aboriginal welfare.

Like Western Australian Lock hospitals, the Ordinance controlling Aboriginal lepers was draconian and ignored all civil rights. The police were empowered to locate lepers and bring them back to Darwin. Many police treated patients humanely, but bush rules were harsh. Neck-chaining was usual, even though patients were not criminals. Because lepers feared detection, they hid when police were seen, so many cases were not diagnosed early. Police sometimes raided camps to prevent escape, but such a rule of law encouraged fear and animosity. Those chained unfortunates often made long forced walks, spent days in hot railway trucks, or voyaged in confined spaces. (The first Channel Island patients voyaged some 1,700 kilometres from Cossack, Western Australia.)

The lot of any leper was horrifying during this period, but it was even worse for Aborigines plucked arbitrarily from a community. They were aware of the stigma of the disease, which their society knew as the "Big Sickness". Scientists still groped towards a cure. Little wonder, therefore, that to the trauma of physical suffering, Aboriginal patients contributed their own spiritually worrying explanations of its causes. These factors added psychological dimensions, including sorcery directed at the patient, retribution for the patient's own failure to perform mortuary or ceremonial obligations correctly, or for eating incorrect food.

Debilitated in body and mind, the patient endured Channel Island living conditions. Some patients of 1931 were there still when the leprosarium closed in 1955. Yet this tiny imprisoning isle was too small to permit traditional hunting and gathering activities, except in the sea. Its soil was totally unsuitable for cultivation, and during the dry season water was so short that it was transported there. Consequently, health-promoting physical activities virtually were impossible. This boring desolation soon became magnified when most trees were cut down for necessary cooking fuel. Thereafter, even wood was brought from the mainland.

The Channel Island Quarantine Station in 1921. On the left is the medical clinic, and on the right, probably the male ward. This complex later served as the leprosarium hospital and part-Aboriginal quarters. Aboriginal patients lived in a row of huts some distance away on a treeless, exposed landscape. (National Library of Australia, Newlands Collection)

A recent view of the 10m x 5m water cistern, Channel Island. Local catchment from buildings often proved inadequate and water had to be transported by boat and pumped into this tank. Water shortage added to the discomfort of isolation. The vegetation has regenerated. (Suzanne Saunders)

Patients were segregated permanently from their kin; they were unable to fulfil ceremonial obligations; they mixed with people of diverse traditions and unknown languages, for they came from as far distant as the Pilbara and the Gulf of Carpentaria. Regrettably, deaths of patients were not communicated to their kin, so they lived, died and were buried in awful spiritual isolation.

Living conditions were not conducive to ease. Aboriginal patients were housed in fourteen huts on the exposed central ridge, where wind and sun on the unlined galvanised iron must have been acutely uncomfortable. Each hut measured less than three metres by four, yet forty-five people inhabited them in 1946. Seven people occupied one hut in 1948. Three former quarantine buildings were used as a hospital and for housing part-Aboriginal patients. As the few European patients received somewhat better quarters, these divisions imply that even within the leprosarium a segregated system applied. Given the minimal government investment in this system, however, it could not have worked at all without the voluntary dedication of a few white Australian managers and nurses — chiefly a Catholic religious order.

The mangroves and scrub have reclaimed much of Channel Island today. Its buildings were stripped of useful materials or scattered by Cyclone Tracy. Twisted metal, concrete slabs and stumps, and other debris are strewn about. This is not a place whose past attractions would make Aboriginal people feel nostalgic. However, they sense spiritual connections with the unfortunate people who died there.

Although leprosy is endemic now, it is curable and the stigma should pass. Once forceful retention in a leprosarium was replaced by an enlightened approach which preferred patients to remain with their communities, people came forward to admit infection and to seek medical assistance. Leprosy does not separate people today, nor should it conjure up fear or loathing. Channel Island merits registration as an Aboriginal place, because it symbolises a medical consequence of racial encounter, involving Asian carriers and emotional European social and scientific attitudes.

CHAPTER TWENTY-EIGHT

The Cootamundra Home for Girls

Henry Parkes laid the foundation stone of the solid brick hospital on the hill above Cootamundra in 1887. It was built to last, but it served only twenty years as a hospital. As community needs expanded, another district hospital was built in a less remote locality. The original building was vacated in 1910. It re-opened in 1911 as the Cootamundra Domestic Training Home for Aboriginal Girls. The Aborigines Welfare Board maintained the Cootamundra Home until its closure in 1968, a year before the Board was abolished. Today, Bimbadeen College is administered by the Aboriginal Evangelical Fellowship as a Christian vocational, cultural and agricultural training college.

Because of its great but tragic significance in the lives of so many Aboriginal women, it is listed in the Register. The forced removal of children from their Aboriginal parents was a major policy device in most states for over half a century. It was carried out on a relatively systematic basis in New South Wales, Queensland and Western Australia. Because this programme was implemented widely in New South Wales, the Cootamundra complex exemplifies that unjust and disturbing aspect of racial encounter.

The scale of family disruption in that state may be gauged from the fact that between 1916 and 1934, around 1,400 children were removed from parental control and were declared to be wards of the state. The statistics are even more startling when the period from 1883 until 1969 is evaluated. It has been estimated that about 5,625 Aboriginal children were taken from their parents, under different legal categories. If a figure of 5,000 is accepted as probable for the period since 1911, the social and psychological impact should be assessed not only upon the children concerned. Some 10,000 parents were separated from their children. Given the close kinship ties in that society, however, many more grandparents, aunts and uncles were deprived of both the fellowship and the obligations of family bonds. It is not unreasonable to claim that 40,000 people, or more, were directly affected by a policy which was, in many cases, legalised kidnapping. It is certain that few Aboriginal families in the state escaped without a child being taken away.

New South Wales approached its centenary before the government first established a Board for the Protection of the Aborigines, in 1883. Its first general legislation was even more tardy. The Aborigines Protection Act of 1909 was typically authoritarian. A reading of it today prompts the query as to whether it was designed to protect the white community *from* Aborigines. It certainly was framed without any consultation with Aborigines. Revisions of that Act in 1915, 1918 and 1936, paid even less attention to the niceties of civil rights and liberties.

Two salient features of these Acts merit notice. First, government control over Aboriginal reserves tightened. The number of reserves fell from hundreds in 1909 to seventy-one by 1939. Missionaries withdrew or were eased out of control in many instances, so that the employment of salaried government officials diminished dedicated humanitarian concern for their charges. The other relevant feature was the strict control over children, both Aboriginal and the "neglected" children of a person "apparently having an admixture of Aboriginal blood in his veins". The Aborigines Welfare Board had powers to establish institutions for children's maintenance and education. It could charge any parents who committed the "offence" of "enticing" their child away from an institution or work place.

These protective and restrictive powers were related directly to prevailing concepts and assumptions in contemporary racial theory. In the first place, the "pure" Aboriginal race was destined to die out, according to simplistic evolutionary principles. Even prominent Australian anthropologists and social theorists believed in the inevitability of extinction, including scientists Baldwin Spencer and A.W. Howitt, and Lorimer Fison, a distinguished missionary. Popular opinion termed it "the survival of the fittest" (and everybody knew that the white race was the fittest of all). As for the rapidly increasing numbers of people of mixed racial descent ("half-castes"), experts were emphatic that they could be "bred out", to become racially white within two or three generations.

Such ideas were bandied about in the ambient climate of the White Australia policy and elementary notions of eugenics. Many theories were formulated by men who considered themselves to be experts in native welfare, but most of them were ignorant of contemporary overseas research or practice. The historian, Charles Rowley, charitably referred to some of the state officers as "kindly and well meaning", but acting "on the common racist assumptions of the Australian folklore".

The obvious solution to Reserve populations swollen by part-Aboriginal residents was to segregate them from the "pure" population. This latter group could be treated humanely in the assurance that the problem would pass with time. Fewer Aborigines required fewer reserves and less funding. Meanwhile, the part-Aboriginal population should be dispersed around the community so that it would become absorbed into European society, both genetically and culturally. During the years of the Cootamundra Home, this remained the motivating purpose of Aboriginal policy in all Australian states which sought to solve its Aboriginal "problem". The exception was Tasmania which, despite its Straits people, admitted to no Aboriginal "problem". This was an application of the term "dispersal", less bloody than its use in the outback during the previous century. Its social and psychological effects, however, were almost as drastic.

The possibilities for eugenic engineering, more suited to science fiction, were expounded forcibly by Dr C. Bryan to a 1934 Western Australian Royal Commission: "I wish to speak of the half-caste and the breeding out of the half-castes, the black man whose presence irritates us . . . and who is now in addition a standing menace to our dreams of a white Australia."

Charles Chewings shared these notions. A geologist, he visited Tempe Downs in 1881 and formed the pastoral company which stocked the region. In 1936 he published the popular *Back in the Stone Age*. His ethnocentric racialism informed readers that

> . . . the numbers of half-castes, quadroons and octoroons is increasing, and giving the authorities concern. One of the saddest remembrances the writer retains of the Finke was of a young half-caste woman of prepossessing appearance living in the black's camp, with a blackfellow as husband. The missionaries it was said had married them. The Federal Government has now forbidden such unions; half-castes must marry whites and breed the black out, or as commonly expressed "breed them white".

Such notions became formally enshrined as the *Policy of Absorption*, at a conference of Commonwealth and state authorities in 1937. As formulated, this policy "believes that the destiny of the natives of Aboriginal origin, but not of the full-blood, lies in their ultimate absorption by the people of the Commonwealth and it therefore recommends that all efforts be directed to that end".

Although this absorption or assimilation policy (as it was termed later) was officially proclaimed at this conference, its philosophy had guided New South Wales legislation since 1909. The key to its future success was believed to depend upon control of the destinies of the children. They needed the education and socialisation appropriate to entering the European labour force and marriage market as white workers. All training programmes were geared to the goal of working class attainments, so secondary education seldom was necessary. Simple technical trades for boys and housework, cooking and laundry for girls were the objectives. To achieve them, it required total segregation from Aboriginal society. Whether intentional or incidental, institutional indoctrination of children often made them despise Aboriginal culture and feel ashamed of their black connections. Therefore, when they reached adulthood, the products of these homes frequently rejected Aboriginal society, yet experienced profound discrimination from lack of acceptance by the white community.

The Cootamundra Home for Girls opened in 1911 as one of the chief centres for implementing the absorption policy. It was intended for girls under fourteen years of age, too young to enter domestic service. It succeeded a dormitory established in 1893 at Warangesda, near Darling Point. Boys were sent to various institutions, until the Kinchela Home for Aboriginal Boys opened at Kempsey, in 1924. The Board imposed its policies in a more thorough manner from 1915, when regulations applied to all Aboriginal children under eighteen years, whether living on a reserve or elsewhere.

Reserve managers used forms upon which they entered the reasons why children were removed from parental control and committed as wards of the state. While police also prepared a charge sheet, in consultation with the manager, no committal hearing was necessary and there was no appeal.

Obviously, the system allowed the break-up of any family whose lifestyle did not match the manager's opinion of what was appropriate. It also aligned the local police with the manager in actions which were seen by Aborigines to set the state against their communities. It would be foolish to deny that there were many instances where children needed care and protection, due to parental drunkenness or neglect, as in the white community. However, the safeguards against abuses of the system were removed. Indeed, the government favoured this sytem as a means of acculturation, so even when family circumstances improved, children were not returned to their parents.

No European child would have been made a ward for reasons such as those commonly entered on the form by managers. These vague "charges" included, "to be protected from going bad", "to better her prospects", "fourteen years of age and fit to be apprenticed", "unmanageable", and "being an Aborigine". Similarly, a common police charge simply asserted, "neglected and under incompetent guardianship". Such subjective statements opened the way for prejudices or vindictive actions by managers or police.

Managers also were instructed that all half-caste children of "fairer" appearance, or others defined as "quadroons" or "octoroons", were to be denied access to any reserve and be committed to training schools. This was regardless of the fact that parents may have been industrious and caring, and it took no regard of the wishes of the children. Peter Read wrote of the situation after 1915, in the light of these arbitrary rulings, that "Aboriginal girls were about to be saved from their homes, their parents, culture, heritage and race by the ill-disposed, ill-educated and frequently ill-natured managers".

Aboriginal oral tradition contains numerous memories of the means adopted to take children from their parents. Sir Douglas Nicholls was an eyewitness. He was born at Cumeroogunga, near Echuca. His sister was taken by the police, together with a number of other girls, all of whom were said to be "neglected". This was untrue of his sister, and the methods used by the police to round up the group suggest a totally haphazard grab-bag approach. "The police came without warning, except for the precaution of ensuring that the men had been sent over the sandhills to cut timber. Some of the girls eluded the police by swimming the Murray. Others were forced into cars, with mothers wailing and threatening the officers with any weapon at hand." Nicholls recalled, that "it was the crafty way the police handled the matter that rankled".

It rankled with many others. As recently as 1957, Noel Johnson went to Sunday school in Condobolin, followed by an outing. He was taken away and did not see his family for twenty-five years. Around 1917, the police arrived at the school to collect Margaret Tucker, her sister and another girl. As their parents were employed and caring, this was not a case of neglect. Indeed, Margaret's parents had been approached previously by the Board about sending their two daughters to the Cootamundra Home. The offer was rejected outright, although Margaret Tucker remembered "how pleased and proud Mother and Father were to hear them say what lovely little girls they had, how nicely kept, everything so scrupulously clean". The police evidently were ordered to act in any case.

Many parents never learned where their children had been taken. Those who went to Cootamundra were barred from making home visits and all their mail was censored; some claim that letters were withheld. In theory, parents could visit children once a year. In practice it proved more difficult, because their local reserve manager had to make the arrangements. If parents managed to overcome official obstructions and to meet the costs involved in getting to Cootamundra, they were not permitted to stay overnight. While this scheme was paternalistic in its authoritarianism, it is evident that Aboriginal parents were evaluated as incapable of acting or thinking in the best interests of their families. It elevated station managers into dictators. Not surprisingly, Aboriginal opinion rarely classes their rule as benevolent.

Even as late as 1953, the Board continued to justify its policies on humanitarian grounds, although it admitted "that a child's natural heritage is to be brought up in its own home". No mention was made of the Board's wish to assimilate and so breed out the black taint. In the light of the manner in which it still obtained its state wards, its praiseworthy sentiments sound specious. "Unfortunately", the Board officialese continued, "some parents, despite all efforts on their behalf, prove themselves incapable or unsuitable to be entrusted with this important duty, and the Board is forced to take the necessary action for the removal of the child."

The Cootamundra Home had the advantage of size and large grounds. It was a typically solid brick building of the late nineteenth century, ornamented with iron tracery on the front verandah. An adjoining detached building, linked by a trellis wall, provided the kitchen and dining area. The best rooms at the front of the house provided the matron's flat. Behind this were the former hospital wards, where the girls lived. The main long dormitory was crowded with four rows of beds, with five beds in each row. Two smaller dormitories provided the balance of the sleeping area.

There were normally between thirty and thirty-five girls in residence. This number is confirmed by a number of surviving group photographs taken across

Opened as Cootamundra hospital in 1887, today it is Bimbadeen College, administered by the Aboriginal Evangelical Fellowship; from 1911 to 1968, it was the Cootamundra Domestic Training Home for Aboriginal Girls. They were taken there by the police without the consent of their parents, whom many never saw again. (D.J. Mulvaney)

The rear of Bimbadeen College. The kitchen block is to the right, while dormitories were in the main building. The sheds, rear left, provided the only bathroom and wash-house facilities. Girls feared the square structure in the foreground, reputedly the hospital morgue. (D.J. Mulvaney)

the years. An average of thirty-five images of smiling girls stand with the matron. Disciplinary methods varied, but it seems little happened there to smile about. Obviously there was little individual living space and no privacy or quiet, as female ages ranged from infancy to fourteen years normally and sixteen sometimes.

Washing facilities would not meet modern standards. There were only two or three baths and no showers. Any hot water was fetched in dippers from the laundry copper. As an economy, three or four children used the same bath water. The older girls washed the infants. This large brick building with the wooden additions of bathrooms and laundry must have been very cold in the winter, so it is not surprising that former inmates emphasise its coldness. All the exterior structures constitute such a central aspect of life at the Home, that it would prove unfortunate if they were demolished in any future renovations.

A frightening permanent feature of childhood must have been the former hospital mortuary. This is the alleged function of a separate building close to the rear of the residence. During this period it was used as a storeroom, but its associations must have been with dead spirits. Margaret Tucker remembered her terror when she was locked in a dark bathroom as punishment. "We all believed in ghosts", she stated emphatically.

A girl's arrival also proved a traumatic experience. Each child had been either spirited away by the police, or forcibly taken from a protesting mother. Their captors placed them on transport to Cootamundra, where they were met by the local police and taken to the home. Margaret Tucker never forgot her fear when the policeman produced handcuffs at the time her mother was resisting. On her arrival at the Cootamundra Home after a police escort, she was acutely embarrassed. Because she had been refused permission to go home and pack, she arrived without any night wear. Presumably most newcomers came only in the clothes which they wore, without any familiar objects so treasured by children, such as dolls. The break with their past was made even more total by this callous attitude. The girls came from all over the state, so they also had to adjust suddenly to associating with girls from unknown regions, with different traditional backgrounds.

Children had little time to fret, however. They were woken at 6 a.m. and a scramble followed to wash, make beds and scrub dormitory floors daily before a frugal 7 a.m. breakfast. Older girls were rostered to learn cooking, laundry and other domestic duties. A small brick building, with walls badly cracked today, served as a school. In post-1950 times, promising students attended secondary school in Cootamundra. Only about six girls achieved their Intermediate certificate, but it cannot have been an environment conducive to study. Most of them left in second or third year to become shop assistants or telephonists.

Very few girls during earlier decades received any secondary schooling. Margaret Tucker was more typical. Because she was a big girl at thirteen years, officials disbelieved her age. They ruled that she was over fourteen, so she attended school only on her first day. Like her contemporaries, who worked at station homesteads or uban middle class homes, Margaret was placed as a domestic help with a wealthy Sydney family. She received lower wages than those paid to white domestics and she was shamefully treated by her neurotic first mistress.

Some graduates of the home later led happy and well-adjusted lives. Margaret Tucker triumphed over her adversity, which took her from eating rat poison under her first employer to an MBE for her later inspiring example to her people. Some women consider that they were better off than contemporaries who were not taken away from home. They form a fortunate minority. As Cootamundra is within Wiradjuri territory, let the statistics of Wiradjuri children provide the example. Of eighty-three children removed from their parents between 1916 and 1928, seven died, ten spent periods in mental hospitals and ten became pregnant while still wards of the state. Through the archival records of the Aboriginal Welfare Board, numerous case studies have been made. There is a sad procession of lonely and mentally unstable people. Many girls were rejected by their white peers, but because of the instilled shame at being black, or because of fear of rejection by Aborigines, or from sheer ignorance of their family origins, they shunned black society.

An Aboriginal organisation, *Link-Up*, was founded in 1980 to work with adults who had been taken from their parents as children. Its success is remarkable. Between 400 and 500 people have been put in touch with their families. Its co-ordinator is Coral Edwards, herself an inmate of the Cootamundra Home, who only found her family when she was thirty. *Link-Up* is a great humanitarian movement.

Let another Cootamundra Home girl, Margaret Tucker, reflect on this episode of racial encounter: "The lack of care and the lack of understanding of our people in those years from my childhood upwards — some called it paternalistic, but it was less than that."

Phillip Ck

CHAPTER
TWENTY-NINE

Shifting Camp to Phillip Creek

The war to preserve civil liberties in the Pacific ended during the week that 215 Warumungu and Warlpiri people were moved compulsorily to Manga-Manda settlement on Phillip Creek. The site of their 1945–56 settlement, over forty kilometres from Tennant Creek, is listed in the Register. Before describing the place, the background to its settlement requires clarification. This was neither the first nor the last transplanting of Warumungu people. The story of their government-arranged moves reflects and typifies the problems facing Aboriginal Australians when their interests conflict with the economic concerns of white settlers. Their troubles began when gold was found at Tennant Creek in 1932. Subsequent government decisions foreshadowed controversies and actions in relations between the mining industry and Aborigines over the past three decades.

For many years after the Tennant Creek Repeater Station opened in 1872, the only Europeans in the area were its small staff. Relations between the two races proved harmonious, with numbers of Warumungu camping on Tennant Creek, just east of the Telegraph Station, on the small telegraph reserve. The creek was dry often, but there were near-permanent rock holes within a few kilometres, especially at Wiitin. An Aboriginal Reserve was declared in 1892, east of the telegraph reserve, so it did not include this popular waterhole. Its 384 square kilometres included important hunting and food collecting country, but although it included some waterholes, it was generally deficient in surface water. As its boundaries followed neat, bureaucratic rectangularity, rather than geographic or social divisions, nobody was clear where they lay. Aboriginal people erroneously assumed that they covered their traditional creekside camps, Wiitin included.

When Spencer and Gillen made their anthropological studies there during 1901, large numbers of people were living near the Telegraph Station. The Warumungu

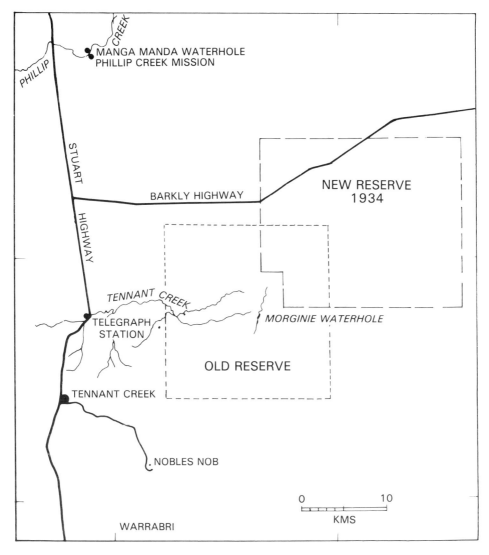

Tennant Creek area

staged an exhausting series of complex ceremonies during the nine weeks stay by the anthropologists. It proved to be a mutually agreeable interaction. Spencer and Gillen recorded invaluable myth, ceremony and material culture. As for the Warumungu, Gillen believed, that "our stay amongst them will never fade from their memories . . . they have had unlimited supplies of Baccy . . . and a liberal allowance of flour besides tea, sugar, tinned meats and other luxuries".

Pastoral settlement was relatively slight in this region for forty years following the declaration of the Aboriginal Reserve, so nobody bothered greatly about its boundaries. Aboriginal traditional life continued, with unrestricted access to significant ceremonial places, while people habitually lived on Tennant Creek, outside the Reserve. Two developments relevant to their future require comment.

The former Tennant Creek Repeater Station, opened in 1872. The shady creek is a few hundred metres to the right. (D.J. Mulvaney)

The Aboriginals Ordinance was passed in 1918. Under its section 21, holders of miners' rights were specifically excluded from Aboriginal reserves. This was reaffirmed by the Mining Ordinance of 1939, so miners were doubly excluded. Secondly, the Telegraph Station greatly increased its stock holding, so that by 1934 it ran about 500 head of cattle. Obviously, such numbers could not be fed on the small telegraph reserve.

A young Sydney anthropology graduate, W.E.H. Stanner, visited Tennant Creek during 1934 and reported on the situation of Aborigines in the aftermath of the gold rush. He found that the cattle grazed heavily on the Aboriginal Reserve lands, that they used and spoiled all waterholes and that even a stockyard was

Posts in the dry sands of Manga Manda waterhole, Phillip Creek, with the ruins of the settlement on the far side. (D.J. Mulvaney)

built at a major Aboriginal ceremonial and watering place. In addition, fifty miners' claims had been pegged in the southern portion of the Reserve, with many more claims pegged elsewhere. Stanner posed the reasonable question: "what actually *is* an 'Aborigines' Reserve'?"

Stanner explained that he had talked extensively with two traditional leaders, who had met with the government geologist and the Northern Territory parliamentary representative, H. Nelson. They had agreed to cede portion of the Aboriginal Reserve to mining interests in return for alternative land, but they asserted that "they were 'hurried' by Mr Nelson to do this and they now wanted to change their mind". As this meeting foreshadowed many such situations reproduced in post-1950 times, it serves as a metaphor for encounters between Aborigines and miners.

The European party sets up a meeting in good faith to formulate policy in a committee-type context. Its representatives are fluent, and capable of special pleading which stresses the advantages of their proposal. Aboriginal participants are in an unfamiliar setting, comprehend only some of the proceedings and politely agree to a proposition which is new to them. The satisfied European negotiators depart, pleased that a democratic resolution has been achieved. In this case, as in many later ones, the Aboriginal participants had no right and no wish to represent all the clan territories involved; no precedent existed under Aboriginal deliberative procedures to make unilateral decisions. Besides, as areas including sacred places were involved, nobody could cede them, because they were inalienable spiritual inheritances from their Dreaming origins. Consequently, under either Aboriginal law or lore, such verbal agreements were unrealistic and unworkable.

As an anthropologist, Stanner appreciated these genuine complexities which mining interests then, and today, largely dismiss as artifices. No simple economic transaction was implied when one parcel of land was exchanged for another, Stanner warned. "They could be given better land from the point of view of food sources, but the sacred affiliations with the actual land in this portion of the Reserve makes this quite impossible." In any case, Stanner criticised the proposed substitute land — "I have no hesitation in saying that the strip of country is mostly of poor quality. It has no permanent surface waters."

Sensing that the loss of the Aboriginal Reserve was inevitable, Stanner suggested some conditions, including the government's affirmation of "the principle of the non-violation of Aborigines' Reserves, and lay down some definite policy concerning them". He recommended temporary mining access as a concession, but not the revocation of the Aboriginal Reserve. Bores were needed as a matter of priority and mining royalties should be paid to the Warumungu.

On 12 July 1934, the Commonwealth government revoked the Aboriginal Reserve and established another large one further east. It was further away from the new Tennant Creek township, distant from many ceremonial places and situated in arid country. Despite untruthful ministerial assertions that the new area was "well-watered", the Northern Territory director of Native Affairs thought differently. In 1952 he described it as "useless country" and waterless. The Warumungu, he added, "have gained nothing from the discovery of gold within their area". Stanner later commented wryly that "the miners won and the Warramunga lost". A less academic visitor to Tennant Creek in the early thirties was the journalist, William Hatfield. He deplored intrusions onto reserve land. "To set aside a reserve for the remnants of a doomed race", he commented, "and then, when gold is discovered on it, order him to move on, is — to put it mildly — shabby."

The 1918 Aboriginals' Ordinance gave the authorities extensive powers. The motive was paternalistic humanitarianism, based on notions that Aborigines were mere children. The aim was to shelter people from the social and economic evils of urban fringe life, but authoritarianism permitted bureaucratic interference and local abuse of power. Those powers directly restricting civil liberties included permission to take Aborigines or part-Aborigines into custody, even if no criminal activity was involved, and even when it necessitated entering premises without a warrant. Places could be declared prohibited areas for that race; Aborigines could be removed from one reserve to another, or restricted to remain within a specified reserve. Such repressive laws had parallels in all states during this period.

Tennant Creek was declared a prohibited area in 1935, at a time when its non-Aboriginal population numbered 600. During the war, Aborigines also were prohibited from going within five miles of the Stuart Highway. As there was little water available on the remote Aboriginal Reserve, it is not surprising that they continued to live on the creek within the Telegraph Station reserve, several kilometres north of the town. They also inhabited fringe camps near mines, where prostitution was rife.

The director of Native Affairs used his powers in 1940 to order the removal of people to Morginie waterhole (Pigeon Hole), twenty kilometres east of the telegraph. His order foreshadowed the impracticality of the action, by accepting that water shortage was probable at Morginie. In any case, his directive failed to budge the people from the vicinity of the Telegraph Station.

Circumstances had increased the Aboriginal population in this region. By this time the Warumungu people had been joined by groups of Warlpiri, Warlmanpa, Alyawarra and Kaytej. Warumungu probably were in the minority. Tennant Creek and the mines had proved lures; there were consequential movements of people following the disruption which accompanied massive punitive raids associated with the murder of a prospector on Coniston Station in 1928; the wartime construction of the Stuart highway and the presence of army camps caused further mobility.

In a subsequent change of location, the Native Affairs Department established a rations distribution depot on Tennant Creek, only ten kilometres east of the telegraph. This was near the important Kalkarti ceremonial site, known to Europeans as Six Mile Depot. Kalkarti may be a bounteous Dreaming place, but its waters are impermanent. As water had to be carted from the Telegraph Station bore during an acute water shortage in 1945, residential control again failed. The Australian Inland Mission authorities who supervised the depot, urged a move to a well watered location with soil suitable for growing vegetables. They favoured Powell Creek, further north. As the government administration also considered that the depot was too close to Tennant Creek town, another shift was inevitable. The theory was that a rations depot was a magnet which held people within each reach, so it was best to be located away from competing magnetic urban influences. Besides, the exclusion of Aborigines from the town conserved its water supply for Europeans.

It is surely a reflection on the ad hoc policies and the lack of economic viability of the two Aboriginal Reserves, that both these wartime attempted solutions lay outside them, in the Telegraph Station Reserve. Despite the perceived need for a permanent relocation, water shortage forced the move to Phillip Creek during August 1945, as another expedient. An interim operation it may have been, but it took eleven years before a decision was reached on a suitable alternative. The people were uprooted again in 1956 and moved over 150 kilometres south of Tennant Creek to Warrabri. Ironically, two bores were sunk at Warrabri in 1954, making occupation there possible. Twenty years earlier, Stanner had urged the drilling of two bores in the Warumungu Reserve. That advice was ignored.

Phillip Creek possessed the advantage of a productive bore. The initial site selected was two kilometres south of the bore, but a week later it was abandoned in favour of Manga Manda waterhole, east of the bore. It was flat, sandy and fairly open country, with heavier bush along the creek. At that time it looked attractive, as the waterhole held about three months supply of water. So did some other stretches further east at Coodna hole. Visited when the riverbed is dry, however, it looks a very thirsty place. The sandy soil, unpredictable rainfall and shortage of natural water, combined with the salinity of the bore water to negate the expressed need for regular vegetable production. Its administrative advantage surely consisted in its remoteness, five kilometres east of the highway and over forty kilometres north of Tennant Creek, where Aborigines still were prohibited visitors. That mining centre was intended to be left free for European habitation.

The period 1945–56 witnessed important changes in official Aboriginal policies, so this abandoned settlement is an artefact and a material manifestation of those policies. It was a sufficiently lengthy period, also, for people to form attachments to the area. The eventual move away must have saddened many people, particularly the Warumungu. At Warrabri they were far south of their territory.

It is revealing that Phillip Creek settlement lay outside the boundaries of both the 1892 and 1934 Reserves. The 1934 Reserve was revoked in 1962, on the grounds that its natural water supply was poor. It was added to a pastoral lease. David Nash acidly observed that, therefore, "the poor natural water supply of the 1934 Reserve, apparent at the time of its proclamation, provided the excuse for its revocation". Sadly, neither the Phillip Creek nor the Warrabri locations assured the chief concern of the Warumungu ever since the gold discovery — access to, and security for, their main ceremonial sites.

It is a mark of the disruption to traditional life that, by mid-1946, there were 275 people congregated at Phillip Creek (78 men, 94 women and 103 children), and that number increased. Such numbers could not possibly live upon traditional hunting and gathering food resources. Further, the Warumungu people were in a minority on their own traditional land, for they were greatly outnumbered by Walpiri people. By 1954 there were 343 Warlpiri residents and only 45 Warumungu. It is a tribute to the rational basis of Aboriginal social organisation that an amicable modus vivendi was achieved. This was Warumungu land, so they remained the hosts. As a resolution of the Walpiri need to validate their residence, however, Warumungu men were permitted to marry Walpiri women and it was accepted that their children were Warumungu. Joint participation in rituals also occurred. Such arrangements averted conflict and are further proof of the fact that Aboriginal society is capable of adjusting to changed circumstances. It is not the monolithic, static and conservative society portrayed by many European commentators. These adjustments, compromises and integrative trends continued when the shift occurred to Warrabri. There, they were in the traditional country of the Alyawara and Kaytej. Warumungu and Warlpiri people maintain their ties and occupy the western areas of Warrabri, while the host people live on the east side of the settlement.

The main settlement at Manga-Manda stretched south of the creek for over 250 metres and there were people living in the bush for several kilometres to the east, particularly near Coodna waterhole. Authorities encouraged this dispersal in order to optimise use of water, but westward movement towards the highway was restricted. This official influence upon settlement pattern is reflected in the surviving traces of occupation.

Phillip Creek settlement was often referred to as a mission. In fact it was a government settlement, although it was supervised initially by the Aborigines Inland Mission. The Native Affairs Branch assumed direct control in 1951. Patricia Davison, who carried out a field survey in 1979, has shown how the material remains of the settlement reflect these different regimes. The early buildings were constructed of material salvaged from the Six Mile Depot and other places. They consisted of corrugated iron over a timber frame, standing on concrete foundations. The surviving concrete floors indicate their presence today.

Mission priorities and assumptions are reflected in the settlement's layout. There was a fenced area, within which there was a structured plan. The staff residences and a separate laundry, bounded by another fence, indicated the privileged status of those in charge by being erected closest to the waterhole, the track and the shady trees. Within the "compound" there were dormitory blocks for school children (one for girls, another for boys), locked for night "security", and another dormitory for part-Aboriginal children. These children had been taken from their families living in the bush near the settlement. The dormitories were within sight of the superintendent's house, as were the dispensary and the rations depot. There was a central ablutions and laundry block and a communal children's dining area and kitchen, which served also as a school and a church.

It is worth reflecting that the two chief official purposes of this settlement were to keep the people out of Tennant Creek and to feed them. There was a direct connection between these functions, as it was assumed that people dependant upon food supplies would concentrate around the settlement. It seems cynical to encourage "handouts" as a device for population control, and then to blame the Aboriginal race for its ready acceptance of handouts as a way of life. Sheer population numbers and lack of available traditional food resources made such local adaptations necessary. Equally cynical was the policy which made Aboriginal communities frequently move to watering points, while water was brought to European settlements, such as Tennant Creek.

Beyond the formally defined and controlled central area at Phillip Creek, whose fence symbolised the barrier between European discipline and the apparent laxity of the Aboriginal encampments, lived the majority. Their windbreaks or brush shelters (wiltjas) were flimsier, more dispersed and outwardly unplanned. This was deceptive, because they were no less structured than the bureaucratic centre, but their symbolism differed. The Aboriginal "settlement" spread for up to twenty kilometres. The placement of each shelter depended upon group, clan and kin affiliations. This subtler pattern of settlement reflected the flexibility, mobility and spatial use of Aboriginal societies. For example, Warumungu families camped only in the southern and southwestern areas, oriented towards their traditional ceremonial places further south. Few European suburban dwellers can feel such an appropriateness of domicile, when separated from their birthplaces.

Although displaced persons, the Phillip Creek people felt a sense of place while maintaining their spiritual links with distant places. The ordered and fenced administrative area at the centre of the settlement purveyed a sense of discipline, paternalism and cultural superiority. As Davison concluded from her conversations with former residents: "To the mission, the spatial configuration of the settlement represented order and control; to many of the Aboriginals . . . it was an alien, inflexible environment."

When the Native Affairs Branch assumed full control from 1951, policy changes were reflected in the surviving remains. The restrictive dormitory system was abandoned and children returned home; buildings performed different functions. As wooden buildings had decayed, rebuilding was necessary, even though a future move elsewhere was intended. Consequently money saving techniques were followed. A number of structures were made of adobe. These sun-dried bricks were made from the innumerable fine-grained termite mounds which dominate this region. This low-cost production was used to build a number of attractive structures. These included two stores, a kitchen and dining complex, an ablution and laundry block. Several houses were constructed by Aboriginal workers at the settlement. This suggests that this pattern of domicile and use of local resources appealed to some Aborigines, who adopted it voluntarily. Adobe was widely used by early settlers and this settlement represented one of its last large scale applications in the outback.

Unfortunately, when the settlement was abandoned, re-usable materials were taken to Warrabri. This resulted in the dismantling of roofing iron, doors and windows. Consequently, the attractive and well constructed adobe buildings have

Adobe walls harmonise with the environment as a successful Aboriginal initiative. (D.J. Mulvaney)

Because roof iron was removed, these buildings are weathering although the courses were laid well.
(D.J. Mulvaney)

a more limited life, exposed as they are to the elements. As the settlement has been invaded by the introduced plant *Parkinsonia aculeata*, the buildings are pleasantly screened by greenery, although this regrowth also is causing destruction of the walls. A management plan which fences the area off from cattle, removes vegetation and arrests adobe decay is needed.

The adobe fortuitously possessed a good combination of grain size (clay, silt and sand) for brick manufacture. Bricks were tempered with chopped-up spinifex grass, which is visible in the eroding bricks. These bricks were well laid in courses, with corners strengthened by metal straps, some of which are visible today. Inside walls were coated with a lime wash. The final result was neat, unobtrusive, functional and cool.

Despite the recent date of the occupation of this place, it in no way diminishes its social and historical significance as a monument to inter-racial policies and to human aspirations. This development constituted an excellent environmental adaptation. Even today, although rain followed by drying has eroded or cracked the walls, they appear in perfect harmony with the environment. They endow this empty place with an aesthetic sense, sadly lacking amongst most white settlements in tropical Australia.

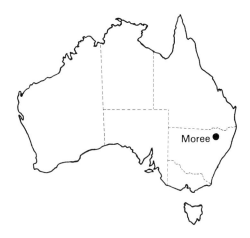

Freedom Ride to Moree

They sank an artesian bore at East Moree in 1895. Water gushed from a depth of 900 metres at the rate of over five million litres a day, at a temperature of 43°C. This bonanza was diverted to irrigation, but minerals in the slightly alkaline water proved unsuitable for plants. Within a year, however, the water was found to possess medicinal properties, so baths were constructed. Bathing, it was claimed by 1896, was "a certain cure for rheumatism and kindred complaints".

More elaborate baths, with a wooden decorative facade, were erected in 1913, owned and operated by the Moree Municipal Council. Although the natural flow of water ceased in 1957, it was then pumped into the baths. They became so important in the social and economic life of the town that, in 1965, the seventy-fifth year of local government, it was stated that "the baths are Moree's main attraction to tourists".

Moree was the subject of adverse criticism during January 1965, from Graham Williams, an *Australian* newspaper journalist. In compiling a major three-part report on the situation of New South Wales Aborigines, he had been accompanied on a 3,000 kilometres tour by two Sydney advisors, the Reverend Ted Noffs and Charles Perkins, then a university undergraduate. Williams reported that Perkins had been refused entry to the Kempsey swimming pool, under a 1949 council by-law, unless he produced written council permission.

The Moree situation was comparable. That council passed a regulation in 1955 excluding Aborigines or part-Aboriginal persons from the facilities of the Bore Baths, as they were known. An amendment approved in 1961 allowed Aboriginal high school children to swim there under supervision on school sports days. Because of Aboriginal needs, however, the local Apex organisation constructed a pool at the Moree Aboriginal reserve, about four kilometres out of town.

Williams concluded that this gesture was seen by Aborigines as "the tangible symbol of their rejection by the white community, as well as an excuse to continue the color bar at the town pool"; in addition, it presumed that all Aboriginal people were dirty.

"Of all the color bars I encountered", Williams continued, "those imposed by the Moree . . . and Kempsey [councils] . . . are the most illogical." At Moree, school pupils could swim there at times, but were debarred at others. "What once may have professed to be a hygiene bar is now in fact more than ever a color bar."

The tensions produced by such regulations need to be considered within the context of Aboriginal demography. More than ten per cent of Moree's 7,000 population was Aboriginal. As only about half actually lived on the reserve, while many occupied shanties on the other side of town, the Apex pool did not serve the whole community. Significantly, also, sixty-five per cent of the 368 residents on the reserve (in November 1965) were aged under twenty. This was precisely the age group most likely to be attracted to the Baths, or to resent their exclusion from them.

Students Action for Aborigines, a society aimed to improve Aboriginal conditions and to lessen racial discrimination, was formed at Sydney University in July 1964. It led to the establishment of the Foundation for Aboriginal Affairs, in which Reverend Ted Noffs was a prime mover. News of the American Freedom Rides encouraged Noffs to attempt some local public activity. He sponsored a sociological survey of Aboriginal conditions in New South Wales. Essentially moderate and fact-finding in its intention, a group of university student volunteers was organised to undertake a coach tour of problem centres. The team leader was Charles Perkins, presumably already briefed through his survey with Graham Williams. In the event, sociological survey was minimal, but the exposure of social inequalities became headline news.

Perkins stated the team's publicity aims before the coach departed in mid-February 1965. "We are concerned at the discrimination . . . much of it subtle and psychological — in some country towns. But generally the main problem is not prejudice so much as apathy and ignorance . . .."

Their survey had achieved media notoriety by the time their coach reached Moree. In Walgett their banners, posters and demonstration had aroused heated confrontation, capped upon their departure by a hooligan truck driver who rammed their coach and forced it off the road.

They arrived in Moree to sympathy from an outraged metropolitan press. In light of its earlier articles, the *Australian*'s support was understandable, but the *Sydney Morning Herald* also was editorially sympathetic to Aboriginal problems. "This is a free country where people have the right of peaceful assembly and protest", proclaimed the *Daily Mirror*. The *Sydney Sun* responded emphatically to a Walgett complaint against Aboriginal drunkenness. "This is the old and famous circular defence by which the whites first debase and exploit the Aborigines to a state of hopelessness and deprivation in which they get drunk and brawl, then blame them for doing so."

Preliminary indications proved more amicable at Moree. On their arrival, Perkins praised the local Services Club for admitting four Aboriginal members, unlike exclusive Walgett. The next morning, however, when some Aboriginal children were escorted to the Moree baths, they were refused admittance by the manager. Following the mayor's arrival they were allowed entrance, as was a second group. The day following the departure of the demonstrators for discrimination centres new, however, Aborigines were barred again. Upon receipt of this news the coach returned to Moree and deposited the students outside the baths.

This demonstration lasted for more than three hours, while entrance to the baths was blocked by the placard-holding students. Scuffles developed into an unpleasant confrontation, involving police and bystanders. Fruit and other missiles were hurled and the demonstrators were spat upon; the coach was plastered with eggs and tomatoes. Four attackers eventually were charged with offensive behaviour. The confrontation ended when the mayor agreed to rescind the discriminating regulation; a decision later supported by a public meeting and the council.

The widespread publicity concerning these events in Walgett and Moree, and the sympathetic reaction of the press, alerted Australians to subtle issues of racial discrimination in country towns. It revealed starkly the fact that white people imposed unjust local laws on black people. "I think the Freedom Ride was the one thing that destroyed this charade", Perkins claimed later. "It sowed the seed of concern in the public's thinking across Australia." There is little doubt that it proved an important factor in influencing public opinion, producing the unprecedented affirmative vote in the 1967 Commonwealth referendum on Aborigines. It played a significant role, also, in alerting disadvantaged Aborigines

A sign of the times? This insensitive signpost pointed the way through Moree in 1962. The spa baths were in Anne Street where Aborigines then were excluded. (D.J. Mulvaney)

No colour bar at the Moree baths today. (D.J. Mulvaney)

in country towns to the need for a more radical approach to public issues, in which Aboriginal grievances were voiced. One of the children who entered the pool during the demonstration was Lyall Munro junior, an important leader today. Munro remarked in 1978, that "he saw the power of direct action that day in Moree".

The Moree baths were rebuilt on a grander cream brick scale not long after the 1965 events. Although the building is new, the place merits its inclusion in the Register for two reasons. The first is local: the social and economic significance of the mineral waters in Moree's development, in which its spa featured. The second reason is their symbolic national significance. Through the Freedom Ride incidents they symbolise a positive action in the civil rights struggle for Aborigines; and *by* Aborigines, for the leader of the bus tour was an Aborigine, and his message got through to other young Aborigines.

Like many other rural centres, Moree still exhibits serious racial tensions. That co-operation rather than confrontation is more appropriate, however, is a lesson learned by many civic fathers. When the new Moree Services Club was built in 1967, an Aboriginal ex-serviceman laid the foundation stone. Years later, when Perkins visited Moree, the mayor shook his hand, "and reflected on what a good thing the Freedom Ride was for the town".

Charles Perkins (left), whose Freedom Ride to Moree in 1965 produced this happy occasion. (News Limited)

Mumbulla Mt.

On Mumbulla Mountain

Mumbulla Mountain's forested and boulder strewn slopes rise to over 700 metres. This prominent peak on the New South Wales south coast, ten kilometres north of Bega, has been the focus of two contrasting encounters, separated by a century, between Yuin people and other Australians. Mumbulla supports thick scrub, fern gullies and messmate and Sydney Blue gum forest. With its enormous tumbled granite boulders eroded into strange shapes, it is a place of great natural beauty. It is in the Register, however, primarily because of the deep significance that this solitary place holds for the culture and dignity of Aboriginal people.

Before European times, the slopes provided secluded initiation ritual locales, associated with the spiritual power of clusters of time-smoothed boulders. Along tracks which had Dreaming origins, and over several weeks, male initiates were led from one sacred place to the next. They were painted with ochre. Traditional law gradually was revealed and explained by appropriate elders as they visited each place in its proper ordained order, and special ceremonies were performed at earthern bora (bunan) rings, set in more open groves; at waterholes other rituals occurred. Yuin communities knew that initiates "go up the Mountain as boys; they come back as men". Doubtless, there also were female roles to play and special places for their veneration. Secrecy about rituals and sacred places was maintained under the threat of death.

Those people attending periodic major ceremonies travelled here from affiliated but scattered clans, until the drastic impact of European settlement. The last publicly revealed ceremony occurred around 1918, but with the exception of the following episode the final occasion on which widely separated clans assembled for a major ceremony occurred during the 1860s. A large gathering also occurred in 1883, involving a significant encounter between black and white culture. It centred round the initiative of A.W. Howitt, police magistrate of Gippsland.

Alfred William Howitt (1830–1908) was a versatile and innovative Australian. An explorer and influential public servant, he made major contributions to geological and botanical science. His most lasting memorial, however, is over sixty publications on Aboriginal society. His interest developed during personal contacts with Kurnai men whom he employed on his Bairnsdale property. He mentioned about twenty Kurnai informants in his papers, including residents at the Lake Tyers and Ramahyuck missions.

Remarkable for his energy and sympathetic approach to Aboriginal society, Howitt corresponded with intellectual leaders overseas in an effort to ascertain what he should do to record traditional beliefs and customs. His two most significant advisors were the founders of modern social anthropology, Lewis Henry Morgan, a lawyer in New York State, and E.B. Tylor, at Oxford. These men were "social Darwinists", in that they subscribed to the tenets of evolutionary science, as they applied to the origins and development of social institutions. They persuaded Howitt to record marriage regulations, kinship terminology and ritual life, on the assumption that they represented fossilised institutions from the early evolution of culture. Because of Howitt's close association with Kurnai people, however, he treated his subjects with dignity.

As Howitt's mentors erred, he interpreted much data incorrectly, while he virtually ignored relevant aspects of Aboriginal society. This is regrettable; yet his research notes and publications constitute the fullest documentary source on what he termed *The Native Tribes of South-East Australia* (1904). Howitt's compilations of his own research and that of his correspondents — pastoralists and police — merit special emphasis. Like James Dawson, Howitt's western district contemporary and author of *Australian Aborigines* (1881), such informants were genuinely interested in and concerned about the welfare of Aboriginal society. Some current critics brand all colonial era settlers as genocides. This is nonsense. Modern Aboriginal people need to draw heavily upon the storehouse of information which Howitt and Dawson, amongst others, accumulated voluntarily and without any financial return.

Over many years, Kurnai informants revealed much secret information to Howitt, whom they treated with the status of an initiated elder. From 1881, he used his influence to promote a kuringal, a major regional initiation ceremony, in order to describe it in the interests of science. A century later it became a basic source used in the interests of Aboriginal culture.

It took twenty months to arrange the gathering of widely distributed, but affiliated groups. Messengers, message sticks and other paraphernalia were circulated as tokens of intent, discussions were held, and elders called upon Howitt to authenticate his standing. In April 1883, between 130 and 150 people assembled near Bega, from places as distant as Queanbeyan, Braidwood, Nowra, the Monaro and eastern Gippsland districts. Unfortunately Howitt did not state the precise locality of the ceremonies, but from his account and sketch plans, it almost certainly was on Mumbulla Mountain. Field survey in the area confirms the existence of artificially raised earth circles — the bora or bunan areas.

When most people had congregated for these ancient rites, Howitt received a telegram instructing him to attend. Aboriginal society had adapted to change, just as Arnhem Land people today use sophisticated telecommunications in arranging ceremonies. Howitt took leave for two weeks, but this included a horseback ride

across the mountains from Walhalla, where he presided in court, to Bega,
followed by his return to Bairnsdale. He actually arrived in Bega ahead of the
Kurnai contingent, on his strenuous and heroic fieldwork.

In order to suit Howitt's timetable, individual ceremonial acts were accelerated
and some rituals were adjusted or curtailed, but the elders were satisfied that
although time was reduced by two-thirds, tradition was upheld. Back home, the
energetic observer wrote an account of proceedings and posted it to Tylor, who
read it at the Anthropological Institute in London that December. Howitt
produced an expanded version of events for his 1904 book, so he recorded events
in remarkable detail. In the following year he performed a similar service for
Kurnai people, when he encouraged them to hold an initiation ceremony, known
as a jeraeil, near Lakes Entrance. That ended Howitt's role as a tribal elder.
Missionaries were concerned about the revival of pagan corroborees and
absenteeism, so Howitt's government minister intervened to prevent any more
activities.

Much of Howitt's material today might be criticised by Aborigines as being
secret/sacred in content and unsuitable for publication. At that time, of course, it
would not have circulated amongst Aboriginal people. That it may do so today
poses problems, as is particularly the case with the Spencer and Gillen books.
Rather than attempt to ban or censor them, however, Aboriginal people need to
consider the extent to which their evidence is invaluable in restoring much of the
detail and the dignity of Aboriginal cultural identity.

About a century after Howitt's ride to Bega, his evidence assisted the protection
of sacred places on Mumbulla Mountain. The New South Wales Government
Advisory Committee on South Coast Woodchipping, advised in 1977, that
archaeological and sacred sites probably existed within the Five Forests area,
including the Mumbulla State Forest. Unfortunately nobody consulted Aboriginal
people before logging commenced on the mountain. Within a few weeks,
destructive logging occurred to within fifty metres of sacred places. Previously,
one of the most significant places, "Mumblers Dreaming Place", amongst the
rocks on the summit, was blasted to site a trig point. Prominent Aborigines had
historic associations with the mountain. It was a tribal elder, Jack Mumbulla (or
Mumbler), who led initiation ceremonies early this century, while "King
Mumbulla" was given a brass plate by Governor Bourke in 1834.

South Coast Aboriginal people mounted a campaign to prevent further
destruction. Amidst heated controversy, logging was suspended during the first
half of 1979, to allow an anthropologist to gather and sift information. Cynics who
supported the timber industry claimed that the sites were inventions, because
nobody had heard about them previously. The most active Yuin elder, Guboo Ted
Thomas, aptly outlined the problem in a letter to the premier, indicating a
fundamentally different attitude to country and resources.

> These are sacred matters which must be kept quiet. We do not talk about these things
> even among ourselves unless it is absolutely necessary. These are our laws that come to
> us from the mountain. We only talk . . . when we are forced to do so in order to protect
> our sacred places from ignorant white people to whom only the dollar is sacred. So you
> can see why these things never became public knowledge until early 1978. It is not a
> question of making up stories, it is a question of our sacred heritage which we are trying
> to protect and to build up once again.

A prospect from Mumbulla Mountain, with one of its many prominent boulders. Many weathered rocks possess deep relevance for Aboriginal ceremonial life. (Wes Stacey and Ted Thomas, courtesy AIAS)

A time-worn rock with "faces" on its right side, Mumbulla Mountain. (Wes Stacey and Ted Thomas, courtesy AIAS)

During the period when the consultant, Brian Egloff, was investigating the evidence, the situation was muddied by provocative actions and words. Several ministers and timber industry officials donned hard hats and toured the mountain. Members claimed that they saw no sacred sites. Hardly surprising as they are not signposted! As Gubbo Ted exclaimed, "they would not recognise a sacred site if they tripped over one". The minister for Conservation grumbled about "frivolous complaints", while another minister urged the speeding up of the already hurried reporting process; and he demanded the precise location of sites. That all the places might form a complex, connected by integral Dreaming tracks, and that the concealing forest was part of the mountain's "power", escaped appreciation. That rituals occupied weeks, involving many different locations, also was an alien concept. Judging from newspaper comments, however, they appreciated the grilled steak served at the picnic ground, adjacent to a ceremonial site.

Comparison with regions where traditional life survives strongly establishes that a sacred site is more extensive than the ground on which the symbolic object stands; paths invariably link places over wide areas; dominant landmarks such as this mountain are central features; unusual geological formations become components of Dreaming landscapes.

Apart from analogy, two chief sources of information existed for any assessment of the spiritual content of Mumbulla Mountain. There was the oral testimony, traditions and deep commitment of Yuin leaders, but opponents dismissed this source as fictitious. This left Howitt's evidence. His publications were supplemented by his handwritten notes. These papers had been deposited by Howitt's family in the Museum and the State Library of Victoria. This writer located Howitt's 1883–84 correspondence with E.B. Tylor in Oxford's Pitt Rivers Museum, and years before the controversy, reconstructed Howitt's role in the Kuringal.

Quite independently of Aboriginal oral traditions, therefore, Howitt's papers confirmed their general reliability. Critics might complain that Aborigines derived their knowledge from Howitt, in any case, but such prejudices could only invoke the printed sources. The manuscript material was new. Most importantly, Howitt drew a sketch map of the 1883 ceremonial grounds, covering a hillside and a valley, more than three kilometres south to north. He annotated twenty widely dispersed locations of camps or activity places which featured in the events which he witnessed. He noted that the women retired to places eight or more kilometres distant, so a large area was involved in sustaining or concealing participants.

Egloff concluded from such evidence, that "all the necessary elements are present in the area immediate to Mumbulla Creek. The all important setting is identical, particularly the required seclusion, rocky outcrops, glens, waterholes and flowing creeks. In other words all elements are consistent with the Yuin Tribal assertion that sacred sites are present in this area."

The government agreed in 1980 to declare 7,508 hectares of state forest an Aboriginal Place. No logging would be permitted within the central core of 1,100 hectares, within which are the sacred sites. It was declared in 1984, so the precise identity and location of most sacred places remains concealed. Further good flowed from the encounter. The New South Wales Forestry Commission supported archaeological surveys in other forests and developed closer consultation processes with Aboriginal people.

A spiritual concept of place may prove to be Aboriginal society's greatest contribution to multi-cultural Australia. As the *Canberra Times* observed of the Mumbulla confrontation in 1979: "For an Anglo-Saxon it is a hard argument. Rocks are rocks, mountains are mountains." The world's largest rock, Uluru, raised the meaning of place to a national level.

CHAPTER THIRTY-TWO

Uluru Returned

Katatjuta's conglomerate domes on the distant horizon beckoned Ernest Giles in 1872, across a thirsty expanse of salt flats. Water scarcity prevented this first white party in the area from approaching further. Giles spattered the map with esoteric names, having added Glen Helen, the Tarn of Auber and the Vale of Tempe. Now the salt depression became Lake Amadeus and Katatjuta, Mount Olga, honouring the Spanish king and queen.

Approaching eagerly from the south a year later, Giles found that W.C. Gosse, a South Australian surveyor, had beaten him to Mount Olga. Consequently, other prominent features received more prosaic names, as Gosse converted flat-topped Atila into Mount Connor and Uluru became Ayers Rock. During this feast of naming places , nobody asked Aborigines about their existing names.

On 19 July 1873, Gosse and Kamran, his Afghan cameleer, climbed Uluru, at the spot where tourists now ascend. Gosse expressed his "astonishment" at its size, declaring it "the most wonderful natural feature I have ever seen". He judged well, because Uluru and Katatjuta meet the criteria for inclusion in the World Heritage List. Despite his wonderment, Gosse entered in his diary only twenty lines of general comment about his day there, and wrote nothing about the view. He added a further eight lines on old Aboriginal campsites and rock paintings. "They amuse themselves", he noted, drawing in caves; some were "very cleverly done". Gosse returned briefly a few days later and met Aboriginal people there. He sought their word for "water", in this thirsty land.

Gosse's simple rituals of renaming and climbing to the summit, constituted a symbolic flag of possession planted in Australia's heart. The agents of transfer were a young European and a barefoot Asian. Scientists later would describe this nine-kilometre circumference red monolith as a 348m high inselberg consisting of coarse arkose grit, which suffered violent folding 600 million years ago. Ever since, it has been weathering into weird shapes and cavities, caused when rain cascades down its sides, or when hot winds blast it with dust. Around its base moisture promoted vegetation, while rock pools attracted fauna. This allowed a couple of Aboriginal families to occupy it seasonally and tend its ritual places, as their territorial focus. Away from the rock a waterless sea of spinifex and sand stretches in all directions until other life-giving watering places are reached. Such to the west is Katatjuta, and to the east stands the mesa, Atila (Mount Connor).

The Yankuntjatjara and Pitjantjatjara people who are the traditional owners of Uluru perceive that rock very differently. It has existed unchanged in every superficial detail and inner essence from Tjukurpa, their more adequate concept for "Dreaming". Virtually every feature on its time-worn face has an identity and a mythological association. Not surprisingly, the network of pathways taken by these ancestral creatures and persons are inextricably linked to Katatjuta and Atila. The tracks of Mala (hare wallaby), Kuniya (harmless carpet snake) and the venomous reptile, Liru, all cross and mingle here. At such a meaningful place, alien visitors, their horses and camels, all impacted upon its spiritual essence and unintentionally disturbed sacred places.

Uluru typifies the different intellectual perceptions which distinguish black from white Australians. Aboriginal people possess a basic sense of certainty about their identity and relationship with this place, because all relevant incidents, ritual associations and clan bonds have existed since the Dreaming. Curiosity about its physical or aesthetic properties is absent amongst traditionally oriented people. Europeans feel impelled to explore, identify, touch; photographs are an essential record; they are dared to climb and boast about it on their T-shirts or to perform stunts. To the one, it is sufficient that it is there as part of pre-ordained nature; to the other, the challenge exists because it *is* there.

Extrovert schemes for rock concerts at the rock, rolling off boulders, paint bombing, or hang-gliding, were in the future, however, when Gosse and Kamran made their climb. The region is so arid that pastoralists avoided it and the traditional owners enjoyed some undisturbed years before Uluru effectively became Ayers Rock. It was 1889 before another exploring party passed by.

Five years later, two scientists arrived. They were a geologist and a biologist on the Horn expedition. The biologist was Baldwin Spencer, whose anthropological interest blossomed on this journey. Spencer probably was the first of the legion of visitors to be captivated by the changing play of light and colours; he was its first photographer. The party camped at Kantju soak, a pool on the western side rich in Dreaming associations. Both there and at Mount Olga, they met people who never before had seen Europeans. They overcame fears and maintained friendly relations, as Spencer recorded details of everyday activities by men and women. He praised their help and cheerful character and sketched in colour a number of rock paintings. His comments on the art were more sympathetic than was then common, noting that some designs were geometric, others schematic or naturalistic. He later grasped the fact that while some art was secular in character, even the same motif within a different context could be symbolic and sacred.

These percipient observations may constitute the first objective account of Aboriginal art in Central Australia. His hurried freehand sketches of motifs in a

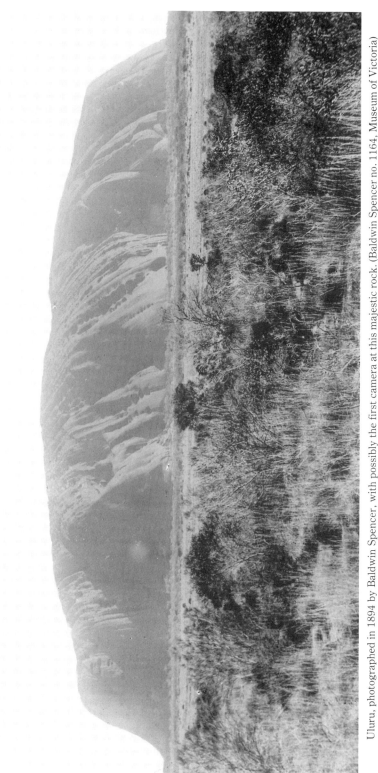

Uluru, photographed in 1894 by Baldwin Spencer, with possibly the first camera at this majestic rock. (Baldwin Spencer no. 1164, Museum of Victoria)

Kantju soak, on Uluru's western side. Water at the base of the rock permitted Aboriginal families to pass time here. The Horn expedition camped by this pool in 1894. (D.J. Mulvaney)

cave near Kantju (one visited today by tourists), were so accurate that they can be identified in recordings made there almost half a century later by C.P. Mountford.

Despite the objectivity of Spencer's ethnographic observations and his art recording, his intellectual preconceptions were those of a post-Darwinian evolutionary biologist. Such opinions influenced government racial policies. Spencer expressed his excitement and sense of privilege to "have enjoyed an experience such as now falls to the lot of few white men. We had actually seen, living in their primitive state, entirely uncontaminated by contact with civilisation, men who had not yet passed beyond the paleolithic stage of culture."

Spencer here voiced his subjective sense of racial and cultural superiority, virtually an onlooker in a human zoo, based upon current notions of progress. He confused a complex intellectual society of fully modern people, whose alternative economy relied upon hunting and gathering, with Old World societies. These ancient world people also centred life around a hunter-gatherer economy, but their cultural inheritance was more elementary and, for the early period which interested Spencer, their cranial capacity was less. He was not comparing like with like. He wrongly assumed that a "primitive" (that is, non-agricultural) economy reflected a more rudimentary mind-set and a less developed society. It was a fundamental error which persists even today.

The Commonwealth government appointed Spencer, in 1912, as its special advisor on Northern Territory Aboriginal policy. He urged the establishment of Aboriginal reserves, sufficiently extensive, rich in natural food resources, and located so that affiliated groups could occupy contiguous areas. He stressed the importance of the Hermannsburg reserve, but made no reference to needs further south.

It was 1920 before the large South West Reserve was declared. It was presented as a holding operation, utilising an area not required for pastoralism. It offered "sanctuaries of a temporary nature. The Aboriginal may here continue his normal existence until the time is ripe for his further development."

For the following twenty years the South West Reserve served that purpose, but it was a fragile situation, as those who intruded did so with impunity. Doggers moved freely and impacted upon Aboriginal groups. Lasseter, the latter-day Midas, who claimed to transform rock into a golden reef, perished there in 1931. His propaganda encouraged others; airstrips constructed in the northern sector facilitated aerial survey. After a confused series of events in 1934, which involved both a traditional punishment killing and cattle spearing, an escaped Aboriginal prisoner was shot dead by a policeman at an Uluru cave. That man was a traditional owner.

On 26 October 1985, the traditional owners of Uluru stand proudly at the centre of the transfer ceremony, flanked by (left) the governor-general, Sir Ninian Stephen, the minister for Aboriginal Affairs, Clyde Holding, and (right) the minister for Arts, Heritage and Environment, Barry Cohen. (Australian Information Service)

Improved postwar vehicle performance and affluence brought increased activity. A track reached Uluru in 1948; application for an airstrip here was lodged in 1951, although planes already landed there. Tourism pressure led to the excision of Ayers Rock and the Olgas from the Reserve in 1958; its area already had been reduced previously in the interests of pastoralism and mining. The excision became the Ayers Rock-Mount Olga National Park. Indications are that Aborigines were discouraged from camping there. Obtrusive tourist facilities clustered close to the rock's eastern face, adjacent to the airstrip. Tourists clambered over sites of sacred meaning or entered painted caves of enormous spiritual power.

In 1973 the Commonwealth Government Standing Committee on Environment and Conservation acted positively, recommending that the traditional rights of people who had associations with the area should be protected, and that they should play a determining role in park management. Traditional owners had impressed investigators by their sincerity. Paddy Uluru had made an impassioned appeal two years before, after a female tourist entered a place sacred to Mala rituals.

"Ayers Rock is my camp", he asserted, "Ayers Rock is holy. I am Ayers Rock and these things are mine. And now white people have broken . . . our Laws, ours, our great ceremony, the ceremony of the Mala wallaby . . . And I am speaking truly to you."

During subsequent years, many meetings occurred, elders wearied of reiterating the same eternal truths and false hopes were raised. Even the 1976 Land Rights Act was judged, in 1979, not to apply to Uluru. Its title had been alienated from the Crown by the National Parks and Wildlife Service. The frustrations of incomprehending traditional owners continued until November 1983, when Prime Minister Hawke promised that ownership would be restored to them.

Finally, it was agreed that the Uluru Katatjuta Aboriginal Land Trust would hold title for the 200 traditional owners, but the land would be leased back to the Commonwealth for ninety-nine years. Traditional owners receive rental and play a major role in managing the park. Areas of Uluru are barred to visitors, while the construction of Yulara village removed the unsightly clutter of buildings near the rock and facilitated easier visitor control.

On 26 October 1985, hundreds of Aboriginal people assembled at Uluru for one of the most significant events in Australian history. It was a close racial encounter of a special, and unfortunately, rare kind. Henceforth, Aboriginal people, who never ceased owning this area under their own Law, also own it in white law. The governor-general, Sir Ninian Stephen, successor of Governor Arthur Phillip, handed over the title deeds. He observed, that the traditional owners became "the custodian of this heartland of Australia. The Trust, by the Deed which is to be handed over today, acquires inalienable freehold title under Australian law to this place which is so special to its members. At the same time, recognizing, too, the special significance of Uluru to *all* Australians, and the appropriateness of its remaining as a National Park."

Afterword

This account referred to fifty-seven "contact" places in, or proposed for, the Register of the National Estate, forty-seven of them in some detail. Many places are of such outstanding importance for the history of race relations that they might feature in the selection of any author, Aboriginal or white Australian. Others reflect my interests and fieldwork. Except for the Northern Territory, featuring thirteen major places, distribution was fairly even. Tallies ranged from the four Victorian places, through five each for Tasmania and New South Wales, eight in Queensland including three places in Torres Strait, to six major places each in South and Western Australian. It is impossible to assign clear-cut chronological segments. As an approximation, seven chapters concerned Australia before 1800, six prior to 1850, eleven in the period 1850–1900, while eight belonged to this century.

What other places in the Register should have been included? Myall Creek's claims are outstanding, but it has been subjected to numerous studies. The book's structure had been decided before Lake Condah gained a higher profile in 1987, by its welcome return to Aboriginal ownership. The police station ruins associated with Pigeon's Kimberley saga were sacrificed to space limitations, as was Fannie Bay gaol. The case for including further mission stations is accepted, including Lake Tyers.

Other places not in the Register merit further treatment. They include Mapoon, Arukun and Palm Island in Queensland, Cumeroogungah in New South Wales, the Noonkanbah drilling site, the first Pindan Company mine, Wattie Creek, and Papunya, an exemplar of the worst in official "welfare", yet the focus for a remarkable art movement. High on my personal list are the banyan tree at Gove, so celebrated during the sixties, and Galiwinku. As Elcho Island Methodist Mission, the latter had two significant associations. The first was the public display of ritual objects thirty years ago, as a symbol of an adjustment movement between traditional religion and Christianity. Elcho was then the base for Reverend H. Shepherdson, who initiated from here the first Outstation (Homelands) settlements in Arnhem Land. By 1965, he supplied four or five outstations from his plane. All these original places merit inclusion in the Register.

Research is essential to locate and document places where important encounters occurred between Aboriginal people and Melanesian Kanakas, Japanese and Chinese. Popular Palmer River goldfields accounts abound in improbable and racially prejudiced tales of the fate of Chinese. I could not accept this nonsense or link it closely with documented localities; this needs to be examined.

The co-operation and advice of many people is gratefully acknowledged. To my colleagues in the History Department, I am grateful for the opportunity in my retirement to occupy a congenial workplace. Typing and other assistance proved generous, from Beverly Gallina, Anthea Bundock, Janice Aldridge, Helen Macnab and, in particular, Marie Penhaligon. Dr Barry Smith saved the text from many infelicities.

Jean, my wife, proved an invaluable research assistant during more than 20,000 kilometres drive to visit places ranging from New Norcia and Albany, to Marree, Uluru, Tennant Creek and Cloncurry. She has not complained, although my "retirement" continues as a daily office routine.

I am grateful to the following for expert advice: Jeremy Beckett, Anne Bickford, Carol Cooper, Brian Egloff, Peter Forrest, Luise Hercus, Mary Anne Jebb, Dick Kimber, David Moore, Howard Pearce, Don Ranson, Suzanne Saunders, Mike Smith, Moya Smith, Peter Sutton, Daniel Thomas and Ron Vanderwal.

Staff of the following libraries assisted my research: Australian Institute of Aboriginal Studies, Canberra; Australian National Library; J.S. Battye Library of West Australian History, Perth; Mitchell Library, Sydney; Mortlock Library of South Australiana, Adelaide; Oxley Library, Brisbane; State Library of Tasmania, Hobart; National Gallery of Victoria; and Museum of Victoria.

The generous co-operation of many photographers provided a range of excellent images. I acknowledge the cameras of: Richard Baker, Clare Bassett, George Chaloupka, Robert Edwards, Dick Kimber, Darrell Lewis, Campbell Macknight, Suzanne Saunders, Moya Smith, Wes Stacey, Jim Stockton, Paul Tacon, the late Donald Thomson (courtesy Mrs D. Thomson), and Grahame Walsh.

The staff of the Faculties Photographic Laboratory, ANU, particularly Bob Dowhy and Warren Hudson, developed and printed all my photographic needs. Their prompt and efficient co-operation proved important. I am grateful to the Curator, Whakatane and District Museum, New Zealand, for advice and photographs, and also, to the Curator of Pictorial Collections, National Library of New Zealand. The assistance of Mrs N. Samson, Friends of First Government House is acknowledged, together with the co-operation of the British Museum (Natural History). The Naval Historical Library, Ministry of Defence, London assisted with great consideration.

For the reproduction of the Namatjira painting of Hermannsburg, I am indebted to Mr A.D. Hickinbotham, Adelaide, and to Elizabeth Williams and the Ntaria Council Inc. Ntaria. All maps were drawn by Irene Jarvin.

The project has been assisted by the Australian Heritage Commission, whose officers always prove willing to advise. I thank Denise Robin and Marilyn Truscott in particular. I am indebted to the staff of the University of Queensland Press for their prompt and sympathetic assistance, especially Clare Hoey.

D.J. Mulvaney
Department of History
Research School of Social Sciences
September 1987

Sources and Further Reading

Note: The sources are given chapter by chapter, in the order and pagination in which they appear in the text.

Chapter 1   The Protocol of Aboriginal Encounters

ABORIGINAL VERSIONS: Two outstanding presentations of history according to Aboriginal oral sources are: L. Hercus and P. Sutton (eds), *This Is What Happened: Historical narratives by Aborigines* (Canberra, 1986); and Jennifer Isaacs (ed.), *Australian Dreaming: 40,000 years of Aboriginal History* (Sydney, 1980).

ABORIGINAL PROTOCOL: An illuminating discussion of the protocol of Aboriginal society is presented by Sylvia Hallam, "A view from the other side of the frontier", in Moya Smith (ed.), *Archaeology at ANZAAS 1983* (Western Australian Museum, Perth, 1983), pp. 95-121.

CEREMONIAL EXCHANGE NETWORKS: D.J. Mulvaney, "The chain of connection", in N. Peterson (ed.), *Tribes and Boundaries in Australia* (Canberra, 1976), pp. 72-94; Isabel McBryde, "Goods from another country: exchange networks and the people of the Lake Eyre Basin", in D.J. Mulvaney and J.P. White (eds.), *Australians to 1788* (Broadway, 1987), pp. 253-73.

WIVES: B. Spencer and F.J. Gillen, *The Arunta* (London, 1927), p. 444.

STURT: C. Sturt, *Narrative of an Expedition into Central Australia*, 2 vols (London, 1849), *II*, p. 275.

WILLIAM THOMAS: T.F. Bride (ed.), *Letters from Victorian Pioneers* (Melbourne, 1898), p. 68.

WARNER: W.L. Warner, *A Black Civilization* (New York, 1958), pp. 155, 163, 148.

THE MUDLUNGA: L. Hercus, " 'How we danced the Mudlunga': memories of 1901 and 1902", *Aboriginal History* 4 (1980), pp. 5-32; B. Spencer and F.J. Gillen, *Across Australia* (London, 1912), pp. 245-46; D.J. Mulvaney, "the chain of connection", in N. Peterson (ed.), *Tribes and Boundaries*, pp. 91-92.

ALICE SPRINGS: Encounter 1: B. Spencer and F.J. Gillen, *Across Australia* (London, 1912), p. 232. Encounter 2: pp. 248-54.

THE ROM CEREMONY: S.A. Wild (ed.), *ROM, An Aboriginal Ritual of Diplomacy* (Canberra, 1986).

EYRE: E.J. Eyre, *Autobiographical Narrative of Residence and Exploration in Australia 1832-1839* (London, 1984), p. 136.

MITCHELL: T.L. Mitchell, *Journal of an Expedition into the Interior of Tropical Australia* (London, 1848), pp. 182, 313, 321.

ABORIGINAL RESPONSES: Mitchell, pp. 144, 240; L.A. Wells, "Journal of the Calvert Scientific Exploring Expedition 1896-7", *Western Australian Parliamentary Papers*, 1902, no. 46, p. 16.

"MORAL INDIFFERENCE": W.E.H. Stanner, *White Man Got No Dreaming* (Canberra, 1979), p. 190.

Chapter 2   Confrontation near Cape Keerweer

EARLY VOYAGES: The evidence for the voyage by Jansz is assembled by Gunter Schilder, *Australia Unveiled: The Share of the Dutch Navigators in the Discovery of Australia* (Amsterdam, 1976), pp. 43-49. An Aboriginal oral version of "Dutchmen at Cape Keerweer", is brilliantly transcribed by Peter Sutton, in L. Hercus and P. Sutton (eds), *This Is What Happened* (Canberra, 1986), pp. 83-107. The evidence for Torres and Prado is cited by A. Sharp, *The Discovery of Australia* (Oxford, 1963), pp. 23-31, and by H.N. Stevens (ed.), *New Light on the Discovery of Australia* (Hakluyt Society, London, 1930), pp. 231-33. Their route through Torres Strait is investigated by Brett Hilder, *The Voyage of Torres* (St Lucia, 1980).

DUTCH ON CAPE YORK: The full translation of the Cape York journal of Jan Carstensz is in J.E. Heeres (ed.), *The Part Borne by the Dutch in the Discovery of Australia 1606-1765* (Luzac, London, 1899), pp. 34-44. All the incidents referred to relate to pp. 36-41. A good popular account is J.P. Sigmond and L.H. Zuiderbaan, *Dutch Discoveries of Australia* (Adelaide, 1976). The Aurukun elder on Dutch eviction: J. Roberts and D. McLean, *Mapoon — Book Three* (International Development Action, Fitzroy, 1976), p. 35.

ABORIGINAL CAPE YORK: The classic description of Cape York coastal economy is Donald Thomson's "The seasonal factor in human culture", *Proceedings of the Prehistoric Society* 5 (1939), pp. 209-21. The number of Aboriginal sites is inferred from the Aurukun Mapping Project 1985–86, by R. Cribb and P. Sutton (pers. comm.). These sites are mapped in J.C.R. Camm and J. McQuilton, *Australians, A Historical Atlas* (Sydney, 1987), pp. 36-37.

GONZAL: The voyage of J.E. Gonzal is described in Heeres, p. 94.

MONBODDO: J. Burnet, *Of the Origin and Progress of Language* (Edinburgh, 1774), vol. 1, p. 201.

OTHER VISITORS?: For a discussion of possible early contacts with Australia, D.J. Mulvaney, *The Prehistory of Australia* (Penguin, Ringwood, 1975), pp. 19-51. The voyages of Ch'eng Ho and the Darwin figurine are discussed, pp. 41-44.

PORTUGUESE: The literature on alleged Portuguese contacts is voluminous. For the latest evaluation of the Dieppe maps and their apparent inclusion of southeastern Australia, Helen Wallis, "The Enigma of Java-la-Grande", in I. Donaldson (ed.), *Australia and the European Imagination* (Canberra, 1982), pp. 1-40. The claims for Portuguese archaeological finds, including the mahogany ship, are detailed by K.G. McIntyre, *The Secret Discovery of Australia: Portuguese Ventures 200 Years Before Cook* (Medindie, 1977).

PORTUGUESE LANGUAGE AND MELVILLE ISLAND: Mulvaney, *Prehistory*, pp. 46-47; J. Urry and M. Walsh, "The lost 'Macassar language' of Northern Australia", *Aboriginal History* 5 (1981): 91-108.

NAPIER BROOME BAY: G. Henderson, *Unfinished Voyages* (Perth, 1980), pp. 51-56; armaments in 1920, V. Hall, *Outback Policeman* (Adelaide, 1973), p. 25.

THE MAHOGANY SHIP: An extensive literature exists, for which see McIntyre. See also *The Proceedings of the First Australian Symposium on the Mahogany Ship* (Warrnambool, 1982).

ASSISTANCE: For details of the C14 date and the wood identification, I acknowledge the help of the Preservation Services Branch of the National Library of Australia.

GEELONG KEYS: McIntyre, *Secret Discovery*, pp. 257-58.

EXOTIC CONTACTS: A proponent of an array of foreign influences in Australia was Michael Terry. For example, see his articles in *Walkabout* August 1965 and August 1967.

Chapter 3   A Dampierland Tercentennial

DAMPIER'S 1688 VISIT: A. Gray (ed.), *A New Voyage Round the World* (London, 1927), pp. 311-16.

1699 VISIT: R.H. Major (ed.), *Early Voyages to Terra Australis, now called Australia* (London, 1859), pp. 134-64. The same volume reproduces the Australian section of the Sloan Ms 32361, "The Adventures of William Dampier, with others . . . ", pp. 108-11. The attempt to capture a man, Major, pp. 158-59.

BANKS: J.D. Hooker (ed.), *Journal of Sir Joseph Banks* (London, 1896), pp. 262, 297.

DAMPIER QUOTATIONS: "miserablest", 1927, p. 312; Sloan Ms, p. 109; flies, 1927, p. 312; fish trap, 1927, p. 313.

KARRAKATTA BAY: The basic source is Moya Smith, "Joules from Pools: social and techno-economic aspects of Bardi stone fish traps". M. Smith (ed.),

Archaeology at ANZAAS 1983 (Perth, 1983), pp. 29-45. I also acknowledge Moya Smith's assistance in supplying photographs.

Chapter 4 Praus to Carpentaria

MACASSANS: The basic account of Macassan contact is C.C. Macknight, *The Voyage to Marege* (Melbourne, 1976). For details of relations with Aboriginal society, see Macknight, "Macassans and Aborigines", *Oceania* 42 (1972), pp. 283-321. D.J. Mulvaney, *The Prehistory of Australia*, ch. 1, presents a general account.

KIMBERLEY: *The Journal of Post Captain Nicholas Baudin* (Adelaide, 1974), pp. 539-41.

ARNHEM LAND: M. Flinders, *A Voyage to Terra Australis* (London 1814), vol. 2, pp. 228-33.

PELLEW ISLANDS: Flinders, vol. 2, pp. 168-73. A more detailed description of the North Island stone lines was provided by the naturalist, Robert Brown, who accompanied Flinders. It is quoted by Macknight, *Voyage*, p. 52.

COMMANDANT'S DESCRIPTION OF ACTIVITIES: The account was recorded by Leichhardt during his stay at Port Essington in December 1845 — E.M. Webster (ed.), *An Explorer at Rest* (Melbourne, 1986), p. 25.

L. LAMILAMI: *Lamilami Speaks* (Sydney, 1974), p. 72.

PORT ESSINGTON: Quoted in Macknight, *Oceania*, p. 309.

VISITS TO MACASSAR: *Lamilami Speaks* pp. 70-71; Macknight, *Voyage*, pp. 85-87, and plates 18-19.

ABORIGINAL RITUALS: Macknight, *Oceania*, p. 314; D. Thomson, *Economic Structure and the Ceremonial Exchange Cycle in Arnhem Land* (Melbourne, 1949), pp. 89-90.

STONE PICTURES: C.C. Macknight and W.J. Gray, *Aboriginal Stone Pictures in Eastern Arnhem Land* (Canberra, 1970).

Chapter 5 Adventure Bay: "A Convenient and Safe Place"

TASMAN'S VISIT: A. Sharp, *The Discovery of Australia* (Oxford, 1963), pp. 74-77.

BOUGAINVILLE'S VISION OF TAHITI: Bernard Smith, *European Vision and the South Pacific* (Oxford, 1960), p. 25.

MARION du FRESNE: Accounts of expedition members are quoted in N.J.B. Plomley (ed.), *Friendly Mission* (Tasmanian Historical Research Association, 1966), p. 37-39; quotations 38.

"IT WAS SCIENTIFIC CURIOSITY": N.J.B. Plomley, *The Baudin Expedition and The Tasmanian Aborigines 1802* (Hobart, 1983), p. 208. SKIN COLOUR AND FIRES: H.L. Roth, *Crozet's Voyage . . . in the years 1771-1772* (London, 1891), p. 20.

BANKS: J.D. Hooker (ed.), *Journal of Sir Joseph Banks* (London, 1896), p. 308.

BLIGH'S OPINION OF ADVENTURE BAY: W. Bligh, *A Voyage to the South Seas* (London, 1792), p. 54; M. Flinders, *A Voyage to Terra Australis* (London, 1814), p. clxxxii.

FURNEAUX: Three different accounts of the 1773 Furneaux visit are consistent: J. Beaglehole (ed.), *The Journals of Captain Cook* (London, 1961), vol. 2, p. 165 (Cook), pp. 733-35 (Furneaux), pp. 746-48 (Burney). The 1777 visit draws upon J. Beaglehole (ed.), *The Journals of Captain Cook* (London, 1967), vol.3, pp. 784-94 (W. Anderson); pp. 991-94 (D. Samwell).

OMAI: Samwell, pp. 991-92.

MEDALS: L.R. Smith, *The Resolution and Adventure Medal* (Sydney, 1985), p. 11; for details of the Tasmanian medal, I thank the former caretakers of the Bligh Museum, Adventure Bay, Jill Hall and Jim Mitchell.

BLIGH'S *BOUNTY* VISIT: *A Voyage to the South Seas* (London, 1792), pp. 46–54.

BLIGH'S 1792 VISIT: W. Bligh, *The Log of HMS* Providence (Guildford, 1976), entries for 9-22 February 1792.

D'ENTRECASTEAUX VISIT: J.J. Labillardière, *Voyage in Search of La Perouse, performed by order of the Constituent Assembly, during the years 1791, 1792, 1793 and 1794 (London, 1800), vol. 11, p. 82.*

NUENONNE: An account of the Nuenonne people of Bruny Island is given by Sandra Bowdler and Lyndall Ryan, in D.J. Mulvaney and J. Peter White (eds), *Australians to 1788* (Broadway, 1987), pp. 309-27. It is illustrated by four of George Tobin's watercolours of Adventure Bay, while on HMS *Providence*, in 1792.

ASSISTANCE: I am indebted to the Naval Historical Library, British Ministry of Defence, for permission to reproduce the painting *Captain Cook's interview with the natives in Adventure Bay, Van Diemen's Land, January 29, 1777*. It was photographed by Clare Bassett. It is in the Fannin collection of drawings and sketches. Fannin was master of arms on the *Resolution*. The artist almost certainly was John Webber. Aboriginal men in the foreground have scars (cicatrices) on their bodies, which match very closely with those on a drawing of a "Man of Van Diemen's Land", by Webber. It is illustrated in J.C. Beaglehole (ed.) *The Voyage of the* Resolution and Discovery (Cambridge, 1967), part 1, pl. 12A.

Chapter 6   British Ceremonial at King George Sound

VANCOUVER: G. Vancouver, *A Voyage of Discovery to the North Pacific Ocean* . . . (London, 1798), vol.1, pp. 35-50; Point Possession, p. 35.

FISH TRAPS: Vancouver, p. 38; W. Dix and S. Meagher, "Fish traps in the southwest of Western Australia", *Records of the Western Australian Museum* 4 (1976), pp. 171-87.

FLINDERS: M. Flinders, *A Voyage to Terra Australis* (London, 1814), vol. 1, pp. 54-61.

AMERICAN SEALER: Nicholas Baudin, *The Journal* (Adelaide, 1974), pp. 488-89.

CEREMONIES: Flinders, pp. 60-61; Isobel M. White, "The birth and death of a ceremony", *Aboriginal History* 4 (1980), pp. 33–42; Bates quotation, p. 35.

NYUNGAR: For a general history of the Nyungar, see N. Green, *Broken Spears* (Perth, 1984). A brilliant essay on the King George Sound clans, highly illustrated, is by W. Ferguson, "Mokare's Domain", in D.J. Mulvaney and J.P. White (eds), *Australians to 1788* (Sydney, 1987), pp. 120-45.

Chapter 7   The House That Phillip Built by Sydney Cove

PHILLIP'S HOUSE: This chapter draws upon my *A Good Foundation, Reflections on the Heritage of The First Government House, Sydney* (Canberra, 1985), Special Australian Heritage Publication Series no.5. Another relevant study is R.H.W. Reece, *Aborigines and Colonists* (Sydney, 1974).

PHILLIP'S INSTRUCTIONS: *Historical Records of Australia, (HRA)*, series 1, vol. I, pp. 13-14.

MACQUARIE: *HRA*, ser.1, vol. VIII, p. 338. Barron Field's view was expressed later, in his *Geographical Memoirs on New South Wales* (London, 1825), p. 224.

DARLING: *HRA* ser. 1, vol. XII, p. 125. For Blacktown I am indebted to advice from Anne Bickford; see also J. Woolmington, *Aborigines in Colonial Society 1788-1850* (Sydney, 1973).

BOURKE: *HRA*, ser.1, vol. XVIII, pp. 811-12 — a proclamation of 26 August 1835.

PHILLIP: W.E.H. Stanner, "The history of indifference thus begins", *Aboriginal History* 1 (1977), pp. 3-26; quotation p. 23.

KING: *HRA*, ser. 1, vol. IX, pp. 141-45; N. Gunson (ed.), *Australian Reminiscences and Papers of L.E. Threlkeld* (Canberra, 1974), vol. 1, pp. 49-50.

SYDNEY CLANS: J.L. Kohen and R. Lampert, "Hunters and fishers in the Sydney region", in D.J. Mulvaney and J.P. White (eds), *Australians to 1788* (Sydney, 1987), pp. 343-65.

ARABANOO: References for the remainder of this chapter are provided in D.J. Mulvaney, *A Good Foundation*.

GRIEVANCE: T. Watling, *Letters of an Exile at Botany Bay to his Aunt in Dumfries, 1794*. Reprinted, Sydney, 1945, p. 28.

SMALLPOX: See two articles by Judy Campbell, in *Historical Studies* 20 (1983) and 21 (1985), and one by N.G. Butlin, also in 21 (1985). N.G. Butlin, *Our Original Aggression* (Sydney, 1983) is an important though provocative study.

BLIGH: I am indebted to Helen Proudfoot for directing me to the King Papers, vol. 8, pp. 244-45 (Mitchell Library).

CHAPTER 8   Terror at Cape Grim

BASS STRAIT, MUTTON BIRDS, AND CAPE GRIM: M. Flinders, *A Voyage to Terra Australis* (London, 1814), pp. clxx–clxxiii. His journal reference to "dismal" cliffs. A. Sharp, *The Discovery of Australia* (London, 1963), pp. 213–14.

CAPE GRIM: The basic source for this essay is N.J.B. Plomley (ed.), *Friendly Mission, The Tasmanian Journals and Papers of George Augustus Robinson 1829-1834* (Hobart, 1966), pp. 174-97, 602-25. For "tribe" names, p. 973; territory name, p. 957.

NUMBER OF DEATHS IN NORTHWEST: L. Ryan, *The Aboriginal Tasmanians* (St Lucia, 1981), pp. 263–66.

CAPE GRIM MASSACRE: Shepherd's version, p. 175; Aboriginal version, p. 181; Chamberlain, pp. 175–6; Gunshanan, p. 196.

GOLDIE AND CURR: pp. 192, 197, 235, 432–33, 603.

ROBINSON: Golgotha, p. 183; prophecy, p. 612.

ASSISTANCE: I acknowledge use of a manuscript report by Dr Jim Stockton, "Cultural Resources Information for Cape Grim", prepared under contract for the Australian Heritage Commission, June 1979. Illustrations are also from Stockton's camera.

Chapter 9 "Civilized off the face of the earth" at Wybalenna and Oyster Cove

WYBALENNA AND OYSTER COVE: The indispensable reference is N.J.B. Plomley, *Weep in Silence: A History of the Flinders Island Aboriginal Settlement* (Hobart, 1987). A more general survey is by Lyndall Ryan, *The Aboriginal Tasmanians* (St Lucia, 1981). This chapter draws heavily upon Plomley's masterly survey, but also upon my own impressions from visits to The Lagoons, Wybalenna and Oyster Cover.

BACKHOUSE ON WYBALENNA: Plomley, p. 232; Robinson's impressions, 17 October 1835, Plomley, p. 303.

WALLABY TABOO: Plomley, p. 231.

MINDERS: Plomley, e.g. pp. 303, 633.

FRANKLIN VISIT: Plomley, pp. 542–25.

OYSTER COVE: Plomley, pp. 171–201; Ryan, pp. 205–21; G. Lennox, "Oyster Cove Historic Site: A Resource Document", *Occasional Paper* no. 9, 1984 (National Parks and Wildlife Service Tasmania).

ARCHAEOLOGICAL POTENTIAL: J. Allen and R. Jones, "Oyster Cove: archaeological traces of the last Tasmanians . . .", *Papers and Proceedings, The Royal Society of Tasmania*, 114 (1980), pp. 225-33.

REMOVAL OF BURIALS: W.E.L.H. Crowther, "The final phase of the extinct Tasmanian race 1847-1876", *Records of the Queen Victoria Museum*, Launceston, no. 49 (1974), p. 28.

Chapter 10   Across Torres Strait

DATES: D.R. Moore, *Islanders and Aborigines at Cape York* (Canberra, 1979), pp. 14-15; Michael Rowland, pers. commun.

TORRES STRAIT CULTURE: Moore, 1979; J.R. Beckett, "The Torres Strait Islanders", in D. Walker (ed.), *Bridge and Barrier: The Natural and Cultural History of Torres Strait* (Canberra, 1972), pp. 307-26.

MORILAG ECONOMY: Moore, 1979, pp. 301-6; D.R. Moore, "Cape York Aborigines: fringe participants in the Torres Strait trading system", *Mankind* 11 (1978), pp. 319-25; D.R. Moore, *The Torres Strait Collections of A.C. Haddon* (London, 1984), pp. 35-37.

KWOIAM: The chief source is A.C. Haddon (ed.), *Reports of the Cambridge Anthropological Expedition to Torres Straits* (Cambridge, 1904-1935), vol. 5, pp. 3-5, 67-83, 368-69. For supplementary information, M. Lawrie, *Myths and Legends of Torres Strait* (St Lucia, 1970), pp. 88-101. Variant stories are contained in W. Laade, "Further material on Kuiam, legendary hero of Mabuiag", *Ethnos* 33 (1968), pp. 70-96. For details of the sites on Mabuiag and Pulu, see Haddon, vol. 5, pp. 3-5, 82-83, 368-69, and Lawrie, pp. 98-100.

JANIE CREEK: D. Thomson, "Notes on a hero cult from the Gulf of Carpentaria, North Queensland", *Journal of the Royal Anthropological Institute (JRAI)*, 64 (1934), pp. 217-35; U. McConnell, *Myths of the Munkan* (London 1957), pp. 207-27; A.C. Haddon, *Reports of the Cambridge Expedition* vol. 1, pp. 270-72. For details of relics at Janie Creek, see especially Thomson, pp. 226-29 and McConnell, pp. 20-24. Other Papuan and Torres Strait Island influences on northeastern Queensland are described by D. Thomson, "The hero cult, initiation and totemism on Cape York", *JRAI* 63 (1933), pp. 453-537.

ADVICE: I acknowledge assistance from David Moore and Dr Jeremy Beckett, Sydney, Dr John Taylor, Townsville, Michael Rowland, Brisbane, and Dr Ron Vanderwal, Melbourne. Vanderwal conducted an archaeological survey of some Torres Strait Islands in 1972. His report is, "The Torres Strait: Prehistory and beyond", *Occasional Papers*, Anthropology Museum, University of Queensland, 2 (1973), pp. 157-94.

Chapter 11   Port Essington: A Friendly Frontier

LEICHHARDT: E.M. Webster (ed.), *An Explorer at Rest* (Melbourne, 1986), p. 30.

THE SETTLEMENTS: The fullest published account is by P.G. Spillett, *Forsaken Settlement* (Melbourne, 1972). The archaeological evidence is presented in an unpublished doctoral thesis, F.J. Allen, "Archaeology, and the History of Port Essington", 2 vols (ANU, Canberra, 1969). See also *Fort Wellington Raffles Bay*, published by the Historical Society of the Northern Territory, 1971.

CRITICAL VISITOR: H.S. Melville, *Adventures of a Griffin* (London, 1867), p. 133. Naturalist opinion: J. MacGillivray, *Narrative of the Voyage of H.M.S.* Rattlesnake (London, 1852), vol. 1, p. 138.

DEATH RATE: J. Allen and P. Corris (eds), *The Journal of John Sweatman* (St Lucia, 1977), p. 137.

CONDITION OF BUILDINGS: MacGillivray, p. 136; Webster, p. 23.

RAFFLES BAY MASSACRE: The figure of thirty dead was given by Sweatman (p. 135), at Port Essington fifteen years later. For an account of this episode and of Barker's success, see J. Harris, "Contact languages at the Northern Territory British military settlements 1824-1849", *Aboriginal History* 9 (1985), pp. 151-61.

PORT ESSINGTON DEATH: Harris, pp. 163-67; Allen "Archaeology and the History of Port Essington", vol. 1, p. 397.

LEICHHARDT AND CHILDREN: Webster, p. 23.

MELVILLE AND DOCTOR: H.S. Melville, *Adventures of a Griffin* (London, 1867), p. 136.

ARCHAEOLOGICAL EXCAVATIONS: Allen, vol. 1, pp. 58-61, 398.

SWEATMAN'S EXPERIENCES: *Journal*, pp. 130-32, 146-47.

SMALLPOX: Allen, p. 399.

NEWSPAPER AND SUPPLIES: *Sydney Morning Herald*, 22 June 1840.

ABORIGINAL SEAMEN: Sweatman, p. 144; McGillivray, vol. 1, pp. 154-57.

VD: McGillivray, vol.1, p. 159.

"MERRY PEOPLE": Sweatman, pp. 146-47.

CONFALONIERI: Sweatman, pp. 114-16.

DOMESTIC ANIMALS: H.J. Frith and J.H. Calaby (eds), *Fauna Survey of the Port Essington District . . .* CSIRO, Division of Wildlife Research Technical Paper, no. 28 (Melbourne, 1974). For an evocative survey of the ravages of buffalo, see Carmel Schrire, *The Alligator Rivers prehistory and ecology in western Arnhem Land* (Canberra, 1982), pp. 13-16.

Chapter 12   Moorundie: "Tranquillity everywhere prevails"

MOORUNDIE: The basic account is by E.J. Eyre, *Journals of Expeditions of Discovery . . .* (London, 1845), 2 vols; vol. 2, pp. 147-512, passim. Geoffrey Dutton, *The Hero as Murderer: The Life of Edward John Eyre* (London, 1967), pp. 145-65, describes Eyre's life at Moorundie. The place is set into the Aboriginal history of the region, in [G. Pretty], *Ngaiawong Folk Province* (South Australian Museum, 1977).

"RUFUS": Edmund Morey, who settled at Euston in 1846, claimed blood discolouring — Morey Papers, Mitchell Library MSS 883, p. 201. Eyre's muddy water: J. Waterhouse (ed.), E.J. Eyre, *Autobiographical Narrative of Residence and Exploration in Australia 1832-1839* (London, 1984), p. 186; large population, p. 157.

RETALIATION: Apprehensive stockmen, Eyre, *Autobiographical Narrative*, p. 179; surgery, pp. 182-83; reflections, p. 184.

RUFUS ATTACKS: All four incidents are fully reported in *Papers Relative to the Affairs of South Australia — Aborigines*, Colonial Office, Great Britain, documents, nos 87-105, 1841-42. Larger casualties — J.C. Hawker, *Early Experiences in South Australia* (Adelaide, 1899), p. 79.

BUCHANAN: Diary entries quoted in G. Jenkin, *Conquest of the Ngarrindjeri* (Adelaide, 1979), pp. 283-84.

EYRE'S AIMS: Eyre, *Journals*, vol.2, pp. 149, 463.

"A JUST RIGHT": Eyre in *Papers Relative to . . . Aborigines*, no. 101, 10 January 1842.

"ESSENTIAL" AIM: Eyre, *Journals*, vol. 2, p. 480.

MUSTERS: Eyre, *Journals*, vol. 2, pp. 372-75; Hawker, *Early Experiences*, p. 82.

DIGNITY: *Papers Relative to . . . Aborigines*, no. 101, 10 January 1842.

VD: *Journals*, vol. 2, pp. 379-81. I acknowledge the assistance of Dr Stephen Webb.

MOORUNDIE TODAY: *Ngaiawong Folk Province*, pp. 90-95.

TRANQUILLITY: C. Sturt, *Narrative of an Expedition into Central Australia* (London, 1849), 2 vols, p. 215.

Chapter 13   A Wiradjuri Memorial near Molong

MITCHELL: T.L. Mitchell, *Journal of an Expedition into the Interior of Tropical Australia* (London, 1848), provides the basic source for Yuranigh. Mitchell's tribute to Yuranigh, pp. 414-15. Mitchell's visit to the grave on Sunday, 3 August 1851, is recorded in the Mitchell Library, MSS no C.71, "Sir T.L. Mitchell's Diary 1851 Visit to Bathurst Gold Field". I am indebted to D.W.A. Baker, Department of History, Faculty of Arts, Australian National University, for drawing my attention to this entry.

THE GRAVE: Details of the fences and the headstone are provided by W.R. Glasson, "Yuranigh", *Queensland Geographical Journal* 54 (1950), pp. 54-65.

CARVED TREES: David Bell, "Aboriginal Carved Trees in New South Wales. A Survey Report" 2 vols, NSW Parks and Wildlife Service, 1979 (in Australian Heritage Commission library).

YURANIGH'S ACTIVITIES: 91 separate references to Yuranigh have been counted, the first on p. 25.

NATURAL HISTORY OBSERVATIONS: e.g. pp. 36, 224-25, 285, 321, 352, 371-72; artefacts, p. 104, 374.

MITCHELL'S RELIANCE ON YURANIGH: e.g., pp. 66, 113, 143, 163-66, 178-79, 193, 214, 262, 265, 325-27.

ECOLOGY: quotation, pp. 412-13. See also pp. 69-70, 90, 98, 170, 306. It is necessary to add a caution, however, about Mitchell's reliability in view of B. Finlayson's study, "Sir Thomas Mitchell and Lake Salvator: an essay in ecological history", *Historical Studies* 21 (1984), pp. 212-28.

Chapter 14   Two Innovative Missions: New Norcia and Poonindie

New Norcia

A useful article is by S. Livings, "The New Norcia Heritage Trail", *Heritage Australia* 6 (1987), no. 1, pp. 20-21. *The Story of New Norcia* (New Norcia, 1973) is a booklet available at the New Norcia museum.

SALVADO: E.J. Stormon (ed.), *The Salvado Memoirs* (Nedlands, 1977), pp. 45-88, recount Salvado's experiences up to 1849. The quotations by Salvado, pp. 65, 82. Other details, including population numbers, P. Hasluck, *Black Australians* (Melbourne, 1970), pp. 97-99, 219. Modern criticism of Salvado is made in a review of Stormon's edition, by T. Stannage, *Studies in Western Australian History* 7 (1984), pp. 33-5. Salvado is defended by Muriel Berman in the same journal — "Bishop Salvado: a reappraisal", *Studies* 7 (1984), pp. 36-41.

ROWLEY: C.D. Rowley, *The Destruction of Aboriginal Society* (Canberra, 1970), p. 106.

MUSIC AND CRICKET: G. Russo, *Lord Abbot of the Wilderness* (Melbourne, 1980), pp. 242-44.

Poonindie

The essential account is by Bishop [M.B.] Hale, *The Aborigines of Australia* (London, [1889]). Useful comment is made by G. Jenkin, *Conquest of the Ngarrindjeri* (Adelaide, 1979), pp. 65-66, 115, 215-16, 222, 232, 241.

HALE IMPROVISES: Hale, pp. 12, 27, 43, 53, 74-75. The critical inspector was quoted in K. Hassell, *The Relations Between the Settlers and the Aborigines in South Australia* (Adelaide, 1966), pp. 158-59.

POONINDIE IN THE 1870s: J.W. Bull, *Early Experiences of Life in South Australia* (Adelaide, 1884), pp. 242-43; p. 239 states that Hale used his personal funds; Hale, pp. 74-75, 77, 100.

MUSIC: Hale, p. 93.

CRICKET: Hale, pp. 56, 97; J. Tregenza, "Two notable portraits of South Australian Aborigines", *Journal of the Historical Society of South Australia* 12 (1984) pp. 22-31. This important article contains much other material on Poonindie. The illustration of a match in progress, p. 28.

DISEASE: Hale, pp. 48, 92; Tregenza, p. 29; E. Richards (ed.), *The Flinders History of South Australia — Social History* (Adelaide, 1986), p. 305; Hassell, p. 141.

BRICKS AND BUILDING: Hale, pp. 44, 51-53, 87; the church, p. 87.

EVICTION: Richards (ed.), p. 306; Jenkin, pp. 215-16, 232.

Chapter 15   Massacre and Dispersion at Cullinlaringo

RECENT STUDIES: There are many secondary accounts of the Wills massacre and related incidents. The most useful are Lorna McDonald, *Rockhampton* (St Lucia,

1981), pp. 183-97; Gordon Reid, *A Nest of Hornets* (Melbourne, 1982), pp. 123-40; Judith Wright, *The Cry for the Dead* (Melbourne, 1981), pp. 94–129; David Carment, "The Wills massacre of 1861: Aboriginal-European conflict on the colonial Australian frontier", *Journal of Australian Studies* 6 (1980), pp. 49-55.

CONTEMPORARY SOURCES: There are some eye-witness accounts of the massacre scene, particularly the unpublished memoirs of Jesse Gregson (especially pp. 49-63), which were written, however, in 1906 (ML MSS 1382, item 1). Tom Wills wrote a hurried letter: T.W. Wills to H.C.A. Harrison, 24 October 1861 (Oxley Library OM 66/2/f2). An account appeared in the Rockhampton *Morning Bulletin*, 26 October 1861. Cedric Wills published an important statement in the Rockhampton *Daily Record*, 8 November 1912.

I am grateful to T.B.S. Wills, Minerva Creek, for permission to use family letters, copies of which he deposited in the library of the Capricornia Institute of Advanced Education, Rockhampton, and to Carol Gistitin of that library.

OSCAR DE SATGÉ: *Pages from the Journal of a Queensland Squatter* (London, 1901), pp. 152-61, was in the area at the time of the massacre. The participant in the Hornet Bank posse was E.C. Davies, "Some reminiscences of early Queensland", *Royal Historical Society of Queensland Journal* 6 (1959), p. 39.

THE CRITICAL BRISBANE EDITORIAL: *The Courier*, 8 November 1861.

REPORTS OF THE ABDUCTION OF ABORIGINES TO SYDNEY: *Sydney Morning Herald*, 12 December 1861, *The Courier*, 20 December 1861. An important statement by C.B. Dutton was published at Ipswich, *The North Australian*, 13 December, 1861, p. 3. Landsborough's comment: *Journal of Landsborough's Expedition* . . . (Melbourne, 1862), pp. 102–3.

SIR GEORGE BOWEN'S DESPATCHES: These are in the Queensland State Archives (QSA) GOV/22, 16 December 1861 (massacre report) and GOV/23, 8 July 1862 ("grass and water"). See also J.C.H. Gill, "Governor Bowen and the Aborigines", *Queensland Heritage* 2, no. 7 (1972), pp. 3-29.

THE REPORT OF THE SELECT COMMITTEE ON THE NATIVE POLICE FORCE: *Votes and Proceedings. Legislative Assembly*, 17 July 1861. C.B. Dutton's and F. Walker's complaints, QSA Col. A21/2545; this file also contains the responses of Bligh and Patrick.

OFFICIAL RESPONSE: Bligh's report on Patrick's actions at Rainworth, QSA Col A18/1889, 29 July 1861. Documents reporting the Wills massacre and its aftermath, Q.S.A. Col A23/3051.

THANKS: I am indebted to Mrs Lorna Smith, Burnside, Springsure, for assistance in the field.

Chapter 16   A Madimadi Cricketer at Lord's

MULLAGH: The evidence relating to Mullagh and Aboriginal cricket within his period is drawn together by the author in *Cricket Walkabout: The Australian Aboriginal Cricketers on Tour 1867-8* (Melbourne, 1967). A much enlarged, revised edition, with many illustrations, has been published in 1988 by Macmillan, Melbourne. Rex Harcourt is the co-author.

Chapter 17   Anthropology Along the Overland Telegraph Line

THE PINCH: B. Spencer and F.J. Gillen, *Across Australia* (London, 1912), p. 222.

IRON ADZE TIPS: C.E. Cowle to W.B. Spencer, 31 August 1900. Copy in Australian Institute of Aboriginal Studies library.

GOYDER: M.G. Kerr, *The Surveyors* (Adelaide, 1971), p. 177.

CHAMBERS PILLAR: T.G.H. Strehlow, *Journey to Horseshoe Bend* (Sydney, 1969), pp. 114-15; Spencer and Gillen, *Across Australia*, pp. 87-89; J.McD. Stuart, *Explorations Across the Continent of Australia* (London, 1863), pp. 151-52.

"DREAM TIMES": B. Spencer (ed.), *Report on the Work of the Horn Scientific Expedition to Central Australia* (London, 1896), vol.1, p. 50; W.B. Spencer and F.J. Gillen, *The Arunta* (London, 1927), pp. 589-96- for a discussion of Hermannsburg concepts.

ETHNOGRAPHIC COLLECTIONS: D.J. Mulvaney and J.H. Calaby, *So Much That Is New* (Melbourne, 1985) pp. 249-50. The major Spencer and Gillen books concerned with Overland Telegraph areas were all published by Macmillan. They are: *The Native Tribes of Central Australia* (London, 1899); *The Northern Tribes of Central Australia* (London, 1904); *Across Australia* (London, 1912), 2 vols; *The Arunta* (London, 1927), 2 vols; Baldwin Spencer, *Wanderings in Wild Australia* (London, 1928), 2 vols.

IMPORTANCE OF *Native Tribes:* Mulvaney and Calaby quote Malinowski (p. 396) and Frazer (p. 180).

BARROW CREEK: Spencer and Gillen, *Across Australia*, pp. 318-22; T.G.H. Strehlow, *Songs of Central Australia* (Sydney, 1971), pp. 588-93; A. Powell, *Far Country* (Melbourne, 1982), pp. 131-32.

ABORIGINAL PHASE OF TELEGRAPH STATION: C.D. Rowley, *Outcasts in White Australia* (Ringwood, 1972), p. 57 — removal of children; V. Hall, *Outback Policeman* (Adelaide, 1976), pp. 198-200; Charles Perkins, *A Bastard Like Me* (Sydney, 1975) p.7. The figures for Aboriginal army employment come from R. Hall, "Aborigines, the Army and the Second World War in Northern Australia", *Aboriginal History* 4 (1980), pp. 73-96; numbers, p. 81.

GILLEN NOSTALGIA: *Gillen's Diary: The Camp Jottings of F.J. Gillen* (Adelaide, 1968), p. 46.

Chapter 18   Central Australia: "Land of the Dawning"

CENTRAL MT STUART: W. Hardman (ed.), *The Journals of John McDouall Stuart* (London, 1865), p. 165.

SOURCES: I acknowledge the assistance of Dick Kimber and Howard Pearce, Alice Springs. The evocative account by T.G.H. Strehlow of the *Journey to Horseshoe Bend* (Sydney, 1969), places events on the Finke River into their anthropological context. For Willshire, see especially pp. 32, 43-48, 78, 154. The basic historical survey of the region is by M.C. Hartwig, "The Progress of White Settlement in the Alice Springs District and its Effects upon the Aboriginal Population

1860-1894'', Ph.D. thesis, University of Adelaide, 1965. For details of police, N.A. Richardson, *Pioneers of the North-West of South Australia* (Adelaide, 1925).

PUBLICATIONS BY W.H. WILLSHIRE, IN ORDER OF PUBLICATION: *The Aborigines of Central Australia* (Port Augusta, 1888); *The Aborigines of Central Australia* (Adelaide, 1891); *A Thrilling Tale of Real Life in the Wilds of Australia* (Adelaide, 1895); *The Land of the Dawning* (Adelaide, 1896). His letter concerning Pompey's skull, 4 December 1896, South Australian Museum, AD 43.

WILLSHIRE'S OBITUARY: *The Observer* (Adelaide), 5 September 1925, pp. 39, 45. For an essay which sets Willshire's literary work into context, J.J. Healy, ''The Lemurian Nineties'', *Australian Literary Studies*, 8 (1978): 307-16.

QUOTATIONS FROM WILLSHIRE: Citations are referred to by the year of publication: Women and the Almighty, 1896, pp. 18, 6; Oleara and harem, 1895, pp. 26, 40; vocabularies, 1888, pp. 19-25; ''good Winchester'', 1896, n. 50; Anna's Reservoir, 1896, p. 20; sadism, 1888, pp. 10, 12, 1896, pp. 54, 20, 45; ''working'' the Daly, 1888, p. 5; carbines ''talking English'', 1896, pp. 40-41; police ''never commence hostilities'', 1891, p. 32; on Wurmbrand shooting, 1891, p. 34; ''country J.P.'', 1896, pp. 22-23; *Kadina and Wallaroo Times* quoted, 1895, p. 63; for his account of his trial, 1895, pp. 56-57; sixteen deaths in Territory, 1896, pp. 19-20.

SPENCER AND ANNA'S RESERVOIR: B. Spencer, *Wanderings in Wild Australia* (London, 1928), p. 412.

DEATHS: The estimate that from 500 to 1,000 Aborigines died comes from Dick Kimber's research. The attack on 150 to 170 Aborigines is reported in A. Russell, *A Tramp-Royal in Wild Australia 1928-29* (London, 1934), pp. 254-55.

BLACKFELLOW'S BONES: T.G.H. Strehlow, *Songs of Central Australia* (Sydney, 1971).

Chapter 19   Sacred Storehouses: Illamurta's Role

COWLE: Background to the career of C.E. Cowle and the Horn scientific exploring expedition is provided by D.J. Mulvaney and J.H. Calaby, *So Much That Is New: Baldwin Spencer 1860-1929* (Melbourne, 1985), ch.7. Cowle's letters to Spencer are in Oxford's Pitt Rivers Museum. Copies were deposited in the library of the Australian Institute of Aboriginal Studies by Mulvaney, together with copies of Gillen's letters.

DATES OF LETTERS CITED: snakes, 18 March 1899; ''shooting in the old style'', 10 June 1899; sixteen arrests, 18 March 1899; ginger beer, 21 January 1903; care for troopers, 10 June 1899; diseases, 15 April 1899, 28 May 1900; ecology, 12 March 1896 (rabbits); ruined pools, 9 October 1896; biological impact, 22 August 1896; tjurungas, 5 October 1895, 9 February 1897, 18 March 1899, 13 April, 13 August, 23 November 1900, 14 April 1901, 25 November 1902; ''Grimm's Fairy Tales'', 18 March 1899.

THE 1929 POLICEMAN AND CHAINS: A. Russell, *A Tramp-Royal in Wild Australia* (London, 1934), p. 244.

GILLEN'S DESCRIPTION OF COWLE: *Gillen's Diary: The Camp Jottings of F.J. Gillen on the Spencer and Gillen Expedition Across Australia 1901-1902* (Adelaide, 1968), p. 82.

STIRLING AND TJURUNGA: B. Spencer (ed.), *Report of the Work of the Horn Scientific Expedition to Central Australia. Part IV Anthropology* (Melbourne, 1896), pp. 76-78, 179; C. Winnecke, "The Horn Scientific Exploring Expedition", *S.A. Parliamentary Papers*, vol.2, 1896, paper 19, p. 16.

SPENCER'S ACCOUNT OF CONSEQUENCES: Spencer and Gillen, *The Arunta* (London, 1927), p. 101. Excellent anthropological insight into this incident is given by T.G.H. Strehlow, in R.M. Berndt (ed.), *Australian Aboriginal Anthropology* (Nedlands, 1970), p. 120.

SPENCER ON TEMPE DOWNS: Spencer and Gillen, *Across Australia* (London, 1912), p. 143.

DUFFING: For insight into the extent of cattle duffing and horse stealing early this century, see the experiences of Walter Smith, in R.G. Kimber, *Man From Arltunga* (Carlisle, 1986). The chief "borrower" was Billy Colter (Coulthard), whose brother, Bob Coulthard, then managed Tempe Downs station: he "borrowed" hundreds of beasts. (e.g. pp. 9-14, 16-17, 26-31).

ASSISTANCE: I am grateful to Howard Pearce, Conservation Commission of the Northern Territory, for guiding me to Boggy Waterhole, Illamurta and Old Tempe Downs, during August 1986.

Chapter 20   Hermannsburg

HERMANNSBURG: There were two main sources for this account. N. Amadio (ed.), *Albert Namatjira: The Life and Work of an Australian Painter* (Melbourne, 1986), especially the chapter by Anne Blackwell; E. Leske (ed.), *Hermannsburg: A Vision and a Mission* (Adelaide, 1977). There is an illustrated article on Hermannsburg by Penny Watson in *Heritage*, 6 (2) 1987, pp. 31–4.

STREHLOW: The character of Carl Strehlow is poignantly portrayed by T.G.H. Strehlow, *Journey to Horseshoe Bend* (Sydney, 1969).

Chapter 21   Self-determination at Coranderrk

BASIC SOURCE: The late Diane Barwick will always be identified as the historian of Coranderrk. Her research forms the basis for this essay, but for the details it is essential to consult her publications. In particular, see her "Coranderrk and Cumeroogunga: Pioneers and Policy", in T.S. Epstein and D.H. Penny (eds), *Opportunity and Response* (London, 1972), pp. 10-68. See also her essays, "And the lubras are ladies now", in F. Gale (ed.), *Woman's Role in Aboriginal Society* (Canberra, 1974), pp. 51-63; "This most resolute lady", in D.E. Barwick, J. Beckett, M. Reay (eds), *Metaphors of Interpretation* (Canberra, 1985), pp. 185-239. Her discussion of medical aspects is provided in "Changes in the Aboriginal population of Victoria, 1863-1966'', in D.J. Mulvaney and J. Golson (eds), *Aboriginal Man and Environment in Australia* (Canberra, 1971), pp. 288-315.

CORANDERRK UNDER GREEN: Especially Barwick 1972, pp. 24-35; ''Presbyterian rigour'', p. 25; Barak and Birdarak quotations, p. 34.

OTHER SOURCES: Another useful source for Coranderrk and its context is M.F. Christie, *Aborigines in Central Victoria 1835-1886* (Sydney, 1979), pp. 157-204. Aldo Massola, *Coranderrk* (Kilmore, 1975), is a popular account containing numerous excellent photographs and appendices which quote accounts by visitors there. For H.N. Moseley and cricket, pp. 68-69. For causes of death since 1875, see pp. 83-100. A popular account of William Barak is S.W. Wiencke, *When the Wattle Blooms Again* (Woori Yallock, 1984).

Chapter 22   The Peppers of Ebenezer

WIMMERA RIVER: E.J. Eyre, *Autobiographical Narrative of Residence and Exploration in Australia 1832-1839* (London, 1984), pp. 139-40.

SELECT COMMITTEE: ''Report of the Select Committee of the Legislative Council on the Aborigines'', *Votes and Proceedings Legislative Council of Victoria* 1858/9 pp. III-IV.

EBENEZER: There are two undocumented general accounts. A.B. Werner, *Early Mission Work at Antwerp, Victoria* (Dimboola, 1959), concentrated upon the missionaries. Aldo Massola, *Aboriginal Mission Stations in Victoria* (Melbourne, 1970), pp. 31-62, summarised Board reports.

NATHANIEL PEPPER: Phillip Pepper, *You Are What You Make Yourself To Be* (Melbourne, 1980), pp. 9-29, provides an Aboriginal perspective.

CAUSES OF DEATH: Based upon analysis of Returns of Death published in Mossola, pp. 54, 59-61.

ABORIGINAL APPRECIATION: Pepper, p. 15.

ANNUAL REPORTS: Third Report of the Central Board for 1863, *Victorian Parliamentary Papers (VPP)* 1864, no.8, pp. 6, 14, for Ebenezer details.

1877 POPULATION: Report of Royal Commission into Aborigines, *VPP* 1877-78, vol. 3, p. 95.

1884 ''HALF-CASTES'': ''Twentieth Report . . . Board . . . for 1884''. *VPP* 1884, vol. 4.

1890: Twenty-sixth Report, *VPP* 1890, vol.4, p.4.

1902 ACTIONS AND PREDICTIONS: Thirty-eighth Report, 1902, p. 7.

Chapter 23   Epitaphs of Friendship: Camperdown, Esperance, Bichero

CAMPERDOWN: J. Dawson, *Australian Aborigines: The Languages and Customs of Several Tribes of Aborigines in the Western District of Victoria, Australia*

(Melbourne, 1881). This important book was reprinted by the Australian Institute of Aboriginal Studies (Canberra, 1981). The monument is discussed in the introduction to the facsimile, by Jan Critchett [p.3]. Dawson's own dedication is on p. v; his population estimate, p. 3.

NOONGALE: L. Tilbrook, *Nyungar Tradition* (Perth, 1983), pp. 24-26. A photograph of the headstone is on p. 26. A more critical attitude towards Forrest's Aboriginal sympathies has been argued in a recent reappraisal — E. Goddard and T. Stannage, "John Forrest and the Aborigines", *Studies in Western Australian History* 7 (1984), pp. 52-58.

WINDIITJ: J. Forrest, *Explorations in Australia* (London, 1875) contains many references, e.g. pp. 115, 266-7; Windich Springs, p. 180; *Dictionary of Australian Biography*, vol. 6, pp. 426-33; H.W. Wood, *Bushman Born* (Perth, 1981).

GRAVE: Illustrations of its original location are reproduced in J. Rintoul, *The History of Esperance* (Kalgoorlie, N.D.), p. 28. It is described on p. 27; see also J. Rintoul, *Esperance Yesterday and Today* (Perth, 1964), p. 30.

WAUBADEBAR: Tasmanian Tourist Council brochure "Let's talk about Bicheno", collected in 1985. I acknowledge the assistance of Ian Farrington, Canberra. Solid data proved impossible to locate.

Chapter 24   Battles in the Bush: Pinjarra and Battle Mountain

Pinjarra

FEWER THAN 1,000 DEATHS: A major symposium on Australian culture was published in *Daedalus*, the journal of the American Academy of Arts and Sciences, Winter 1985. The quotation comes from Richard Walsh, "Australia Observed", p. 421.

YAGAN: See the account by N. Green, *Broken Spears* (Perth, 1984), pp. 79-88.

CALYUTE: For the background to the Pinjarra expedition, Green provides a helpful survey, pp. 89-98, the quotation, p. 98. The role of Peel is outlined by R. Richards, *The Murray District of Western Australia: A History* (Shire of Murray, 1978), pp. 80-87. Stirling's despatch to E.G. Stanley, 1 November 1834- Battye Library Despatches to Colonial Office, 14 Sept. 1834 – 6 Dec. 1838, no. 14.

PINJARRA: All quotations from Stirling are taken from the above despatch. J.S. Roe's diary is quoted in Richards, *Murray District*, pp. 88-93. G.F. Moore, *Diary of Ten Years: Eventful Life of an Early Settler in Western Australia*, 1884 (Perth, 1978), pp. 239-43, provides another account. A clear presentation is by Green, *Broken Spears*, pp. 99-108. For an analysis of numbers killed, see N. Green, "Aboriginal and settler conflict in Western Australia 1826-1852", *The Push From the Bush*, no. 3 (1979), pp. 70-94.

GRAVES: Richards, *Murray District*, p. 95.

BUSSELL: Quoted in E.O. Shann, *Cattle Chosen*, 1926 (Perth, 1978), p. 176.

"HUMANE POLICY": Moore, *Diary*, p. 237.

Battle Mountain

OLD ACCOUNTS: The two chief sources are S.E. Pearson, "The Prospector of Argylla", N.D., MS Oxley Library, Brisbane, OM74-8; Hudson Fysh, *Taming the North* (Sydney, 1950) [1933]. Pearson also published a general article, "In the Kalkadoon country — The habitat and habits of a Queensland Aboriginal tribe", *Journal of the Historical Society of Queensland* 4 (1949), pp. 190-205.

RECENT STUDIES: The most detailed modern account is R.E.M. Armstrong, *The Kalkadoons* (Brisbane, N.D.). Unfortunately it contains a number of errors, and mistakes in the references. N. Loos, *Invasion and Resistance: Aboriginal-European Relations on the North Queensland frontier 1861-1898* (Canberra, 1982), sets regional issues into broader perspective, although reference to Battle Mountain is limited to p. 58.

LIGHT BRIGADE: Armstrong, p. 144; "number of riflemen", p. 142.

URQUHART: Fysh, p. 186.

PROSPECTORS: G. Blainey, *Mines in the Spinifex* (Melbourne, 1960), pp. 18-23; Armstrong, p. 88.

PALMER: E. Palmer, *Early Days in North Queensland* (Sydney, 1903), pp. 213–14. Palmer corresponded with A.W. Howitt, the Victorian ethnologist, who encouraged him to publish "Notes on some Australian Tribes", in the London *Journal of the Anthropological Institute* 13 (1884). He also published in E.M. Curr, *The Australian Race* (Melbourne, 1886).

EVENTS 1878-84: Armstrong, pp. 116-47; Fysh, pp. 92-149. "Deadly carbines", Fysh, p. 96; 300 dead, Armstrong, p. 128.

NORMANBY DEATHS: Fysh, p. 185.

PANIC AND BRISBANE VISIT: Fysh, p. 125; Loos, pp. 58, 78.

POWELL'S MURDER: Pearson, MS, p. 135; Fysh, pp. 140-49.

THE BATTLE: Fysh, pp. 184-85; Pearson, MS, p. 135; Pearson, 1949, pp. 199-200; Armstrong, pp. 140-45.

AFTERMATH: Cannibalism — Fysh, p. 184. Armstrong, p. 145, quotes Pearson's claim (MS, p. 135), that "on Prospector Creek there is a spinifex gully among the rugged schistose hills that for years after was whitened by their bones". Blainey (*Mines in the Spinifex*, p. 23) evidently elaborated this to read, "that for decades a hill was littered with the bleached bones of warriors, gins, and piccaninnies". This may be, but hard evidence is lacking. A reader of Fysh's lurid account of the sequel to Powell's murder, might conclude that this previous massacre involved more people than the encounter at Battle Mountain (Fysh, pp. 144-45).

Chapter 25   Afghans and Aborigines at Marree

CAMELS: Information about camel numbers and Afghan cameleers is derived largely from T.L. McKnight, *The Camel in Australia* (Melbourne, 1969), especially pp. 22-24, 57-72.

AFGHAN-ABORIGINAL RELATIONS: Aboriginal attitudes are expressed by oral accounts reproduced by Luise Hercus, "Afghan stories from the northeast of South Australia", *Aboriginal History* 5 (1981), pp. 39-70, and by Ben Murray and Peter Austin, ibid., pp. 71–80; L. Hercus and P. Sutton, *This Is What Happened* (Canberra, 1986), pp. 128-32. Some general comment is provided by M. Cigler, *The Afghans in Australia* (Melbourne, 1986).

WALTER SMITH: R.G. Kimber, *Man From Arltunga* (Victoria Park, 1986), pp. 33-39.

SYED GOOLAMDEEN: L. Litchfield, *Marree and the Tracks Beyond in Black and White* (Marree, 1983), pp. 71-72 — quoting an interview in 1962.

BEJAH DERVISH: *Australian Dictionary of Biography* (Melbourne, 1979), vol. 7, p. 250. George Farwell must have visited Marree around 1948 and retold his story vividly, but always without precise dates or other relevant details. See G. Farwell, *Traveller's Tracks* (Melbourne, 1949), pp. 66-9; G. Farwell, *Land of Mirage* (Melbourne, 1950), pp. 25-28; G. Farwell, "Camel town", *Walkabout*, February 1948, pp. 16–21; R. Robinson, *The Shift of Sands* (Melbourne, 1976), pp. 18–19.

WELLS: The quotations by L.A. Wells are from, *Journal of the Calvert Scientific Exploring Expedition, 1896-7, Western Australia Parliamentary Paper* 1902, pp. 18, 55.

JACK BEJAH: C.T. Madigan, *Crossing the Dead Heart* (Melbourne, 1946), p. 14. I am indebted for advice to Mrs B.N. Bejah, of Port Augusta, and Mrs I. Mahomet, of Alice Springs.

LAKE HARRY: L. Litchfield, *Marree*, pp. 93-95; H. Pearce, *Homesteads of the Sandy Desert* (Adelaide, 1978), pp. 43-45; F. Ratcliffe, *Flying Fox and Drifting Sand* (Sydney, 1948), pp. 256-57; C.T. Madigan, *Central Australia* (Melbourne, 1944), pp. 53, 152.

DATE PALMS: D.J. Gordon, *Handbook of South Australia Progress and Resources* (Adelaide, 1908), pp. 215, 227; Farwell, *Traveller's Tracks*, pp. 62-69.

ARABANA RECOLLECTIONS: Mona Merrick, quoted in Hercus, *Aboriginal History* 5 (1981), p. 48.

FILM: Roger Sandall made an excellent film on contemporary Aboriginal society and camels, "Camels and the Pitjantjara", Australian Institute of Aboriginal Studies, Canberra, 1969 (50 minutes).

Chapter 26   Bernier and Dorre: "Isles of the Dead"

HISTORICAL EVALUATION: The fullest analysis is Mary Anne Jebb, "The Lock hospitals experiment: Europeans, Aborigines and venereal disease", *Studies in Western Australian History* 8 (1984), pp. 68-87. A short account is Peter Biskup, *Not Slaves Not Citizens* (St Lucia, 1973), pp. 111-14.

OFFICIAL: The annual reports of the Chief Protector of Aborigines between 1903 and 1920, mostly published in Western Australia *Parliamentary Papers*. Some typed reports were consulted in microfilm at the Australian Institute of

Aboriginal Studies. The Roth Royal Commission on the Condition of the Natives is in *Parliamentary Papers*, 1905.

ASSISTANCE: My study was facilitated by the staff of the integrated State Archives of Western Australia and the Battye Library of Western Australian History, and Mary Anne Jebb's assistance is acknowledged.

LACK OF MEDICAL CARE IN LAST CENTURY: J.E. Hammond, *Winjan's People* (Perth, 1933), pp. 60, 71-72.

SCIENTIST AT WYNDHAM: H. Klaatsch, "Some notes on scientific travel", *Australasian Association for the Advancement of Science* XI (1907), p. 583.

BERNIER AND DORRE: "The results of an expedition to Bernier and Dorre Islands . . . in July, 1959", *Fauna Bulletin* no.2, Fisheries Department no. 2, Fisheries Department, Perth, 1962.

BERNIER AND DORRE: "The results of an expedition to Bernier and Dorree Islands . . . in July, 1959", *Fauna Bulletin* no. 2, Fisheries Department, Perth, 1962.

DAISY BATES: *The Passing of the Aborigines* (London 1966 [1938]), pp. 95-104.

ROEBOURNE TELEGRAMS: State Archives AD 612/12, 17 April 1912.

GRANT WATSON: E.L. Grant Watson, *Where Bonds are Loosed* (London, 1920, [1941]), especially pp. 20-35; *But to What Purpose* (London, 1946), pp. 105-22; *Journey Under the Southern Stars* (London, 1968), pp. 43-54.

CONTAGIOUS DISEASES ACTS: Jebb, pp. 68-9; F.B. Smith, "Ethics and disease in the later Nineteenth Century", *Historical Studies* 15 (1971), pp. 118-35.

NECK-CHAINS: C.D. Rowley, *The Destruction of Aboriginal Society* (Canberra, 1970), p. 199. Roth's Royal Commission Report, *Parliamentary Papers* Western Australia, 1905, pp. 13-19, 54, 104. The government's response was included in the report of the Aborigines Department, 1907, p. 6.

ADMISSIONS AND DEATHS: Presented in tabular form by Jebb, p. 81.

EXPERIMENTAL TREATMENT: Jebb, pp. 76-80. For Salvarsan, see Archives file AF760/11, 23 Aug 1911, 8 Mar. 1911.

COMPULSORY TREATMENT: See the interesting account of the hospital by the Chief Protector in a letter to Queensland's Chief Protector, on 15 May 1912, from which "free to roam" statement comes. AD 702/12. This letter explains some of the costs of running the hospital. For punishments, see Jebb, p. 80.

BONE CRUSHER: Biskup p. 113 has misread the file AF 58/11 2 Jan. 1911, which is a serious error.

Chapter 27   "I am no loathsome leper" on Channel Island

SHAKESPEARE: The quotation from Shakespeare, "I am no loathsome leper", was spoken by Queen Margaret, *Henry VI*, Part 2, Act III, Scene *11*.

ACKNOWLEDGMENTS: The assistance of Suzanne Saunders is gratefully acknowledged. Her penetrating thesis " 'A Suitable Island Site': Leprosy in the Northern Territory and the Channel Island Leprosarium", Honours thesis,

Murdoch University, 1986, provided the basic information. Anne Bickford, consultant archaeologist, Sydney, kindly supplied information concerning her field survey on Channel Island.

LEPROSY: The basic medical assessment of leprosy in the Northern Territory is J.C. Hargrave, *Leprosy in the Northern Territory of Australia* (Darwin, 1980). Apart from details in Saunders and Hargrave, for Western Australia, see P. Biskup, *Not Slaves Not Citizens* (St Lucia, 1973), pp. 114-15; for Queensland reactions, R. Evans, K. Saunders, K. Cronin (eds), *Exclusion, Exploitation and Extermination* (Sydney, 1975; St Lucia, 1988), pp. 306, 348.

Chapter 28   The Cootamundra Home for Girls

BASIC SOURCE: Peter John Read is the authority on New South Wales Aboriginal history during this period. This account drew upon his ANU doctoral thesis, "A History of the Wiradjuri people of New South Wales 1883–1969" (1983). See also his moving pamphlet, *The Stolen Generations: The Removal of Aboriginal Children in New South Wales 1883 to 1969*, New South Wales Ministry of Aboriginal Affairs, [1982]; also " 'A rape of the soul so profound': some reflections on the dispersal policy in New South Wales", *Aboriginal History* 7 (1983), pp. 23-33.

NUMBER INVOLVED: The estimate of the number of children involved comes from *The Stolen Generations*, p. 9.

LEGISLATION: Further commentary on the 1909 and 1936 legislation is by C.D. Rowley, *Outcasts in White Australia* (Ringwood, 1972), pp. 56, 66.

"KINDLY AND WELL MEANING": Rowley, p. 28.

ABSORPTION POLICY: P. Jacobs, "Science and veiled assumptions: miscegenation in W.A. 1930–1937". *Australian Aboriginal Studies*, no.2, 1986, pp. 15–23; quotations pp. 1, 19.

CHEWINGS: C. Chewings, *Back in the Stone Age* (Sydney, 1936), p. 155.

CHANGES IN 1915 ACT: P. Read, thesis, pp. 149–53.

CHARGE SHEETS: Read, thesis, p. 152; quotation, Read p. 151.

NICHOLLS: M.T. Clark, *Pastor Doug* (Adelaide, 1975), p. 40.

JOHNSON: *Link-Up* (Canberra, N.D.), p. 3. This booklet was written by Peter Read and Coral Edwards, to describe the "Link-Up" organisation.

TUCKER: M. Tucker, *If Everyone Cared* (Sydney, 1977), pp. 81, 88–95.

1953 BOARD STATEMENT: *Dawn* 2, no. 12, December 1953, p. 13.

GHOSTS: Tucker, p. 104.

ARRIVAL TRAUMAS: Tucker, pp. 97–98.

WIRADJURI STATISTICS: Read, "A rape of the soul", p. 27.

CASE HISTORY: See Coral Edwards, "Is the ward clean?", in B. Gammage and A. Markus (eds), *All That Dirt: Aborigines 1938* (Canberra, 1982), pp. 4–8.

PATERNALISM: Tucker, p. 202.

THANKS: I am indebted to Mrs Jennifer Baldry, "Milbey" Wallendbeen, for assistance.

FILM: Coral Edwards produced a film on the Cootamundra Home and its impact upon the lives of girls. *It's a Long Road Back* (Australian Institute of Aboriginal Studies, 1981).

Chapter 29   Shifting Camp to Phillip Creek

PHILLIP CREEK: This chapter draws heavily upon two sources: Patricia Davison, *The Manga-Manda Settlement Phillip Creek* (James Cook University, 1985), and David Nash, "The Warumungu's Reserves 1892–1962: a case study in dispossession", *Australian Aboriginal Studies*, no. 1, 1984, pp. 2–16.

GILLEN QUOTATION: *Gillen's Diary* (Adelaide, 1968), p. 265.

W.E.H. STANNER: "Report to Australian National Research Council upon Aborigines and Aboriginal Reserve at Tennant Creek 1934", *Australian Institute of Aboriginal Affairs Newsletter* 13 (1980), pp. 43–48.

ORDINANCES: J.C. Altman, *Aborigines and Mining Royalties in the Northern Territory* (Canberra, 1983), pp. 3–4.

MINISTER'S AND DIRECTOR'S STATEMENTS: Quoted in Nash, "The Warumungu's Reserves", pp. 6–7; Altman, p. 4.

STANNER: "Report", p. 48, note 2. Stanner made this comment in 1968.

HATFIELD: Quoted by Nash, p. 7; from *Australia Through the Windscreen* (Sydney, 1936), pp. 105–6.

PHILLIP CREEK MOVE: Nash, p. 11; P. Davison, *The Manga-Manda Settlement*, pp. 8–9.

RESERVE REVOCATION: Nash, pp. 12–13; Stanner, "Report", p. 46.

WARUMUNGU-WARLPIRI RELATIONS: Davison, pp. 22–23, 42; M. Meggitt, *Desert People* (Sydney, 1962), pp. 31, 39.

1954 POPULATION: Meggitt, pp. 31, 39.

SPATIAL CONTRAST: Davison, p. 61.

Chapter 30   Freedom Ride to Moree

MOREE: *The Sydney Mail*, 15 Aug. 1896, pp. 341–42; R.J. Webb, "*The Rising Sun*", A History of Moree and District (Moree, 1962); *Moree "North-West Champion" Feature:* A supplement to celebrate 75 years of local government, 18 November, 1965.

G. WILLIAMS SURVEY: Three feature articles in *The Australian*, 4–7 Jan. 1965.

KEMPSEY: C.D. Rowley, *Outcasts in White Australia* (Canberra, 1970), pp. 264–65.

ABORIGINAL DEMOGRAPHY: J.P.M. Long, *Aboriginal Settlements* (Canberra, 1970), pp. 68–70.

FREEDOM RIDE: This account is based upon the *Australian*, 15, 20 January, 4, 12, 19, 20, 22 February, 1965; *Canberra Times*, 13 February 1965; *Daily Mirror*, 16 February 1965; *Sydney Sun*, 16 February 1965; *Sydney Morning Herald*, 17, 18, 20, 21, 22 February 1965. Praise for the Services Club by Perkins is quoted in The *Northern Daily Leader*, Tamworth, 17 February 1965.

LATER COMMENTS BY PERKINS: C. Perkins, *A Bastard Like Me* (Sydney, 1975), pp. 74, 89. Perkins presents a vivid account of the Freedom Ride, pp. 74–91. The Moree visit is telescoped into only one visit.

MUNRO: Quoted in R. Broome, *Aboriginal Australians* (Sydney, 1982), p. 176.

SERVICES CLUB: *Sydney Morning Herald*, 24 November 1967.

Chapter 31   On Mumbulla Mountain

MUMBULLA MOUNTAIN: The basic source for this study was Brian J. Egloff, *Mumbulla Mountain: An Anthropological and Archaeological Investigation* (Sydney, 1979), New South Wales Parks and Wildlife Service, Occasional Paper no. 4. A popular but scholarly account is by Denis Byrne, *The Mountains Call Me Back* (Sydney, 1984), New South Wales Ministry of Aboriginal Affairs and New South Wales NPWS.

HOWITT: His biography was written by his grand-daughter, Mary Howitt Walker, *Come Wind, Come Weather* (Melbourne, 1971). D.J. Mulvaney contributed pp. 285–329, on Howitt's anthropological work.

KURINGAL: The sequence of events was reconstructed by Mulvaney, "The anthropologist as tribal elder", *Mankind* 7 (1970), pp. 205–17. Howitt's account — A.W. Howitt, "On some Australian ceremonies of initiation", *Journal of the Anthropological Institute* 13 (1883), pp. 432–59; *The Native Tribes of South-East Australia* (London, 1904), pp. 516–62.

JACK MUMBULLA: Egloff, pp. 13, 24.

GUBOO TED THOMAS: His letter to Premier N. Wran is quoted in Egloff, p. 13; his comment on politicians and sites, Egloff, Annexure 2.

MINISTERIAL COMMENT: Quoted in Egloff, from *Bega and District Times*, 14 March 1979.

HOWITT'S MAP: Egloff, p. 51. Egloff's conclusion, p. 34.

CANBERRA TIMES: 16 September 1979. An attempt to convey the spiritual sense of Mumbulla Mountain is provided by Guboo Ted Thomas, in the photographic essay (by Wes. Stacey), *Mumbulla — Spiritual — Contact* (Canberra, 1980).

Chapter 32   Uluru Returned

GILES: R. Ericksen, *Ernest Giles* (Melbourne, 1978), p. 80. See p. 133, Giles originally named the lake, Ferdinand, and the mount, Mueller, in honour of his patron, who instructed him to change them to Amadeus and Olga. This royal couple abdicated in February 1873, so the naming was a close call!

GOSSE: "W.C. Gosse's Explorations 1873", *South Australian Parliamentary Papers*, No. 48, 1874, p. 9.

PEOPLE OF ULURU: Robert Layton, *Uluru* (Canberra, 1986), a book which has been used extensively in this account.

SPENCER: B. Spencer and F.J. Gillen, *Across Australia* (London, 1912), 2 vols. Spencer described his 1894 visit in vol. 1, pp. 111–32. His study of art, pp. 116–20 and Pl. *11*, 6; on "primitive" people, pp. 131–32.

MOUNTFORD: C.P. Mountford, *Ayers Rock* (Sydney, 1965), pp. 187–9. Compare his fig. 39, A, R, with Spencer Pl. *11*, 11, 6; fig. 40, A, B, with Spencer Pl. *11*, 1, 7.

RESERVES: B. Spencer, "Preliminary report on the Aboriginals of the Northern Territory", *Bulletin of the Northern Territory* 7 (1913), pp. 24–26. South West Reserve: Layton, *Uluru*, p. 73.

EVENTS OF 30S: Layton, pp. 70–1. An important new Aboriginal source on the Lasseter episode is R.G. Kimber, *Man From Arltunga* (Victoria Park, 1986), pp. 86–103.

LATER HISTORY: Layton, pp. 74–76.

PADDY ULURU: J. Isaacs (ed.), *Australian Dreaming* (Sydney, 1980), p. 40.

GOVERNOR-GENERAL: Layton, p. 118.

Index

Colour illustrations are indexed by plate number in bold type